GETTING FIRED

GETTING FIRED

What to do if you're fired, downsized, laid off, restructured, discharged, terminated, or forced to resign

Steven Mitchell Sack

WARNER BOOKS

A Time Warner Company

344.01
51219

This publication is designed to provide competent and reliable information regarding the subject matter covered. However, it is sold with the understanding that the author and publisher are not engaged in rendering legal or other professional advice. Laws and practices often vary from state to state, and if legal or other expert assistance is required, the services of a professional should be sought. The author and publisher specifically disclaim any liability which is incurred from the use or application of the contents of this book.

Warner Books, Inc., 1271 Avenue of the Americas, New York, NY 10020
Visit our Web site at
http://warnerbooks.com

 A Time Warner Company

Printed in the United States of America
First Printing: January 1999
10 9 8 7 6 5 4 3 2 1

Library of Congress Cataloging-in-Publication Data

Sack, Steven Mitchell
    Getting fired : what to do if you're fired, downsized, laid off,
restructured, discharged, terminated, or forced to resign / Steven Mitchell Sack.
        p.   cm.
    Includes index.
    ISBN 0-446-52215-5
    1. Employees—Dismissal of—Law and legislation—United States—
Popular works. 2. Layoff systems—Law and legislation—United
States—Popular works. 3. Employees—Dismissal of—United States—
Popular works. 4. Layoff systems—United States—Popular works.
I. Title.
KF3471.Z9S23   1999
344.7301'2596—DC21   98-3796
                                                                                                                 CIP

Book design by Giorgetta Bell McRee

To abused and fired workers everywhere

Acknowledgments

I would like to thank many individuals for assisting me in the preparation of this book.

First, gratitude is extended to my publicist, Donna Gould, at Phoenix Media. Her enthusiasm for my work has never wavered through the years, and I appreciate her talent and wisdom. She is the best in the business.

I also thank my literary agent, Alex Hoyt, for his capable efforts and skills. Alex has played a major role in my success as an author and I am grateful to receive his counsel and advice.

Of course my editor and senior vice president at Warner Books, Mel Parker, deserves much credit for his interest in and support of my work and for choosing this book as the catalyst for our Warner Books relationship. I also thank his assistants, Sharon Krassney and Dan Ambrosio, for their capable efforts.

Kudos are also extended to Faith Hanson for her great copyediting skills and to Stanley A. Spiegler, Esq., for his legal guidance and suggestions over the years.

Thanks are given to my wife, Gwen, who provides the nourishment and support that enable me to work such long hours "stress free" during my writing activities; and to my sons, Andrew and David, for their companionship and devotion. I also thank my brother and law partner, Jonathan Sack, Esq., for his capable guidance and assistance; my mother, Judith; Dr. Subhi Gulati, Philip Sassower and family, Sidney Pollack, and my extended family and friends for their encouragement.

As always, I wish to express my appreciation and gratitude to my father, Bernard, whose insights and dreams helped make this book a reality.

Finally, special thanks must be given to all the legislators, lobbyists, lawyers, judges, and others who have enacted and enforce legislation to protect employees in the workplace.

Contents

Fired in Violation of a Company Rule
Fired Inconsistent with a Verbal Promise
Fired in Breach of Contract Rights
Right to Be Warned Before a Massive Layoff

PART II. Negotiating the Best Severance Package After You Are Fired

Recognize the Warning Signs
Review Your Contract
Accumulate and Save Copies of All Pertinent Documents and
    Records
Maintain a Diary
Consider Meeting with a Lawyer Before You Resign or Are
    Fired
Start Looking for New Employment
Remove Personal Documents from Your Office
Talk to Fellow Employees
Analyze Your Financial Situation
Consider Sending Demand Letters
Avoid Resigning
Practice What You Will Say and How You Will Act

Learning Why You Were Fired
How to Properly Handle the News
Stay Calm
Stall for Time
Always Ask for More
Appeal to Decency and Fair Play

Wages
Other Compensation
    Bonus
    Retirement and Savings Plans
    Stock Options

List of Sample Forms, Letters, Legal Documents

INTRODUCTION

Why You Need This Book

This book was written to save you money and help you survive a stressful event in your life with the least emotional trauma possible.

When AT&T announced close to one Christmas that it planned to lay off more than 32,000 workers in one fell swoop, Wall Street applauded the move. The public's reaction to this drastic layoff was not as positive, however, and caused the company to scale back its plans and hire a public relations firm to minimize the negative effects of the decision.

The timing of the firing proves that the taboo against laying people off during the holidays is no longer valid as more and more companies, for business and accounting reasons, opt to trim payrolls instead of trees during the holiday season. This fact was borne out, for example, by released government figures demonstrating that 55,237 layoffs occurred in December 1995, the second highest month's total of 1995.

When the Supreme Court ruled several years ago that older workers would not necessarily have their age discrimination lawsuits thrown out of court after a firing merely because they were replaced by someone over forty, experts predicted that the more than 150,000 cases filed each year around the country in federal and state courts would double in subsequent years. While employers were not thrilled by the ruling, older Americans and their lawyers rejoiced in the decision.

WHAT THE NUMBERS SAY

Layoffs are constantly in the news these days. Whether it involves an announcement of a massive downsizing effort by a large company or a seven-figure verdict won by a terminated executive, more people are faced with this growing problem than ever before. In the past, longevity and security of employment were benefits competent and loyal workers could count on. Not anymore. As a result, legal proceedings arising from job eliminations have drastically increased.

Suppose that you are concerned about keeping an important job, especially after receiving a subjective and unfavorable written warning. If you are close to retirement, what steps can you take to reduce the chances of losing a large pension benefit soon to vest? How do you avoid a forced resignation? Is it better to resign from a job than be fired? Most important, how do you evaluate the merits of a severance package? What are the proper steps to take to financially increase an employer's offer when you are forced to depart?

Like most Americans, you probably know little about the way the law affects your life. But without this knowledge, there is a good chance you will be exploited, especially in your employment and business dealings.

Most people are not aware of the rights they *do* possess and how to use them effectively. But knowing the right moves to make can protect you in many ways. In addition to achieving greater financial success, you may actually feel better knowing that you took positive steps to right a workplace wrong.

We all know how awful it is to be fired even in the best of circumstances. Most people are so disillusioned and shell-shocked after receiving the news that they merely bow their heads and shuffle their feet out the door. However, by questioning the firing and demanding more benefits, or by anticipating a layoff and acting properly, you can gain enhanced financial benefits and the confidence to look for and find a new job.

An executive recently consulted me at my New York City law office. The woman had worked for a large publishing company for almost eight years and was burned out. She felt her efforts were not appreciated and her career with the firm was going nowhere. This was confirmed when she had been squeezed out of a promotion by a younger, unqualified associate the year before.

Frustrated, the client told me she was planning to throw in the towel and resign. I strongly advised her not to do this. I told her that by resigning she would forfeit a large amount of severance pay and other benefits she deserved from her years of loyal and dedicated service.

Instead, I advised her to schedule a meeting with management to discuss why she was unhappy with her job and how her positive attitude might be restored. This bit of posturing was merely a ploy to get the company to fire her (since we both believed that was what her employer desired). We rehearsed what she should say and how she should respond tactically to issues the company would raise at the meeting.

The result? Not only did my client get to leave the company with dignity and on her own terms, but she received eight months' severance with full benefits. During the time she was unemployed, she started her own business and became independently successful with the help of the financial security derived from her severance package.

The experience of this woman is not unique. Although no one should take a job and start anticipating an eventual firing, this book explains the steps you can take during your working years with a company that will help you in the event that you are someday fired. It gives you the information you need to obtain money when you have been wronged and the best possible termination agreement when you are fired. These benefits can go a long way toward restoring your confidence and keeping you going until you find a new job.

Statistics reveal that approximately four out of every one hundred workers are fired or resign from their jobs each month. It is also estimated that more than 1 million workers are fired from their jobs each year.

Government statistics also reveal that the ratio of permanent layoffs to temporary layoffs is rising. For example, in 1980, 61 percent of people who lost jobs reported that the layoffs were permanent. In 1995, the number was 70 percent. It appears that layoffs now have hit workers fifty-five years old and older the hardest. (In the past, younger workers were the ones more likely to bear the brunt of layoffs.) Unfortunately, laid-off workers who find jobs now make 10 percent less on the average than they would have made at their previous jobs.

A PERSONAL EXPERIENCE

These numbers explain why people don't feel secure about their jobs anymore. I personally learned this the hard way. In my first job out of law school, I was fired by a company after working only a few months. The manner in which I was discharged was vicious. Despite thinking (and being told) that I was doing an excellent job, I was called into a vice-president's office and suddenly terminated. No reason was given for the firing. I later learned that the decision was political and that the vice-president feared I was being groomed to replace him.

I was offered two weeks' severance and told to clear out my desk, return my company ID and Rolodex, and vacate the premises within an hour. I was so shocked by the news that I accepted what the company offered and left.

Later, because it had taken me a while to find that job and because I was furious at the company's behavior, I decided to start my own law practice and help others who suffer similar mistreatment.

My career was fueled, in part, by a book I wrote in law school called *The Salesperson's Legal Guide*, which was published in 1981. Additionally, I was fortunate to be interviewed by the *Wall Street Journal* for an article in November 1984 about the rights of terminated managers and workers. Dozens of terminated employees who read the article began calling me to find out if they had any legal rights after being fired.

As a result of that article, my appearances on television and radio programs throughout the country, and seminars I began conducting, I started negotiating post-termination benefits for a large number of clients and was surprised to learn that cash settlements and other perks could be obtained in a large percentage of cases through my intervention. Over the years, I have become convinced that the vast majority of private employers fear the repercussions of most firings and are willing to explore amicable solutions to avoid additional legal expenses, bad publicity, and potential damages that sometimes arise.

In the early 1990s, I wrote *The Employee Rights Handbook*, which was read by tens of thousands of people. The success of that book and the fact that many interviewers were interested in my comments on termination rights and strategies prompted me to focus my energies on writing a book devoted to the unique problems and aspects of separations, layoffs, discharges, firings, and resignations. And that is how this book came about.

Armed with the strategies in *Getting Fired*, you will be in a better position to know how to maximize post-termination compensation and benefits and avoid potential legal complications after a firing. Whatever your experience, compensation level, type of job, or the industry you work in, the valuable sample letters to send, checklists to consult, actual agreements, and names and addresses of important agencies and contacts included in this book will help you learn the proper steps to take on your own and the right moves to make before contacting a lawyer if one is needed.

If litigation becomes necessary, your chances of success and the value of a claim will increase substantially because you will recognize potential exploitation and know what to do about it.

THE LAWYER'S VIEWPOINT

One of the most frustrating aspects of practicing law is telling clients that they waited too long before taking action or that a case could have been worth a great deal of money if the right moves had been made. In fact, millions of dollars are lost each year by workers who have valid claims but fail to take appropriate or timely action. Conversely, significant damages can be obtained by taking the proper steps.

As an example, a New Jersey judge upheld a $7.1-million sex discrimination jury verdict against a company after the plaintiff successfully alleged that senior managers removed her from accounts she had helped build and gave them to male brokers. After twelve years with the company, the woman was accused of poor productivity and fired. The verdict included a $5-million punitive damages award. You will learn what action this woman took to preserve and strengthen her case before filing a claim.

I have tried to reduce complicated court rulings, regulations, and labor law concepts to simple strategies you can follow. These guidelines are intended to give you a practicing lawyer's expertise when you need it. By sharing my experiences in consulting with and/or representing more than twelve thousand fired workers in my nineteen-plus years of practice as a labor and employment lawyer, I have hoped to provide you with invaluable tips and advice.

This information will be quite useful when, after a traumatic firing, you don't know where to turn. All the subjects covered were chosen because they are important areas where people are frequently misinformed. And the glossary at the end of the book will help you understand the meaning of many legal terms and concepts and apply them properly.

Although *Getting Fired* is not meant to replace a lawyer, it will help you understand when you have a problem that requires a lawyer's assistance. You will learn how to eliminate potential misunderstandings with your lawyer after you hire one. In addition, information in the book will tell you how to make an employment lawyer work effectively on your behalf, as well as suggest courses of action to take before consulting a lawyer. Your having taken such actions may prove invaluable to your lawyer once you have retained one.

It doesn't matter whether you have been intimidated or discouraged by the legal process or disappointed by other how-to legal books in the past. If you keep an open mind when reading this book, you will discover that it is a very valuable resource.

Throughout the text, you will be shown how to complain effectively and assert your rights, no matter what your problem. You will learn about a variety of strategies that will enhance your claim in small claims court, arbitration, or mediation, and you will discover effective ways to help maximize and successfully argue your case with or without a lawyer before an appropriate state or federal agency, such as an unemployment insurance board or the Equal Employment Opportunity Commission (EEOC).

Lawyers have been providing successful clients with information on how to take the proper steps to prove and maximize a claim ever since the profession began. That is what preventive law is all about. Just as businesspeople keep lawyers on retainer to obtain ongoing advice, you, too, will now have access to this information.

This book provides you with all the practical information my clients receive at a fraction of the cost. Thus, keep this book in an accessible place and refer to it to avoid problems before they arise. Read the applicable sections before you are fired or decide to resign; it's that simple.

The benefits of applying this information can be significant. The following true stories demonstrate why.

A client attended a lecture I gave in Las Vegas to members of his business association. The man introduced himself after I finished speaking. He told me he had recently been fired from his job, and based on something he heard me say, believed he had been treated unfairly. After investigating the facts, I determined that he had been fired illegally to deprive him of the commissions he would earn from a large contract he was on the verge of closing with a major customer. I told him that I was not surprised by the company's actions, since it was another example of how employers choose to exploit workers for their own gain and that I witness such conduct daily. We also discussed how he, like hundreds of thousands of other workers annually, are victims of a cold-blooded mentality in the business world that has unfortunately become commonplace in American society.

After learning that the customer had signed a contract and paid for the large order, I contacted the ex-employer and demanded that my client receive his expected commission plus a substantial amount of previously due commissions and post-termination benefits.

Within four weeks, I received a check in the amount of $80,000 on his behalf. To this day, the client cannot believe the size of the settlement or the speed with which it was obtained.

The experience of this individual is not unique. People throughout the United States can obtain similar recompense provided their eyes are open.

It is also important to take the proper steps to ensure that you do not receive negative references from ex-employers, that you can possibly use the law to obtain copies of your personnel records, retrieve your personal property after a discharge, and maintain your dignity during this unsettling time.

In one case, I obtained a cash settlement of $37,500 for a man who was fired after being falsely accused of drinking too much at lunch. Another executive with nine-plus years of accumulated work time was fired suddenly one late November day. During negotiations, I determined that the firing was unjustified and done to deprive him of a large year-end bonus he was anticipating and a pension due to vest at the beginning of the following year. The company eventually paid me, on my client's behalf, a bonus of $50,000, severance pay totaling $75,000, representing one month's salary for each year of service, and agreed to keep him on unpaid leave for the duration of the year so that he would qualify for the pension that was about to vest.

There are three simple rules to follow to help yourself survive in corporate America these days: be flexible, be prepared, and be informed. Experts suggest that when you are fired, it will take approximately one month for every $10,000 of compensation you were earning to procure suitable new employment.

Getting Fired can help you recover money when you need it the most and restore your confidence and pride when you are treated unfairly or illegally. Knowledge is power, but if you don't know that you are being exploited or mistreated, you can't or won't fight back!

Steven Mitchell Sack, Esq.
New York, N.Y.

PART I

Determining When
You Are Being Treated
Illegally or Unfairly

CHAPTER 1

An Overview of Current Law and Trends

Radio and television interviewers frequently ask me why I say that a job is like a romance. My answer is that companies woo applicants with promises of security, fulfillment, and riches. Then, when the honeymoon is over, even highly qualified people often find themselves being treated unfairly. Many don't receive promised benefits, such as year-end bonuses, commissions, and overtime. Others are fired without cause or notice through no fault of their own.

Being fired is never good news, and the fact is that hundreds of large companies throughout the United States continue to announce major layoffs. In a layoff (also called a downsizing or a restructuring), many members of a company, a division, or a department are terminated en masse due to the company's perceived financial constraints, budget considerations, or merger with another company. These layoffs differ from one-on-one firings, where only one or several individuals are let go.

In the past, younger workers with less seniority were generally the first to be laid off in a corporate downsizing to reduce payroll costs. But because younger workers were typically at the low end of the wage scale, companies learned they would have to make substantial cuts to achieve meaningful savings. They realized it was more effective to offer early retirement and severance packages to older workers at the top of the wage scale as the way to reduce costs and stay competitive. This enabled them to fire fewer workers but achieve the same result.

Although this tactic appears to be discriminatory because it targets older workers, some employers found that it was legal when disguised as an offer of an early retirement package. Federal and state discrimination laws often approve early retirement programs because they are perceived as an offer of an employee benefit, which employees have the choice of voluntarily accepting or not.

Companies learned how to survive charges of discrimination provided they based reduction-in-force decisions on legitimate business reasons and used objective criteria, such as demonstrable economic necessity, performance reviews, and productivity evaluations, when selecting the employees to be discharged. This caused the burden to fall on employment lawyers to try to prove that in many major layoffs the choice of individuals to be fired was based on gender, race, national origin, religion, or other categories protected under the Civil Rights Act of 1991, the Age Discrimination in Employment Act, or state human rights laws. This is often difficult to prove. The result is that the majority of terminated individuals cannot make such a claim and prove that illegal discrimination entered into the selection process.

Many individuals who are offered early retirement packages want and need to continue working and don't consider the package a gift. They face a dilemma: If they refuse the offer, they feel that the next step, in six months or a year, will be a notice that their job is being eliminated with no offer of enhanced benefits. Wouldn't it be better to accept the package now?

Companies also recognized that if they needed to hire more workers after business conditions improved, they could do so at less cost by hiring "contingency" workers. These are part-time, temporary, freelance, and contract workers who agree to accept less pay and job security and a lack of health insurance and other benefits because, in today's job market, many are unable to find permanent full-time work. Commentators suggest that this development has significantly altered the landscape of the U.S. working world.

The net result is a business climate that can be very cruel. Anyone can get the ax these days. According to a report by the outplacement firm Challenger Gray & Christmas, layoffs surged 74 percent in the first three months of 1996, compared with the same period the year before, claiming nearly 170,000 jobs.

Furthermore, what is often not considered is the effect that layoffs, firings, and cutbacks have on the people that remain at a company. When workers feel the process was handled tactlessly or cruelly, they are certain to wonder if they will be the next asked to leave. This climate of uncertainty can demoralize entire departments.

People will always be fired for the usual reasons, such as poor performance, habitual lateness, excessive absences, insubordination, or disobeying work rules, regulations, and policies. What has changed the rules of the game, however, is being fired because of corporate greed, to satisfy a manager's desire to cut costs, or merely as a result of general business conditions.

THERE IS AN UPSIDE

While these developments are depressing, you should not despair. Some of my clients, out of frustration and anger, cry when they relate the facts of their firing to me in my office. This is understandable. Since most of us equate self-worth with our work, it's not surprising that losing a job can cause anxiety, self-doubt, depression, and even mental illness. But the experience doesn't have to leave you shattered.

Once you deal with the initial pain, you can use your time wisely to examine your goals, discover what you really want from a career, and find a new job that makes you happy. Being fired can be a benefit both financially and personally in many ways, as I will explain later. For example, after negotiating a large severance package for a client, I sometimes recommend that he or she not begin a job search immediately, but rather travel for three months or take the summer off. Later, after they have spent rewarding time "smelling the roses," many clients have thanked me for this advice.

While large numbers of corporate layoffs continue, the law fortunately has changed for the better in many respects. Up until twenty years ago, employees had few options when they received a pink slip. This was because of a legal principle called the employment-at-will doctrine, which was generally applied throughout the United States. Under this rule of law, employers hired workers at will and were free to fire them at any time with or without cause and with or without notice. From the nineteenth to the late twentieth centuries, employers could discharge individuals with impunity for a good reason, a bad reason, or no reason at all with little fear of legal reprisal.

During the 1960s, however, some state legislatures began scrutinizing the fairness of this doctrine. Courts began handing down rulings to safeguard the rights of nonunionized employees. Congress passed specific laws pertaining to occupational health and safety, civil rights, and the freedom to complain about unsafe working conditions.

The net effect has been a gradual erosion of the employment-at-will doctrine in many areas. Now, in most states, there are probably many exceptions that make it illegal for you to be fired. For example, it was recently reported that a state circuit jury in Miami returned an $850,000 judgment against Sears, Roebuck & Co. after a former store manager alleged that officials fired him for filing a workers' compensation claim. The Florida workers' compensation statute, like statutes in many other states, prohibits this kind of retaliation.

As a result of the passage of the federal Worker Adjustment and Retraining Notification Act (WARN), you must be given at least sixty days' notice before being let go or comparable financial benefits (i.e., at least sixty days' notice pay) if you are part of a large layoff that affects fifty or more workers at a plant site or company office.

Some courts have ruled that statements in company manuals, handbooks, and employment applications constitute implied contracts that employers are bound to follow. In many states, handbooks have been transformed into legally binding contracts of employment. Thus, every word counts when companies draft or revise employee manuals. This is a consideration they sometimes forget, and it can be a costly mistake.

Other states now recognize the obligation of companies to deal in fairness and good faith with longtime workers. This means, for example, that they are prohibited from terminating workers in retaliation when they tattle on abuses of authority (i.e., whistle-blowing) or denying individuals an economic benefit (a pension, commission, bonus, etc.) that has been earned or is about to become due.

A few states are even allowing wrongfully terminated workers to sue in tort (as opposed to asserting claims based on contract) and recover punitive damages and money for pain and suffering arising from a firing. Some employees who have sued under tort theories for wrongful discharge have recovered seven-figure jury awards as a result. Innovative lawyers are asserting federal racketeering (RICO) claims, seeking criminal sanctions and triple damages against companies. This is in addition to asserting fraud and misrepresentation claims against the individuals responsible for making wrongful-termination decisions.

A number of recent court decisions have also favored people whose employer-paid health benefits or monthly pension checks were reduced or taken away after a firing. In 1995, Pittsburgh-based USX Corp. agreed to pay $47 million to seventeen hundred steelworkers after a federal district court judge ruled that the company, in closing its Provo, Utah, plant in 1987 simply to avoid paying pension benefits, was in violation of the federal Employee Retirement Income Security Act of 1974 (ERISA).

After six years of litigation, a federal jury in 1995 took less than an hour to decide that Pfizer Inc. had unfairly persuaded a lifelong employee to take an early retirement package just weeks before it offered subsequently downsized employees a more lucrative buyout. And in another case, the U.S. Supreme Court ruled in 1996 that a large company must restore health benefits to individual employees who, in the eyes of the Court, had been tricked into transferring their benefits to an undercapitalized dummy subsidiary and eventually lost the benefits. The workers were awarded $8.3 million in the case.

Various commentators are now suggesting that in situations where employers manipulate employees unfairly, judges and juries are going to find a way for the wronged to win. Thus, given the changing legal climate, it is understandable that more people are seeking information about their rights and are fighting back after being fired. They are requesting enhanced benefits after a one-on-one firing or major departmental layoff and are receiving greater severance pay than the company's initial offer. As a result of successful negotiations, they are also obtaining accrued bonuses; continued medical, dental, and life insurance coverage; unemployment benefits; office space with use of a telephone, secretarial help, résumé preparation, and outplacement guidance while looking for a new job; a mutually acceptable cover story to tell prospective employers; and favorable letters of reference.

Mismanaging the termination process can result in hard feelings, loss of company prestige from bad publicity, a decline in loyalty and morale within the firm, difficulty in attracting new talent, more turnover, and litigation. As a result, employers are now beginning to see a clearer picture of what they are potentially up against when they handle terminations improperly.

Employers are being reminded to carry out terminations in a discreet, consistent, and mature fashion to avoid charges of defamation and/or discrimination. This means, for example, taking all precautions not to embarrass terminated workers in front of coworkers. Companies are also being advised not to fire employees before vacations, during company Christmas parties, or in the presence of a large group of colleagues.

Because a job is closely linked to a person's identity and self-respect and most terminated workers experience feelings of humiliation during a discharge, on-site training is being conducted to help employers understand more clearly how to fire people in a proper and humane manner. In light of the vast number of employment-related lawsuits filed these days, companies are reminded that being fired under humiliating or unfair circumstances is generally devastating to an individual and often brings out vindictive tendencies, which increase the chances that he or she will file a lawsuit to regain a sense of self-respect.

It is not surprising, according to Evan J. Spelfogel, a lawyer and past chair of the New York State Bar Association Section on Labor and Employment, that twenty times more employment discrimination cases were filed in 1990 than in 1970, almost 1,000 percent greater than the increase in all other types of civil litigation combined. The April 1994 issue of *Inc.* magazine reported that workplace discrimination suits have increased more than 2,200 percent close to the past two decades and now represent an estimated one-fifth of all civil suits filed in the United States. There is currently a backlog of close to 100,000 employment discrimination cases at the EEOC and over 25,000 wrongful-discharge cases pending in state and federal courts nationwide. Nearly all these cases involve jury trials with lengthy delays and unpredictable results.

William K. Slate II, president and chief executive officer of the American Arbitration Association, remarks that defending against a wrongful-discharge claim brought by a former employee can cost an employer hundreds of thousands of dollars. He states that the median time between the date an employment lawsuit is filed and the commencement of a civil trial is two and a half years and that fired workers currently win nearly 70 percent of these cases, with the average jury award for a wrongfully fired employee now being approximately $700,000.

One story in the *New York Times* reported that "in almost every industry, unfair discharge litigation has proliferated and the amount of money involved in settlements runs into hundreds of millions of dollars annually." Even more than ten years ago, the *Wall Street Journal* confirmed that more than one third of the New England companies interviewed indicated that they were involved in legal actions with terminated employees.

One reason for this dramatic increase in litigation is that lawyers representing employees have discovered that sympathetic plaintiffs are very appealing to juries in such disputes. Average jurors are lower-level employees themselves. Given the chance, jurors are likely to side with an employee against a deep-pocket employer.

Another reason the number of discrimination cases is soaring is that the stakes have become very high. Due to the enactment of the federal 1991 Civil Rights Act, which made jury trials as well as punitive and compensatory damages up to $300,000 available remedies, more people are now inclined to sue. When the Americans with Disabilities Act (ADA) became effective in 1993, hundreds of thousands of people previously excluded from the legal process who were fired as a result of a physical or mental condition became eligible to sue. The current litigation explosion has also been fueled by an increased public awareness and the large jury verdicts awarded to women who complain they were mistreated or fired after reporting incidents of personal discrimination or sexual harassment.

TAKING CONTROL OF THE REST OF YOUR LIFE

In Chapters 2 through 5, you will learn how to recognize when you are fired illegally. This is the first step on the road to understanding when you have been exploited and collecting what is due. Chapters 6 through 9 stress the correct negotiating strategies to use to maximize severance and other termination benefits. You will learn the right questions to ask and points to make and have clarified at the termination or exit session to increase what you can obtain. Samples of actual letter agreements are included in Chapter 9 to illustrate how you should confirm the deal in writing after it is accepted. You can use these letters as models and tailor them to your own situation.

You will also learn strategies to help you structure a settlement to achieve maximum tax savings. And even if you are not able to negotiate more money in a settlement, structuring the settlement tax-wise can put additional funds in your pocket (see Chapter 9). For example, the amount of any damages received for personal injuries or sickness may be excluded from gross income. Thus, a former employee who develops a physical injury, such as a bleeding ulcer, because of wrongful termination, may be eligible to receive a settlement (or a portion of it) on a tax-free basis.

You will even learn how employment lawyers can structure novel settlements if the need arises. For example, it was reported that a Florida executive, fired after working only six months of his yearlong contract, received a unique settlement. Instead of money, he agreed to accept forty thousand tickets to an animal petting farm, valued at $520,000!

Additionally, you will learn what to look out for when requested to sign a release or settlement agreement prepared by your employer.

Although it is unlikely that you will succeed in getting your job back after a firing, you can discover (in Chapters 8 and 9) how to get a better severance package without hiring a lawyer. You will also learn the steps to take when a satisfactory settlement is not achieved through informal means. If you are victimized and are unable to obtain benefits from your ex-employer and cannot afford a lawyer, you will learn how to obtain assistance through various federal, state, and local agencies. In addition, you will be advised of ways to collect evidence and strengthen a claim before you retain a lawyer.

Chapter 10 will help you learn how to resign from a job properly and gain unemployment benefits after a firing. In Chapters 11 and 12, you will become familiar with various post-termination problems that are frequently encountered. These include protecting your good name and reputation when the employer gives you a poor reference and learning how to stop former employers from enforcing covenants not to compete and other restrictive barriers to future employment.

Chapter 14 gives you valuable information on finding the right lawyer and working with him or her to achieve your goals.

All this information will help you take financial control and seize the opportunity to pick up the pieces of a shattered career. I sometimes remind depressed clients of a personal problem I had to overcome that was far more serious than the sudden loss of a good job. My problem was a life-threatening illness that I had to deal with to survive. Going through that gave me special insights when facing major obstacles, overcoming them, and moving forward with a positive attitude.

Thus, despite all the negative and pessimistic publicity about firings and downsizing, the rules of the game have favorably changed for fired employees in many instances. Keep your chin up and plan ahead. Since there is no use crying over spilled milk, don't get down, get even. The following pages will show you how.

CHAPTER 2

Fired Because of Your Age

Susan was a sixty-one-year-old manager who was fired from her job after fifteen years. She immediately sued the company and the president for age discrimination. The employer argued that her lay-off was due to a budget cut. Susan argued that after the appointment of a new boss in 1990, older workers were systematically replaced and senior positions filled with younger workers.

A jury ruled in her favor. It also found intentional discrimination in the department's failure to rehire Susan for a position that was created several months after her termination. The job was filled by a younger, arguably less-qualified individual, which the jury found to be evidence of retaliation against Susan for having pursued an age discrimination claim.

The jury awarded Susan $500,000 as compensation. Under the federal Age Discrimination in Employment Act, the award was doubled to $1 million because the jury found the discrimination to be intentional, knowing, and willful. According to the *New York Employment Law Letter* (a monthly newsletter published by the law firm of O'Melveny & Myers, which reported this case in the February 1996 issue), the employer is pursuing the post-trial avenues to reduce or set aside the verdict. If these are unsuccessful, it may appeal.

One of the most important aspects of antidiscrimination laws is that they apply anywhere you work or live. And there are no exceptions when workplace discrimination occurs: antidiscrimination laws operate even in employment-at-will states. If you believe you have been fired from a job primarily because of your age, gender, race, national origin, religion, or handicap, federal and state antidiscrimination laws will help you recover damages. You have rights that cannot be waived.

This chapter discusses how to recognize if you, a friend, or a relative has been fired illegally as a result of age and what to do about it. Related issues discussed include forced retirement, the impact on retirement plans and benefits, and reductions in force. You will also learn whether, pursuant to the federal Older Workers Benefit Protection Act, waivers you signed after a discharge legally preclude you from suing the employer for age discrimination. The following overview of antidiscrimination laws gives the background of the current situation.

AN OVERVIEW OF ANTIDISCRIMINATION LAWS

The Civil Rights Act of 1991 implemented a series of sweeping changes in federal antidiscrimination laws. The legislation expanded procedural options and remedies available to workers and overruled a series of important U.S. Supreme Court decisions that limited employees' legal recourse. In doing so, Congress amended six different statutes that together prohibit discrimination based on age, race, color, religion, gender, national origin, and disability. Those statutes are Title VII of the Civil Rights Act of 1964, the Americans with Disabilities Act of 1990, the Vocational Rehabilitation Act of 1973, the Age Discrimination in Employment Act of 1967, the Civil Rights Act of 1866, and the Civil Rights Attorney's Fee Awards Act of 1976. Virtually all employers are covered by these laws.

The 1991 act prohibits discrimination in all aspects of the employment process, including compensation, assignment, classification of employees, demotions, transfers, promotions, wages, working conditions, recruitment, testing, use of company facilities, training programs, fringe benefits, retirement plans, disability leave, hiring, and discharges. An illegal act can be committed by any member of an employer's staff, from the president down to a supervisor or receptionist.

Retaliation and on-the-job harassment are also prohibited. This means that if you file a charge of discrimination in good faith, you cannot be fired, demoted, or reassigned while the case is pending. However, if you knew the claim had no merit and filed it in bad faith, you can be fired legally. (Protection from retaliation is covered in Chapter 4.)

Many states have enacted even stronger discrimination laws with greater coverage and penalties than federal law. For example, although federal law does not recognize discrimination on the basis of a person's marital status or sexual preference, some state laws do. Many small employers (defined as companies employing less than fifteen persons) not covered by Title VII fall within the jurisdiction of state law. Some local laws offer even greater protection; for example, age discrimination protection may apply to the young as well as those who are over forty.

Counsel Comments: A question frequently asked me is: Which law takes precedence? The answer is essentially *the law that is the strictest.* To ensure proper protection of your rights, try to be familiar with federal and state laws as well as those governing employment in your local business community or municipality. If there is a difference in coverage on the same subject, seek to enforce the law that is the most favorable to your situation. To learn whether you have greater protection and how it applies, contact an appropriate state or city agency for further details, or speak to a knowledgeable employment lawyer.

Prior to the Civil Rights Act of 1991, claimants could typically receive only their jobs back, together with retroactive job pay and restoration of seniority benefits. Now, in cases where intentional (i.e., willful) discrimination is proved, the act also authorizes jury trials, witness and attorney fees to be paid to the individual harmed, punitive damages, compensatory damages up to $300,000 depending on the size of the employer, and additional penalties.

Compensatory damages are defined as money paid to compensate individuals for future pecuniary losses, emotional pain and suffering, inconvenience and mental anguish, loss of enjoyment, and physical pain and suffering. Compensatory damages are typically available only for intentional discrimination and unlawful harassment, and do not apply where a job practice is not intended to be discriminatory but nonetheless has an unlawful disparate impact on persons in a protected class, such as workers over forty.

RULES FOR EMPLOYERS

The following are general rules that employers are required to follow. These rules are recommended by Eric J. Wallach, a New York employment lawyer.

1. All employers must review hiring, promotion, and compensation criteria to ascertain whether they are validly job-related and consistent with business necessity. For example, are there statistical imbalances in the workforce that are directly or indirectly traceable to such standards?
2. Proper documentation, including employment forms, job descriptions, and performance evaluations, must be prepared to adequately support any personnel decisions regarding hiring, promotion, compensation, and discharge.
3. Appropriate procedures must be consistently applied in every case, and such decisions must never be made on the basis of a person's age, gender, race, or religion.
4. Employers with overseas operations must be attentive to whether their managers abroad are enforcing the antidiscrimination laws for all employees who are U.S. nationals.
5. All employment strategies must take into account the demographics of the workplace; companies must avoid statistical personnel imbalances.

AGE DISCRIMINATION

Federal and state discrimination laws are designed to promote employment of older persons based on their abilities, irrespective of age. The most important federal law, the Age Discrimination in Employment Act (ADEA), protects workers between the ages of forty and seventy from being arbitrarily fired, refused a job, forced to retire, or treated unfairly with respect to pay, promotions, benefits, health care coverage, retirement plans, and other employment opportunities because of age.

According to Jury Verdict Research, a company located in Horsham, Pennsylvania, the highest median jury awards for wrongful-termination suits between 1988 and 1995 went to individuals claiming age discrimination. The median age discrimination award of $219,000 was $72,201 more than the next highest median award for another type of employment-related lawsuit.

The ADEA governs all private employers with fifteen or more workers. It also protects employees of labor organizations, unions, and local, state, and federal government. Many states have enacted even tougher laws protecting workers by reducing the number of employees an employer must have to be subject to the law or reducing the cut-off age for inclusion into a protected class (i.e., age thirty in a few states).

The following thumbnail sketch outlines what employers *can* generally do under the ADEA and state discrimination laws pertaining to age:

- Fire older workers for documented, inadequate job performance or good cause (e.g., excessive tardiness or absences)
- Entice older workers into early retirement by offering additional benefits, such as bigger pensions, extended health insurance, or substantial severance packages, that are *voluntarily* accepted
- Force employees to retire if the worker is sixty-five or older, has worked as an executive for the past two years, and is entitled to a pension exceeding $44,000, or if the job calls for physical fitness (e.g., airline pilots or police officers) and age is recognized as a bona fide occupational qualification (BFOQ) factor in fitness and job performance. (An employer that sets age limits on a particular job must be able to prove the limit is necessary because a worker's ability to adequately perform that job substantially diminishes after the age limit is reached.)
- Lay off older workers when younger employees are similarly treated
- Make adverse decisions provided the acts are taken as a result of a demonstrated good-faith, reasonable business decision that does not have a discriminatory impact on all older workers at the company.

Tip: Some employers may legally discriminate against older workers when they hire independent contractors (which the law doesn't generally protect) or employ fewer than fifteen workers and there is no state antidiscrimination law to protect the rights of older workers.

Always check the law of your state to see what protection is available if you work for a small employer and are defined as an independent contractor but you disagree. Since some state agencies process discrimination cases more quickly than the EEOC and provide greater damages and remedies under applicable state law, consider pursuing your rights with a state agency or a state court (instead of the overburdened federal EEOC) after discussing your options with an employment lawyer.

The following actions are generally prohibited by federal and state law:

- Denying an older applicant a job on the basis of age
- Imposing compulsory retirement before age seventy
- Forcing older employees into retirement by threatening them with termination or loss of benefits, unless the company has instituted a valid seniority system or retirement plan
- Firing older workers because of age
- Denying promotions, transfers, or assignments because of age
- Penalizing older employees with reduced privileges, employment opportunities, or compensation because of age
- Harassing older workers by, for example, giving them burdensome work, requiring them to work overtime, or ridiculing them in front of other employees

You can recover significant damages if you receive unfair treatment because of age. These may include job reinstatement in the event of a firing, wage adjustments, back pay and double back pay, future pay, promotions, recovery of legal fees, witness fees, and filing costs, compensatory damages up to $300,000 depending on the size of the employer, and punitive damages. Recourse can also include the institution of favorable company policies on behalf of fellow older employees, counseling, and enhanced outplacement assistance.

The U.S. Supreme Court in 1996 made it a little easier for older workers by ruling that when a fired over-forty employee files an age discrimination suit, courts cannot insist that his or her replacement must be under forty to be actionable. In the opinion, Justice Antonin Scalia stated that the fact that the replacement is "substantially younger" is a far more reliable indicator of age discrimination than whether the replacement is older or younger than forty. Thus, for example, an age-discrimination case might now be allowed to proceed if a fifty-eight-year-old employee's job is replaced by someone forty-two years of age.

Counsel Comments: Whenever an older (over forty) employee is fired and consults me, the basic issue I must decide is whether the company's decision was made because of age or was the result of a reasonable nondiscriminatory business decision.

Because direct evidence is often difficult to obtain, the client must typically use circumstantial evidence to prove that an employer's motive was improper. This is sometimes done by demonstrating that the client was between forty and seventy years of age, was doing satisfactory work, was fired, and the position was then filled by a substantially younger employee. In the case of a female employee, if a younger male employee replaces her, she may also have a claim for sex discrimination. However, when employers support firing decisions with documentation of poor work performance or other factors, an older worker's chances of proving age discrimination diminish.

Tip: It is easier to prove age discrimination when age-related statements have been made to or about the claimant (e.g., "You are too old and set in your ways"; "Why don't you retire?") or by using statistics (i.e., that the company fired ten older workers in the past six months and replaced them all with substantially younger employees). This is because courts have been known to uphold age bias suits brought by senior employees because they were subjected to gibes, demeaning jokes, and adverse remarks about their age before being fired. In fact, many companies try to head off such suits by issuing instructions to indoctrinate employees against discriminatory chatter.

But sometimes a valid case can exist when there is no documentation supporting the employer's reason for discharging the older worker. A sudden drop in a performance rating may be viewed with suspicion by juries, particularly when a supervisor failed to give any notice to the employee of his apparent dissatisfaction with the employee's performance. In cases where the worker recently received a raise or bonus for good work and had not been warned, reprimanded, or criticized about his or her performance before being fired, the employer's reason may be a pretext for age discrimination.

Proving age discrimination can be difficult, especially when staff does not make liability-sensitive statements, remarks, or threats with respect to age; the employee is unable to demonstrate statistical proof that the company had a practice of firing older workers and replacing them with younger ones; and there is no direct evidence.

Another Supreme Court ruling that an employer's decision to lay off mostly older workers close to receiving vested retirement benefits did not, in and of itself, constitute age discrimination has not helped the worker's cause. In that case, the Court found that since the employer proffered a rational business justification for firing a large number of older workers (i.e., to save the company money, since older workers with the most seniority had the highest salaries), no illegality occurred even though the older workers were more severely affected by the discharge! (The Supreme Court did say the individuals might consider filing ERISA claims to protect forfeited retirement and severance benefits as a result of the company's actions.)

Progressive Discipline and Warnings

The practice of progressive discipline before a firing, in which notice is given to the employee of alleged work performance dissatisfaction, is frequently used by employers to reduce the risk of discrimination and wrongful-termination lawsuits. By documenting the incidence of employee disciplinary measures through precise records of conferences, warnings, probationary notices, remedial efforts, and other steps, employers sometimes demonstrate that an eventual termination was not due to a discriminatory motive but stemmed from a good-faith business decision.

Many companies, however, apply their system of discipline and warnings in a haphazard fashion and fail to use the same punishment for similar infractions. This may invite a discrimination lawsuit if there are several employees with a chronic problem (e.g., absenteeism) and the older worker is the first to be fired for that reason, while substantially younger workers or those under forty are only given a warning.

If you are an older worker who believes that an employer is treating you more harshly than younger workers for identical infractions, or you are receiving dissimilar, unfair on-the-job treatment with respect to benefits, promotions, or other matters, speak to an employment lawyer for advice.

Tip: When you receive a performance review that is unfair, incorrect, or subjective, write a rebuttal and give it to the supervisor or manager who wrote the review. Send a copy to your company's human resources officer. Keep a copy for your records and store it in a safe place. A rebuttal memo can demonstrate that you did not agree with the review and can come in handy later in the event you sue the company for age discrimination after a firing.

Seniority Rights and Vacation Time

Nothing in the federal laws barring age discrimination prohibits employers from altering the terms of a benefit seniority system provided the new system is not a subterfuge for engaging in arbitrary age discrimination. For example, when companies change vacation pay policies by putting a cap on the amount of annual paid vacation a person can take (this penalizes older workers when all employees regardless of seniority must take the same number of days off) or reduce medical insurance and retiree benefit plans, such acts are legal when justified by significant cost considerations. However, the burden falls on the employer to justify that its actions are lawful.

Retirement Plans and Forced Retirement

This is an area where older workers and executives are sometimes exploited. Most pension or retirement plans require employees to be a certain age or to have worked a minimum number of years before they can begin drawing the maximum pension payment per month. Some plans permit employees to draw monthly pension payments before reaching the age specified in the plan for eligibility of full benefits. When an employee takes "early retirement," he or she generally receives less in monthly benefits. The advantage of taking early retirement is that while monthly payments are less, they are often paid sooner.

A "forced" retirement occurs when companies illegally exert pressure on older employees to opt for early retirement or face firing, demotion, a cut in pay, or poor recommendations. The law requires that employers contemplating a large layoff or seeking to reduce payroll through early retirement incentives must do so carefully to avoid charges of age discrimination.

Under the ADEA and in most states, it is illegal to impose compulsory retirement before age seventy unless the employee is a "bona fide executive" receiving an annual company-paid retirement benefit of at least $44,000 per year after reaching sixty-five or is in a "high policy-making position" during a two-year period prior to reaching age sixty-five. (What constitutes an executive or high policy-making position depends on the unique facts of each case. Thus, speak to an employment lawyer for more details.)

Many states have passed similar laws to protect older employees from being victimized by forced retirement and mandatory retirement plans. For example, New York has a law that prohibits most public employees from being forced to retire, no matter how old they get (except for firefighters, police officers, and other law enforcement personnel). Private-sector employees (with limited exceptions for some executives and tenured college faculty members) are also protected.

It is also illegal to deny early retirement incentives to employees based on their age. For example, an early retirement program limited to workers between the ages of fifty-seven and sixty-two penalizes employees older than sixty-two. Furthermore, eligibility to receive Social Security benefits cannot be used as a factor in deciding which employees will be laid off.

If the employer can show that a retirement plan is "bona fide" (e.g., plan benefits are based on an employee's length of service), that the employee's decision to accept early retirement is voluntary, and that the reasons for the plan are nondiscriminatory (i.e., are not based on age), a plan may not violate the ADEA. Additionally, if an employee can no longer perform the duties of the job, the employer may be allowed to discharge the worker or, alternatively, force him or her to retire (depending on the circumstances).

The ADEA explicitly requires equal treatment in pension plans regardless of age. Employers may, however, set a limit on the maximum number of years of service they will credit to employees. It is also legal for employers who offer retiree health benefits to offset the value of these benefits against an employee's entitlement to severance benefits as a result of a reduction in force, a layoff, or a plant closing. Employers may also reduce life insurance benefits for older workers to keep premium costs equal.

Many executives are willing to retire by the age of sixty-five provided there is sufficient financial incentive. Be sure you understand how much in additional benefits you will be receiving. Speak to your accountant, lawyer, or other professional adviser and do the arithmetic before accepting any early retirement package.

Any retirement incentive program that *forces* older employees to leave is unlawful. The key question is whether the employee voluntarily accepted the incentive. Implied or direct threats that you will be fired or demoted after not taking the benefit can make the offer unlawful. Speak to an employment lawyer immediately if you feel such pressure.

Counsel Comments: Just because you are encouraged to take a severance package does not mean your company has violated the ADEA. Employers have no reason to shy away from discussing severance options with eligible older employees. As long as the severance package is not specifically based on age (e.g., $X for people fifty-five to sixty, $Y for people over sixty), it is probably legal.

In one case, a Texas employer was restructuring its operations. According to *You and the Law*, which reported the case in its December 1996 issue, the company offered voluntary severance packages to a number of employees. Those who did not accept the severance offer were told they could apply for new jobs in the company, but if they were not chosen, they would be fired.

A fifty-seven-year-old employee decided not to take the package. He applied for a new position but did not receive it because it was given to a forty-eight-year-old worker. The fifty-seven-year-old employee was soon laid off. He sued the employer and alleged he was discriminated against because the employer encouraged him to accept the severance and attempted to force him into retirement.

The U.S. District Court for southern Texas ruled that no violation had occurred. The forty-eight-year-old worker had scored better on an objective test given to all applicants. This, among other factors the court determined, constituted a valid reason for not retaining him. The court also commented that the fifty-seven-year-old chose not to accept the voluntary severance offer at his peril.

Tip: If you are fired and the company's pension or retirement plan permits early retirement, investigate whether you qualify and whether the termination can be treated instead as a voluntary early retirement. This is an important consideration to be asserted through negotiation. If you are fired several months before qualifying for early benefits, try to get the company to agree to place you on "unpaid leave status" for the remaining period of time so you can bridge the gap and qualify. I frequently negotiate this point for my clients where appropriate.

You may be able to achieve this benefit if you are fired just before the vesting of a pension. If this happens to you, always argue that the timing of the firing is suspect and that public policy requires the employer to grant your pension. If the employer refuses, consult an experienced employment lawyer immediately.

Another important yet frequently overlooked consideration in deciding whether to accept an early retirement package is whether the employer will honor its promises in subsequent years and be around to pay the benefits. Whatever decision a company makes about retirement benefits, its plan must have the likelihood of standing up in court.

For example, fifty thousand early retirees who took packages between 1974 and 1988 sued General Motors after the company amended their lifetime health benefits plan. The claimants argued that the automaker was required to provide free health care benefits to retirees instead of altering the package a few years later and billing them for copayments.

The company argued that when it made the offer of free health benefits for life, it reserved the right "to amend, modify, suspend and terminate" such benefits. The retirees claimed that the offer of free lifetime medical benefits with no copayment was a compelling factor in why they agreed to retire prematurely in the first place. The court agreed with the workers and ruled that a promise is a promise.

But the opposite result occurred in another important case. As far back as 1946 a company unilaterally provided group life and health insurance for its salaried, nonunion employees. The company's bene-fit literature stated that the company would provide group insurance for all retirees and their dependents. However, the company specifi-cally reserved the right to terminate the insurance "should business conditions warrant it."

Thirty-six years later, retirees were shocked to receive a notice that all retiree health and life insurance benefits would be terminated. The president told them the company could no longer afford to provide the coverage.

The U.S. Court of Appeals ruled that since the company at all times had clearly reserved the right to amend or kill the insurance program and that since no written promise of lifetime welfare benefits was made, the company had not breached any legal obligation to provide continuing benefits.

Tip: The consequence of this case is clear: never assume that retiree benefits you are to receive will continue undisturbed. Many times an offer to pay retiree benefits is merely a gratuitous offer that a company can legally modify or revoke. It is rare that such benefits are guaran-teed (e.g., in certain ironclad union contracts). Remember this and confer with legal counsel for more advice.

Finally, if you sign a release or waiver after voluntarily accepting an early retirement offer, you may have a difficult time repudiating the agreement if you later change your mind. In one case, for ex-ample, a company offered all salespeople over fifty-five an early re-tirement option that included a year's severance pay, medical benefits for life, supplemental life insurance, and retirement benefits com-puted as if the workers had reached sixty-five. Although the em-ployees accepted the package, they later charged that the plan violated the ADEA.

Despite the fact that the salespeople claimed that a supervisor threatened them to take the offer or else their jobs might be elimi-nated, the court ruled that "vague impressions" or threats in the ab-sence of objective factors indicating age discrimination are insufficient to support a constructive discharge claim. The court also noted that the salespeople had signed an acknowledgment stating that the deci-sion to accept the early retirement benefits was made freely with no coercion, that they could have changed their minds shortly after sign-ing the waiver (i.e., within seven days) but didn't, and that the benefits received as consideration for accepting the package were considerable.

TAKING EFFECTIVE ACTION

Ask yourself the following questions if you believe you were fired because of age:

- Did you request a transfer to another position before you were fired? Was it refused? If so, were similar requests granted to younger workers?
- How were you terminated? Were you given false reasons for the termination? Did you consent to the action, or did you protest (such as by sending a certified letter to the company refuting the discharge)?
- Were you replaced by a younger worker under forty (or between forty and forty-five if you are between sixty and sixty-five)? Were younger workers merely laid off and not fired (i.e., rehired several months later)?

Positive answers to these questions may prove you were fired as a result of age discrimination. Your case will be strengthened when fellow employees are also victimized. In one case, for example, 143 persons were forced to retire prematurely from an insurance company at the age of sixty-two. The large number of older employees all the same age made it difficult for the company to claim it was a valid reduction in force (called a RIF), and the workers collectively received more than $6 million in back wages.

Before implementing a RIF, companies must take steps to ensure they have acted properly. For example, if they have a practice of permitting bumping or transfers before a discharge, not extending such opportunities to older workers during a RIF may give rise to a claim of disparate treatment. Moreover, selection of individuals for layoff based on their current cost of retention may be unlawful where wage and benefit rates are found to be a function of length of service and, as such, an arguable product of age.

Recently, a federal court jury found a well-known bank guilty of age discrimination in dismissing five female customer service representatives. The employer was ordered to pay more than $700,000 to the women, who were allegedly dismissed as a result of corporate restructuring. Their ages and seniorities were:

Plaintiff 1: age forty-five, years of service eighteen
Plaintiff 2: age forty-three, years of service twenty-five
Plaintiff 3: age fifty-nine, years of service nineteen
Plaintiff 4: age sixty-two, years of service fourteen
Plaintiff 5: age forty-two, years of service twelve

The lawyer representing the women said there were other positions they could have been offered (but weren't) and that shortly after the dismissals the bank advertised for replacements. Each of the five was awarded $141,000 for back pay (doubled as a result of the jury's finding of "willful" discrimination), $408,750 for lost future wages and benefits, and $25,000 for emotional distress.

Counsel Comments: The employer has appealed the decision. However, the case is instructive in several respects. It demonstrates that you don't have to be in your late sixties to win an age claim when you are fired. Furthermore, a case may be strengthened when, despite having greater seniority, you and other senior workers are terminated (instead of junior employees) in an alleged downsizing, but your jobs are filled by new, inexperienced workers soon thereafter.

Tip: To demonstrate a violation of the ADEA in court, you must be able to prove that you are forty or older, were qualified for or were satisfactorily performing your job, were fired, and that a substantially younger person was put in the position. Once you demonstrate these facts, it is up to the employer to demonstrate that the action was not based on age. Even if the employer's explanation is legitimate, you may still show that the explanation is a pretext or a cover-up for discrimination.

It is always helpful to gather all available information to support your case. Plan ahead if you think you may be fired because of your age. This includes checking your files for documents that show you have been productive and a high performer. Deborah L. Jacobs, in her excellent article "Hurt by Age Discrimination? Here's What to Do" (*San Diego Union-Tribune*, January 24, 1995), writes that these documents include copies of work assignments, notes or letters praising a job well done, favorable performance reviews, and a history of pay increases, raises, promotions, and bonuses.

Ms. Jacobs advises you should make daily notes about relevant events at work, conversations with supervisors, discussions about the company's personnel plans, and offhand remarks that reveal a preference for younger employees. Such remarks might include "You can't teach an old dog new tricks" or "John is less energetic." Such statements, says Ms. Jacobs, might be construed as age discrimination. (It is also a good idea to record the dates, times, and witnesses who overheard such remarks to further substantiate your proofs in court.)

Ms. Jacobs states that you should get names of possible witnesses, collect background about pending lawsuits, and answer any negative reviews in writing. Since it is not always easy to locate this information on your own, discreetly talk to other employees and try to get as much help in collecting information as possible. Your goal is to find information to support a contention that the younger replacement was far less qualified than you in terms of education background, work experience, and career history at the company. Know the company's policies and personnel procedures. Get copies of personnel policies. Find out what a company employee's rights are under existing systems. By asking other employees and personnel officials, determine if the company consistently adheres to its policies.

Ms. Jacobs points out that, to support a decision, your supervisor may be trying to build a case against you. Try not to do your fact-finding on company time or you might be accused of neglecting your job.

After you collect this information, it is a good idea to consult an experienced employment lawyer who has handled many age discrimination cases and obtain an opinion as to whether your case has merit and how to proceed. The lawyer may recommend that you contact the ex-employer on your own to settle the matter or retain him or her to send an initial demand letter to the employer in an attempt to obtain an out-of-court settlement. The letter on pages 28–29 illustrates the kind of letter your lawyer may preliminarily send.

The tone, language, and substance of an initial demand letter will vary depending on your lawyer's style, preference, and the facts. The purpose is to get the company's attention so that the lawyer will receive a favorable response. Hopefully, a dialogue and an appropriate

Law Offices of Sack & Sack
135 East 57th Street 12th Floor
New York, NY 10022
Telephone (212) 702-9000
Telecopier (212) 702-9702

Steven M. Sack
Jonathan S. Sack*
*Also admitted in N.J. & D.C.

Date

Name of Company Officer
Title
Company Address

Re: Termination of (Name of Client, "Wilma Jones")

Dear (Name):

This office has been retained by Wilma Jones concerning her dismissal from employment with your company. On (specify date), Ms. Jones was summarily discharged without cause by (name of supervisor), an officer with your company. Ms. Jones, who is 61 years of age, was dismissed from employment after 12 years of exemplary service in the highly competitive and sophisticated field of publishing. She was replaced by an inexperienced, unqualified, younger woman (specify name).

No articulable reason was provided to Ms. Jones at the time of her discharge other than that the company was downsizing. (Name of supervisor) told my client she was to be terminated, and Ms. Jones was given only one hour to clean out her desk and vacate the premises. Upon further inquiry Ms. Jones learned that your company has not engaged in a downsizing as stated.

My client demonstrated a wide variety of valuable skills in her work. She was never criticized or warned that her job was in jeopardy. The woman who replaced her is much younger (under 40), is not technically skilled in her field, and is inexperienced.

Ms. Jones always received favorable performance evaluations during her tenure.

The manner of my client's discharge was both humiliating and distressful. Ms. Jones is confused, deeply pained, and upset at what prompted her dismissal without explanation or notice. Your offer to pay only four weeks' severance is inadequate in light of my client's long-term contributions and achievements. Furthermore, I have been advised that other executives with similar long-term service have received substantially greater severance packages.

My client's replacement by a much younger, less competent woman causes me to conclude that your company terminated Ms. Jones primarily because of her age. Under this state's laws and federal laws, the circumstances surrounding her discharge and replacement reflect a strong indication of age discrimination. As such, I have advised my client she is entitled to be compensated for the arbitrary manner in which she was treated.

As a result of the termination, Ms. Jones also suffered the loss of the medical, dental, and profit-sharing benefits she was receiving while employed and which she relied on for her future welfare. At her age it is doubtful she will obtain gainful employment soon, and she was counting on working several more years before her retirement. The discharge is even more damaging in view of the fact that Ms. Jones is a widow with little means of support.

Finally, the manner in which she was terminated caused her additional harm and distress in that she was not notified of her continuation of medical benefits under federal COBRA law.

In light of the foregoing, I request that either you or your representative contact this office immediately in an attempt to resolve these and other issues in an amicable fashion to avoid expensive and protracted litigation.

Hopefully this can be avoided, and I thank you for your immediate attention and cooperation in this matter.

Very truly yours,
Steven M. Sack

Sent via messenger

settlement will ensue prior to the institution of further legal proceedings.

If these initial attempts fail, you should consider filing a formal charge of age discrimination. This is typically done at a local EEOC office and/or state antidiscrimination agency. To avoid having your case dismissed, you must file a claim within 180 days of a firing or notification that you were being fired. In some states, you are permitted to file an action within 300 days of the harmful act(s), so check your state's law.

Information on how to present your case properly to the EEOC, what to do once you obtain a finding of probable or no probable cause at the initial administrative level, and how to proceed with a lawsuit in federal or state court are explained in greater detail in Chapters 5 and 13.

Releases and Waivers

To avoid charges that an employee was not given sufficient time to reflect and weigh the options of an early retirement offer and thus was constructively discharged, employers are now required to prepare written releases that give retirees and older workers time to consider the offer, seek advice from a lawyer, and even repudiate the decision within seven days of signing the document. Historically, Congress did not recognize the ability of employers to enforce a waiver of age discrimination claims. As a result, some lucky workers who signed releases prior to 1990 were able to cash their settlement checks and still sue an employer thereafter.

The enactment of the federal Older Workers Benefit Protection Act (OWBPA) in 1991 has eliminated confusion provided its provisions are properly followed. The act makes clear that in relation to the firing or resignation of a worker over forty, a company can protect itself from potential violations of ADEA claims by utilizing waivers, provided:

1. The waiver is part of an agreement that specifically states the worker is waiving his or her ADEA right and is not merely a general release
2. The agreement containing the waiver does not disclaim any rights or claims arising after the date of its execution

3. The worker receives value (e.g., an extra month of severance pay) in exchange for signing the agreement
4. The worker is advised in writing of the right to consult a lawyer of his or her choosing before signing the agreement
5. The worker is advised in writing of his or her right to consider the agreement for a period of twenty-one days before it is effective
6. The worker is given at least seven days following the execution of the agreement to revoke it

When employers request the signing of releases or waivers in connection with mass termination programs and large-scale voluntary retirement programs, the act is even more strict. All individuals in the program must be given at least forty-five days to consider the agreement, and each employee must also be provided with numerous facts, such as the class, unit, or group of individuals covered by the program, any eligibility factors for the program, time limits applicable to the program, the job titles and ages of all individuals selected for the program, and the ages of all individuals not eligible for the program.

The cover letter and release beginning on page 32 illustrate the kind of document that is often prepared by employers to comply with the OWBPA.

A benefit of the OWBPA is that all voluntary early retirement programs are now scrutinized closely to determine that no threat, intimidation, or coercion is directed to the worker to whom the benefit is offered. Older employees must now be given sufficient time to consider the offer and receive accurate and complete information regarding benefits.

Tip: If you are an older worker being terminated after working years for an employer, always try to negotiate a better severance package. Information on how to do this successfully is included in Chapter 8. When companies agree to pay more money in severance and/or benefits, they typically prepare releases for individuals to sign. Carefully review any such document. Question all ambiguous or confusing language. Consult an experienced employment lawyer for advice and guidance where necessary. Do not be afraid to do this, since the release, to be valid, must specifically allow the right to consult a lawyer of your choosing. Take advantage of this provision. The lawyer you consult may advise that the

COVER LETTER AND RELEASE
(SPECIFICALLY WAIVING AN AGE DISCRIMINATION CLAIM)

To: Severed Employee
From: The Company ("The Employer")
Re: Older Workers Benefit Protection Act

This communication apprises you of your rights under the Older Workers Benefit Protection Act ("OWBPA"), which amends the Age Discrimination in Employment Act ("ADEA"), that Congress passed. The OWBPA establishes certain standards as regards waivers that the Employer obtains from its Employees.

The OWBPA amends the ADEA by adding a new section which establishes standards for a "knowing and voluntary" waiver:

(1) The waiver has to be part of an agreement between the Employee and the Employer and it has to be written in understandable English;

(2) The waiver must refer specifically to rights or claims arising under the ADEA;

(3) The waiver cannot cover rights or claims that may arise after the date on which it is signed;

(4) The waiver must be exchanged for consideration, and the consideration must be in addition to anything of value to which the Employee is already entitled;

(5) The Employee must be advised in writing to consult with an attorney before signing the agreement;

(6) The Employee has to be given a period of at least 21 days to decide whether to sign the waiver; and

(7) The Employee is entitled to revoke the waiver within seven days after signing it, and the waiver does not become effective or enforceable until the revocation period has expired.

GENERAL RELEASE

FOR GOOD AND VALUABLE CONSIDERATION, the adequacy of which is hereby acknowledged, in the form of payment to Employee of a severance benefit in the amount of ($XX) _____ salary less withholding for federal and state taxes, FICA, and any other amounts required to be withheld,

Employee agrees that he/she, or any person acting by, through, or under Employee, RELEASES AND FOREVER DISCHARGES (Name of Employer), and its parent company and subsidiaries, affiliates, successors, and assigns, as well as the officers, employees, representatives, agents and fiduciaries, de facto or de jure (hereinafter collectively referred to as "Released Parties"), and covenants and agrees not to institute any action or actions, causes or causes of action (in law unknown) in state or federal court, based upon or arising by reason of any damage, loss, or in any way related to Employee's employment with any of the Released Parties or the termination of said employment. The foregoing includes, but not by way of limitation, all claims which could have been raised under common law, including retaliatory discharge and breach of contract, or statute, including, without limitation, the Age Discrimination in Employment Act of 1967, 42 U.S.C. Sections 621–634, as amended by the Older Workers Benefit Protection Act of 1990, Title VII of the Civil Rights Act of 1964, 42 U.S.C. Sections 2000e et seq. and the Employee Retirement Income Security Act of 1974, 29 U.S.C. Sections 1001 et seq. or any other Federal or State Law; except that this General Release is not intended to cover any claim arising from computational or clerical errors in the calculation of the severance benefit provided to Employee, or retirement benefit to which Employee may be entitled from any plan or other benefits to which Employee may be entitled under any plan maintained by any of the Released Parties.

Employee covenants and agrees to forever refrain from instituting, pursuing, or in any way whatsoever aiding any claim, demand, action, or cause of action or other matter released and discharged herein by Employee arising out of or in any way related to Employee's employment with any of the Released Parties and the rights to recovery for any damages or compensation awarded as a result of a lawsuit brought by any third party or governmental agency on Employee's behalf.

Employee further agrees to indemnify all Released Parties from any and all loss, liability, damages, claims, suits, judgments, attorneys' fees and other costs and expenses of whatsoever kind or individually Employee may sustain or incur as a result of or in connection with matters hereinabove released and discharged by Employee. Employee warrants that he/she has not filed any lawsuits, charges, complaints, petitions, or accusatory pleadings against any of the Released Parties with any governmental agency or in any court, based upon, arising out of, or related in any way to any event or events occurring prior to the signing of this General Release, including, without limitation, his/her employment with any of the Released Parties or the termination thereof.

Employee acknowledges, understands and affirms that: (a) This General Release is a binding legal document; (b) (i) Released Parties advised him/her to consult with an attorney before signing this General Release, (ii) he/she had the right to consult with an attorney about and before signing this General Release, (iii) he/she was given a period of at least 21 calendar days in which to consider this General Release prior to signing, and (iv) he/she voluntarily signs and enters into this General Release without reservation after having given the matter full and careful consideration; and (c) (i) Employee has a period of seven days after signing this General Release in which he/she may revoke this General Release, (ii) this General Release does not become effective or enforceable and no payment shall be made hereunder until this seven-day-revocation period has elapsed, and (iii) any revocation must be in writing by Employee and delivered to (specify), Human Resources, within the seven-day-revocation period.

IN WITNESS WHEREOF, the Employee signs this General Release this _____ day of _____,   (year)

_____

Employee's Name (please print)

WITNESS:

_____

Signature   Date

ACKNOWLEDGMENT

I HEREBY ACKNOWLEDGE that (Name of Employer) in accordance with the Age Discrimination in Employment Act, as amended by the Older Workers Benefit Protection Act, informed me in writing: (1) to consult with an attorney before signing this General Release; (2) to review this General Release for a period of 21 days prior to signing; (3) that for a period of seven days following the signing of this General Release, I may revoke this General Release, and this General Release will not become effective or enforceable until the seven-day-revocation period has elapsed; and (4) that no payment shall be made until the seven-day-revocation period has elapsed.

I HEREBY FURTHER ACKNOWLEDGE receipt of this General Release for my review on the _____ day of _____, (year)

Employee: _____
          (Print or Type Name)

_____
          Signature of Employee

Witness: _____

---

company has violated the ADEA and you are entitled to a greater settlement before signing away your rights. Some workers hire employment lawyers to negotiate a better severance package or to sue the employer in court after an evaluation has been made.

Counsel Comments: If you have signed an employment contract containing an arbitration clause, a claim you make as a fired employee under the ADEA may fall within the scope of the clause and you may be forced to litigate an age discrimination dispute in arbitration rather than in court before a jury. This can work to your disadvantage because in most instances arbitrators are not empowered to award punitive damages, injunctions to stop further harassment, or legal fees. Furthermore, arbitrators are usually businesspeople or lawyers, and their philosophical orientation is often not as closely aligned to an individual's rights as a jury's is. Arbitration awards tend to be smaller than jury awards for discriminatory harms committed. It is important to understand the ramifications of any arbitration clause in an employment agreement before you sign it. Seek legal advice when presented with a comprehensive employment contract for an important job.

Recognize that waivers signed by a departing worker may not protect the employer if the worker later applies for a job. One fifty-five-year-old executive was dismissed in a downsizing move. He accepted an enhanced severance package (twice the usual severance) and signed a waiver relinquishing his right to sue the company. A year later, still unemployed, he saw his old job advertised in the newspaper. With the encouragement of a former superior, he applied for the position. He lost out to a much younger worker under forty with little experience.

The man sued, claiming that he was a victim of age discrimination. The trial court dismissed the case as a result of the waiver he had signed. But the appeals court noted that the ADEA disapproves people waiving age discrimination claims. It ruled that although the waiver would normally preclude the worker from suing the company, it did not cover discriminatory events that occurred *after* the waiver was signed and that illegal treatment had occurred.

Final Tip: The OWBPA provides possible legal protection if your employer offers you the opportunity to participate in a staff reduction program. I frequently represent groups of employees who are told they will be fired as part of a downsizing or reorganization. When you and other departing employees make a counteroffer (e.g., you request that the severance package currently on the table be tripled), your employer may be inclined to settle (e.g., at double the present offer) just to get rid of you and others and avoid a potential age discrimination lawsuit. Thus, if at all possible, try to negotiate the terms of your departure either separately or collectively with coworkers after receiving notification of a staff reduction.

Tax Treatment

Damages received for personal *physical* injury or sickness (e.g., a bleeding ulcer caused by workplace stress) pursuant to an award or out-of-court settlement of an age discrimination claim may be excludable from gross income and therefore not taxable. However, damages for back pay, liquidated damages, and damages for nonphysical personal injuries from emotional pain, sickness, or distress pursuant to the ADEA are taxable. As a result of a federal law enacted in 1996, money received as punitive damages is also taxable. Consult a knowledgeable lawyer for more advice on this subject where applicable.

Since most ADEA awards are not tax-free, they are treated as wages subject to FICA, FUTA, and income tax withholding. Employers who are liable for such awards may also be liable for tax penalties for failing to collect withholding on these awards and failing to pay the employer portion of FICA.

CHAPTER 3

Fired Because of Your Gender or Related Issues (Filing a Sexual Harassment Charge, Being Pregnant, or Taking Family Leave)

Jennifer worked as a salesperson for a successful real estate company. Over a period of time she was excluded from important sales meetings, business lunches, and strategic planning meetings. She observed that her male coworkers were not treated the same way. She claimed that the company made decisions that favored male colleagues and cost her over $400,000 in commissions.

Jennifer complained to management about the discriminatory treatment. She stated that senior managers removed her from accounts she had helped build and gave them to male brokers. Instead of responding sympathetically to her charges and treating her fairly, the employer retaliated by shutting her out of a deal involving a longtime client. The employer also began documenting alleged poor performance and productivity problems.

Jennifer was eventually fired from her job. The reason given was poor performance. Jennifer disagreed and sued her employer for sex discrimination. The court noted that her commission earnings were in the upper half of the sales force and that the employer's reason for discharging her was a pretext. She was awarded $7.1 million, which included a $5 million punitive damages award.

The above true New Jersey case illustrates how women are often treated unfairly by employers. Sex discrimination law encompasses many facets. The law mandates equal pay for equal work. It requires equal treatment, policies, standards, and practices for males and females in all phases of the employment relationship. For example, it is generally discriminatory in all states and under federal law to:

- Require females to resign from jobs upon marriage when there is no similar requirement for males
- Include spouses of male employees in benefit plans while denying the same benefits to spouses of female employees
- Restrict certain jobs to men without offering women a reasonable opportunity to demonstrate their ability to perform the same job adequately
- Refuse to hire, train, assign, or promote pregnant or married women or women of childbearing age on the basis of gender
- Deny unemployment or seniority benefits to pregnant women, or deny granting a leave of absence for pregnancy if similar leaves of absence are granted for illness
- Institute compulsory retirement plans with lower retirement ages for women than for men
- Fire women because of their gender

When a recently fired female employee consults with me, one of the first things I consider is whether she was fired because of gender. For example, I initially ask if the company has a history of laying off predominantly more senior female executives than male executives.

Suppose a company fired a sixty-year-old salesperson because she wasn't meeting quota. Although that sounds like a legitimate reason, the employer may be committing sex discrimination if its sales were down in many of its territories and younger, male salespeople were not fired but merely given a warning or placed on probation.

Suppose a female worker was fired for lateness. In such a case, careful investigation might reveal that male workers with the same record of absences and lateness were merely warned but not fired. What if a female employee was fired in retaliation for complaining that she did not receive the same benefits as her male counterparts? If this is proved, illegal discrimination may have occurred.

Tip: Although this chapter stresses gender-based discrimination problems, other forms of discrimination, including age, race, national origin, disability, and religious discrimination, may also be involved, because women who assert sex discrimination claims after a firing are often victimized by other personal characteristics.

THE LAW

Sex discrimination, also called gender discrimination, is legislated by Title VII of the Civil Rights Act of 1964 as well as by the revised Civil Rights Act of 1991. Gender discrimination covers a variety of subjects and is protected by many laws, including the Equal Pay Act of 1963, which makes it illegal to discriminate against women concerning salary or wages, and the Pregnancy Discrimination Act of 1978, which prohibits discrimination on the basis of pregnancy, childbirth, and related medical conditions and health benefits.

You may be the victim of gender discrimination when you receive disparate treatment (i.e., are treated differently from other employees), when you are denied employment opportunities primarily because you are a woman, or when the effect of a company policy or rule has a disproportionally negative effect on women in your company, causing an adverse impact. In certain cases, illegal sex discrimination arises if you are a woman who is passed over for a promotion and eventually fired because of your gender, because you filed a charge of sexual harassment, or because you were pregnant (and not because of work performance).

In certain instances, it is also possible for you to be constructively discharged from a job even if you quit. Cases have been reported of women who were forced to resign from jobs out of fear they would have to keep working for a supervisor who sexually harassed them. If you are in such a situation and you resign, you may be able to argue successfully that you were a victim of wrongful discharge.

Counsel Comments: A charge of gender discrimination, constructive discharge, and retaliation can be made if you are excluded from meetings, observe that promotions and senior management positions are given to less qualified men, and are fired or resign after complaining about such alleged illegal treatment. Being purposely excluded from new opportunities may constitute workplace bias and gender discrimination if you are fired from a job because of an alleged corporate restructuring or downsizing, are not rehired several months later following the termination, and learn that a less qualified male was offered your position. Consult an experienced employment lawyer for advice where warranted.

SEXUAL HARASSMENT

Another prohibited form of gender discrimination is sexual harassment. In 1986, the Supreme Court ruled that sexual harassment was actionable under Title VII of the Civil Rights Act of 1964. Many thousands of cases are filed yearly with the EEOC and state agencies. In fact, studies indicate that the vast majority of working women (more than 85 percent) believe they have been sexually harassed on the job at one time or another.

In one recent case, the EEOC obtained a $1.85-million settlement in a sexual harassment case on behalf of a group of ten women who had worked for a company as secretaries or executive assistants. The women complained that the company's chairman sought sexual favors in exchange for job benefits and had engaged in a pattern and practice of harassment against them by forcing them to discuss sex acts, touching them in their private parts, and committing other harmful acts. When they complained about the illegal behavior, they were fired.

Sexual harassment cases are on the rise in a variety of nontraditional areas. For example, the firing of a male employee for rejecting the advances of his homosexual male supervisor proved costly to one company. Recently, the U.S. Supreme Court ruled that same-sex sexual harassment is actionable. This clears the way for gay men and women who are sexually harassed by superiors or employees of the same sex to proceed with sexual harassment cases in federal and state courts.

Unwelcome sexual advances, requests for sexual favors, and verbal or physical conduct of a sexual nature all constitute sexual harassment when:

- The person must submit to such activity in order to be hired
- The person's consent or refusal is used in making an employment decision (e.g., to offer a promotion or to avoid being fired)
- Such conduct unreasonably interferes with the person's work performance or creates an intimidating, hostile, or offensive work-

ing environment (e.g., humiliating comments are repeatedly addressed to the complainant)

Defining what constitutes sexual harassment depends on the facts of each particular case. In *quid pro quo* cases (instances when employees of either sex are propositioned for sexual favors in order to receive a job or a promotion or not to be fired), the issue may be clear-cut. If an employee is passed over for a promotion or denied benefits in favor of another who submitted to sexual advances, the passed-over person is considered to be a victim of sexual harassment under federal and state guidelines.

If an employee initially participates in social or sexual contact, but then rejects continued unwelcome advances, that sometimes constitutes sexual harassment as well, and the fact that the employee did not regularly communicate her negative reaction may not exculpate the company from liability.

In hostile, intimidating, and unprofessional work environment cases, the issues are not always clear-cut. Typically, to establish a *prima facie* case, the employee must prove that:

1. She was subjected to unwelcome sexual conduct
2. The unwelcome sexual conduct was based on her gender
3. The unwelcome sexual conduct was sufficiently pervasive or severe to alter the terms and conditions of her employment and create an abusive or hostile working environment
4. The employer knew or should have known of the harassment and failed to take prompt and reasonable remedial action

Courts have ruled that the following constitute sexual harassment with respect to hostile, intimidating work environment cases:

- Extremely vulgar and sexually related epithets, jokes, or crusty language, provided the language is not isolated and is continuously stated to the complainant
- Sexually suggestive comments about an employee's attire or body
- Sexually degrading words describing an employee
- Repeated touching of the employee's body, provided the touching is unsolicited and unwelcome
- Showing lewd photographs or objects of a sexual nature to employees at the workplace

Sandra has a consensual sexual relationship with her boss, the company president. Sandra voluntarily continues the relationship for two years, knowing the president is married. She decides to call off the affair after he refuses to obtain a divorce and marry her.

The boss treats Sandra differently after her decision. He runs after and propositions her in front of coworkers at a company party. He regularly makes demeaning comments about her physical appearance at the office. Eventually, she is fired.

Sandra files a sexual harassment charge. The company argues that since the couple were lovers, no liability should ensue and that Sandra was fired for poor performance. Most important, since Sandra discussed her problems with a supervisor only once and never followed up her complaint or alerted management to more recent acts immediately after they ensued, the company states she contributed to such treatment.

A judge ruled the company failed to investigate her charges and take immediate action (probably because others were afraid to offend the president). All the company's defenses were rejected, and the judge ruled in Sandra's favor. The company fired the president as a result of his harmful, illegal acts and was required to pay Sandra a substantial amount of money and reimburse her for her lawyer's fees and costs.

- Offensive or repeated requests for dates even if such requests are made to the complainant after work
- Continued advances of a sexual nature that the employee rejects even after the parties break off a consensual sexual relationship

How the company investigates and acts on complaints is a major factor in determining whether it will end up in court and incur substantial damages. For example, in one case, after a company investigated a sexual harassment charge and found that it had merit, the employer did nothing further but warn the supervisor only once. When the supervisor continued his unlawful conduct (by showing lewd pictures to the complainant), the female worker quit her job and filed a complaint with the EEOC. She was awarded $48,000 when the court ruled that the company had failed to act on its investigation.

In the June 1998 term the Supreme Court clarified the law on sexual harassment in the workplace, making some lawsuits against employers easier to win while also possibly limiting the legal exposure of companies that have effective antiharassment policies in place (provided the effect of any harassment was not recognizable or severe). In a series of cases decided together, the Court first ruled that employers are *strictly liable* for the acts of their supervisors and managers when the harassment results in tangible harmful action, such as discharge, demotion, transfer, or other retaliation against the complainant. This is so regardless of whether the employer knew or should have known that harassment was taking place. Thus, when you can prove that serious harassment from a supervisor took place resulting in damages (such as a lost job opportunity), the employer will probably lose the case.

However, when there has been no detrimental action taken (for example, an employee, although propositioned repeatedly by a supervisor, refuses his advances and gets promoted anyway), an employee is allowed to proceed with a lawsuit and recover modest damages, but the employer may defend itself by proving it has taken reasonable care to prevent and promptly correct any sexually harassing behavior (such as by adopting an effective policy with a complaint procedure) and proving that the employee failed to take reasonable advantage of such corrective mechanisms by remaining silent instead of coming forward to complain.

As a result of these cases, courts will now carefully look to see if a comprehensive policy against sexual harassment was in place at the time the incidents occurred and whether the employer acted properly and promptly when notified of the complaint. When policies are vague or the complaint is not immediately and adequately investigated, or if the complainant is punished in any way for coming forward, the company may be found liable if the facts are true. Experts suggest that the practical effect of these rulings will be for employers to take a more active role in eliminating workplace harassment, such as by training workers to identify and prevent lewd behavior.

Counsel Comments: EEOC guidelines specify preventive affirmative steps that sometimes shield employers from liability. In determining whether an employer is liable, courts look to see if a comprehensive policy against sexual harassment was in place at the time the incident(s) occurred and whether the employer acted promptly and properly. When policies are vague or the incident is not immediately and adequately investigated, or if the employee is punished for coming forward, the company will probably be found liable if the facts are true.

Sexual harassment cases are dangerous to employers because some courts have ruled that companies are responsible for the acts of their supervisory employees regardless of whether the company knew or should have known of the occurrence. In *quid pro quo* cases involving supervisors, there is a good chance that an employer will be held strictly responsible for the actions of its supervisors, whether or not it knew the acts were occurring. In hostile-environment cases, companies are often liable for incidents they should have known about but didn't, when no effective action is taken to end the harassment, even if the company's official policies prohibit sexual harassment.

To avoid these and other potential legal hazards pertaining to sexual harassment cases, many employers have begun disseminating periodic reminders in policy manuals, journals, and letters distributed to employees that the company does not tolerate sexual harassment of any kind on the job, that anyone who experiences or observes such treatment must report this to management or their immediate supervisor (but not to the one doing the harassing) right away, and that all communications will be held in strict confidence with no direct or indirect reprisals to the informant or complainant.

Tip: Courts consider the nature and frequency of the acts, the conditions under which the conduct occurred, whether the company was promptly notified by the complainant, and what steps, if any, the company took after being notified. To prove a case of sexual harassment, it is *crucial* to take prompt steps to document your claim. For example, if you are being teased on the job, it is wise to complain to a supervisor or manager *in writing* immediately after the incident occurs. Judges, arbitrators, and EEOC hearing officers are more willing to award damages for sexual harassment when a formal complaint was made requesting that the offensive conduct stop and *the request was ignored*.

In one case, a woman was the only female traffic controller stationed at an air traffic center. While working there she was subjected to substantial sexual slurs, insults, and innuendo by other employees, including supervisory personnel. When the woman alerted her super-

LETTER PROTESTING SEXUAL HARASSMENT

Your Name
Address
Telephone Number
Date

Name of Supervisor or Officer
Title
Name of Employer
Address

Dear (name):

While working for the company, I have been the victim of a series of offensive acts that I believe constitute sexual harassment.

On (date), I (describe what occurred and with whom). I immediately (describe your reaction) and ordered that such conduct stop. However, on (date), another incident occurred when (describe what occurred and with whom).

I find such behavior intimidating and repugnant. In fact, (describe the physical and emotional impact on you), causing me to be less efficient on the job. Please treat this letter as a formal protest of such conduct. Unless such conduct ceases immediately, or in the event the company illegally retaliates against me for writing this letter, I will contact the Equal Employment Opportunity Commission to enforce my rights.

I do not wish to take such a drastic measure. All I want to do is perform my job in a professional environment.

Thank you for your cooperation in this matter.

Very truly yours,
Your Name

CONFIDENTIAL

Sent certified mail, return receipt requested

visors of this in a letter, several suggested that her problem might be solved if she "submitted to one of the controllers."

The court held that the woman proved that sexually harassing actions took place, that such acts were offensive and severe, and that the employer did little to stop them after receiving a warning through her letter. She was awarded substantial damages as a result. Thus, by sending a letter similar to the one on page 46, you may be able to prove a repetitive pattern of conduct and demonstrate that the offensive acts were not condoned.

Tip: By sending a letter, you notify the company of the allegations. When an employer does not properly investigate a claim, it can further compound the problem and be legally exposed. Most important, you have proof that you made a formal complaint. If the company then takes any negative action against you in retaliation, such as firing you or claiming that your work has become inadequate, you may be able to prove that the retaliation occurred after and because you sent the letter. (Just because you file a charge of sexual harassment does not mean that you are entitled to lifetime employment. In many circumstances, a court may rule that a subsequent firing is justified, but the burden is on the employer to demonstrate no illegal motive was involved.)

Send a copy of your letter to the president or another high officer of the company. Always keep a copy for your files. Save the receipt to prove delivery. If you think you are the victim of harassment, discuss the incident with other employees you trust to discover if they have suffered similar abuse. By doing so, you may strengthen a claim and be less at risk for making a complaint, since there is some safety in numbers. For example, it was recently reported that a sexual harassment and discrimination lawsuit against a well-known investment firm was amended to include twenty more women in a total of eleven states. The newest plaintiffs joined the action (which was started by one woman only) and alleged they had been subjected to lewd language and unwelcome touching and were denied opportunities and privileges afforded men. The suit seeks class-action status on behalf of all women employed by the firm, in part for the company's permitting the alleged explicit sexual talk to occur in the basement of one of its offices. The case was recently settled, reportedly for several million dollars.

If possible, collect and save evidence (e.g., the pornographic pictures shown to you). Maintain a diary of all incidents of harassment recalling the location, events, time, persons involved, and names of any witnesses who may have observed the illegal conduct. Recall whether supervisors participated in creating or tolerating a sexually poisoned atmosphere.

Speak to an experienced employment lawyer immediately if:

- The matter is not resolved satisfactorily
- You are retaliated against for making a complaint, such as being demoted, reassigned, denied benefits or a promotion, given an unfavorable job evaluation, or fired
- You feel uncomfortable while being questioned about the events (i.e., the company is not conducting a fair and unbiased investigation and is accusing you of contributing to or causing the harassment by your dress, behavior, or language)
- The employer fails to take speedy action to investigate your complaints
- You want to pursue money damages for stress, mental suffering, and physical injuries caused or induced by the harassment
- The company mistakenly determines that no harassment occurred, that the acts do not constitute harassment, that it had no knowledge of the incident and thus is not responsible, or fails to make a decision in an objective manner
- The employer disparages your character, job performance, or family life
- The employer refuses to allow you to grieve the incident through its complaint procedures

An experienced lawyer can tell you whether it makes sense to confront the harasser, use a company complaint procedure, immediately file a claim in court or with an appropriate federal agency (such as the EEOC) or a state agency, or if it is more desirable and/or advantageous to contact the employer and try to settle the matter out of court.

Counsel Comments: Most states have laws that expressly prohibit sexual harassment; there are occasions when it may be advantageous to apply state law and file charges with a state agency instead of the EEOC. Talk to your lawyer about this. Consider filing a private tort lawsuit for assault, battery, or infliction of emotional distress if you are touched, kissed, or rubbed without your consent. The advantage of being able to file a lawsuit is that you may receive greater damages for your injuries and may be able to file a charge more than three hundred days after the acts occurred. Claimants who are not able to file a discrimination charge because the statute of limitations has expired may still be able to commence a private lawsuit in some cases. (By law, you are required to file a charge of discrimination with the EEOC within 180 days of the incident.)

In any event, do not be afraid to assert your rights when subjected to conduct you find uncomfortable. Implement some course of strategy immediately so that you don't suffer more abuse and to protect your rights in this area. If you delay contacting an appropriate agency or a lawyer, your inactivity may be viewed as a waiver of your rights or an acceptance of such illegal acts, which can jeopardize a claim.

SEXUAL BIAS DISCRIMINATION

Some states and municipalities have passed laws that forbid employers from discriminating on the basis of an individual's sexual preference, although such discrimination is not recognized by federal law. A lesbian or homosexual faced with hostile conduct, denied employment opportunities, or fired primarily because of sexual orientation should seek legal advice about relevant state and local ordinances and rulings. Lawyers representing gays and lesbians who practice in states where sexual bias discrimination statutes do not exist are suing employers and supervisors for invasion of privacy and other causes of action.

WORK-RELATED STRESS

Work-related stress caused by on-the-job nonsexual harassment resulting in documented physical and mental injuries can give rise to a valid legal claim, especially when you are forced to resign. Some female claimants have also successfully asserted that such conduct is a form of sex discrimination when the acts complained of were directed to them because of their gender. When the same treatment is not directed to males, a charge of disparate sex discrimination can be asserted.

Tip: It is often easier to win *sex-related* harassment cases because the law specifically authorizes claimants to collect damages for illegal acts and proof of physical or mental injuries is not necessary. For nonsexual harassing acts, you must prove the acts were so severe that they caused you harm (e.g., forced you to quit). This is often difficult to do. I am consulted by numerous female clients each year who request legal assistance as a result of nonsexual harassment (such as for verbal abuse from a supervisor). Most of the time I decline representation because the law does not ordinarily provide protection. In most situations, perhaps the best strategy is to discuss the problem with someone from personnel and request that the harassment stop. Many supervisors are cognizant of the potential causes of action arising from physical and mental distress claims and are instructed to avoid contributing to these problems where possible. You can also write the company a letter protesting such activity. If you do, however, you may be fired for making a complaint and the law may not protect you in this area.

Confer with a lawyer to explore your options if you are the victim of extensive nonsexual harassment. The lawyer may advise you to consult a physician, take prescribed medication, or institute other steps without delay to prove the extent of your injuries and enforce a claim. For example, a workers' compensation claim was awarded to a female employee whose mental troubles arose because she was repeatedly singled out for public criticism and who proved that coworkers were not subjected to this treatment. The employee eventually developed a fear of going to work, which led to a disabling "panic disorder."

DISCRIMINATION IN BENEFITS

Sex discrimination laws also apply to benefits. Retirement, pension plans, and fringe benefits must be equally applied, since any program that favors one sex over another violates federal and state discrimination laws. Be aware that the following practices have been declared illegal in the application of fringe benefits pertaining to vacations, insurance coverage, pensions, profit-sharing plans, bonuses, holidays, and disability leaves:

- Conditioning benefits available to employees and their spouses and families on a particular status (e.g., "head of household" or "principal wage earner")
- Making certain benefits available to wives of male employees but denying them to husbands of female employees

- Basing provisions of a pension plan on norms applied differently according to gender
- Denying a job or benefit to pregnant employees or applicants

These are just some of the ways employers commit violations relating to benefits. If you have doubts about any current practices, seek competent legal advice.

HIRING INTERVIEWS

Many employers ask illegal questions of females at job interviews, particularly with respect to their marital status. EEOC guidelines and most state regulations declare that the only lawful question that may be asked of a female applicant at an interview or on a job application form is "What is your marital status?" It is a good idea to familiarize yourself with the kinds of questions that are illegal at job interviews. If you refuse to answer such questions and are denied a job, you may want to consider filing charges with the EEOC or an appropriate state human rights organization or agency alleging sex discrimination on the basis of such illegal inquiries.

Finally, recognize that female independent contractors (such as insurance agents) cannot sue for sex discrimination under the laws of many states. This means that if you were fired because of your sex but were an independent contractor, you may not prevail regardless of the facts of your case.

PREGNANCY DISCRIMINATION

In 1978, Congress enacted the Pregnancy Discrimination Act (PDA) as an amendment to Title VII. Specifically, the PDA provides that pregnancy-based discrimination falls within the confines of Title VII's prohibition of gender-based discrimination. The PDA prohibits discrimination by employers based on pregnancy, childbirth, or related medical conditions.

Thousands of pregnancy-related discrimination lawsuits are filed each year; the kind of mistreatment varies. Experts suggest that staff cuts and management overhauls have given companies opportunities to save money by unloading workers whose personal circumstances, they think, may require special attention. Some pregnant workers who return to work do not suffer outright terminations, but come back to positions with fewer responsibilities and get pushed off the fast track.

In one recent case, a female lawyer sued her former employer. The case was settled out of court just before the jury gave its verdict. She claimed that the law firm refused to give her work after she returned from maternity leave. Shortly after her return to work, she was told that she was required to leave the Tokyo office where she was stationed. She refused and was eventually fired.

Her employer argued that the decision was purely one of economics, since it could not afford to keep the Tokyo office open. Jury members, however, did not believe that line of defense. The jury was incensed by the law firm's lack of effort in finding another office to which she could transfer. They also heard testimony from fellow employees who overheard a managing partner say that women who have children do not return to work with the same commitment to their jobs.

Pregnant workers also get fired. In one recent reported case, six workers who said they were laid off after asking for lighter duties because of pregnancy sued their employer in federal district court. One of the plaintiffs, a train operator, asked for light-duty assignment when she announced her pregnancy. According to the court papers, she was then placed on involuntary unpaid leave despite the fact that she was ready, willing, and able to continue working and that appropriate work was available. The suit also charged that the women who were laid off were unable to collect unemployment insurance because the employer advised the unemployment insurance department that they had gone on voluntary leaves. The employer argued that no employee is allowed to remain on light duty longer than fourteen days, whether pregnant or disabled by any other condition. The case has yet to be decided by a judge.

Although pregnant workers have been subject to poor treatment from employers in the past, the laws are now attempting to put pregnant women on equal footing with other employees. While it is estimated that approximately 84 percent of women expecting children work into the final month of pregnancy and that approximately one-third return to work within eight weeks and half return within three months after giving birth, millions of women have lost their jobs after giving birth. Fortunately, as a result of the passage of the Family and Medical Leave Act (discussed in the next section), pregnant women who work for employers with more than fifty full-time employees are guaranteed equivalent jobs when they return.

Winning a pregnancy discrimination case after a firing is often difficult, and women lose their claims because they fail to prove their case or fail to ask for accommodations beyond the minimum provided by law. During an economic downturn, employers often attempt to mask pregnancy discrimination as layoffs and downsizing, which often makes it harder to prove the underlying discriminatory motivation.

The following two cases illustrate the problems often associated with winning pregnancy discrimination lawsuits.

In one case, a woman nineteen weeks pregnant asked for reassignment to a job that did not require heavy lifting. She was given a job at the service desk, which required evening and weekend work. She was unable to work those hours because of family conflicts and declined the assignment. The company fired her and she sued for pregnancy discrimination. She lost her case because she failed to prove a disparate impact (i.e., that other employees who were reassigned for medical reasons and objected were not terminated). The judge commented that the law does not *guarantee* that pregnant workers not suffer any adverse employment decisions. He wrote that "the law protects against employment decisions which, for discriminatory reasons, are different from decisions relating to persons who are not pregnant."

In another case, a female salesperson suffered severe morning sickness during her first trimester and was often late in reporting to work. The woman was placed on part-time status but continued to report to work late. After several warnings and being placed on probation, the company fired her. Although she was fired one day before taking maternity leave, the court ruled that fact did not warrant a finding of liability because the company was free to fire anyone who could not work due to a medical condition, whether pregnant or otherwise.

Counsel Comments: This case is significant for several reasons. The salesperson's case might have been strengthened if she had found other nonpregnant workers who had not been fired due to excessive absences or right before taking a leave of absence. And although the company was guilty of poor timing, the woman failed to introduce significant evidence at the trial, including damaging statements made to her indicating that the reason given for the firing (i.e., excessive lateness) was really pretextual (i.e., unfounded) and offered just as an excuse to terminate because she was pregnant. Given the absence of important comparisons and other evidence, she lost her case. This is the kind of evidence you may be required to prove with your lawyer for success in any pregnancy discrimination case.

Speak to a competent employment lawyer if you think you have been discriminated against on the basis of pregnancy. Women who are fired while pregnant should naturally suspect that pregnancy was the reason for the discharge. Consider filing a claim alleging pregnancy discrimination with the EEOC or an appropriate antidiscrimination state agency. This is free and you do not need a lawyer to assist you in the process. How to file a discrimination charge is discussed in Chapter 5.

Employers are often advised that even when a decision to fire has nothing to do with a woman's pregnancy, it may be wise to continue her employment until she voluntarily leaves to give birth, rather than fire her several months before the birth, to avoid the added costs and burdens of contesting a charge of pregnancy discrimination. Employers are also advised by their attorneys that if they must fire a pregnant worker, they should be sure that her file supports the decision (i.e., that unfavorable job performance appraisals and repeated written warnings are present in the file) and that the worker was repeatedly warned about her performance before the company was notified of her pregnancy.

Tip: It is strongly recommended that you tell your supervisor and other bosses immediately after you learn you are pregnant. Some litigants lose their cases because they cannot prove that the company knew they were pregnant before taking adverse action. Once you become pregnant, you enter a protected class under the law, and the company may have to reevaluate any decision to fire you if that was being considered before the news. Thus, recognize that in marginal performance cases, becoming pregnant could give a woman added job security. Do not be afraid to tell key people at the job site that you are pregnant, because this may work to your legal benefit and strengthen a claim.

PREGNANCY AS A DISABILITY

The ability of pregnant workers to succeed in demanding special accommodations has been strengthened by the passage of state and local laws. Although the federal Americans with Disabilities Act does not consider pregnancy a covered disability (since it is classified as a temporary nonchronic impairment with no long-term impact), some state laws have ruled it is a *per se* disability requiring a company to make reasonable accommodation when requested by an employee. Under these state laws, the physical demands of pregnancy may require companies to allow pregnant workers to work at home or to rearrange their work schedules. When a woman seeks reasonable accommodation during pregnancy, an employer should be responsive to the particular physical limitations that the employee brings forward on a case-by-case basis. Employers unwilling to comply with such a request are required to justify their decisions by demonstrating that compliance would create an undue hardship.

Tip: Check your state's law on this issue to understand the extent of protection available to you. If you find the law is favorable, consider requesting reasonable accommodation (such as reporting to work an hour later each day or being allowed to work from bed if you risk losing a baby without extensive bed rest). Speak to a lawyer for more details.

PREGNANCY LEAVE, OTHER UNPAID LEAVE, AND REEMPLOYMENT

Even before the enactment of the federal Family and Medical Leave Act (FMLA) in 1993, the right of pregnant workers to have their jobs back within a certain period of time after giving birth and the ability to enforce the right to take paid maternity leave were being recognized in a number of states. Passage of the FMLA now guarantees that pregnant workers who work for companies with fifty or more employees will get their jobs back after birth. The act affects private and nonprofit employers as well as federal, state, and local government employers. It applies to companies that employed fifty or more employees within a seventy-five-mile radius for each working day for each of twenty or more calendar workweeks in the current or preceding calendar year. This is about half the nation's workforce. Part-time employees and employees on leaves of absence are counted in this calculation provided they are on the employer's payroll for each day of the workweek. Employees who began employment after the beginning of a workweek, were terminated prior to the end of a workweek, or who worked part-time on weekends are not included in the equation.

Since companies with fewer than fifty employees are exempt, analyzing the number of employees who must be counted becomes an important consideration for organizations close to the "magic" fifty number. If a company hires temporary contract employees or part-time workers who work twenty-five or fewer hours a week to get under the number, they will not be subject to the law's provisions.

An eligible employee, defined as someone who has been employed for at least twelve months and worked for the employer at least 1,250 hours during the twelve-month period immediately preceding the commencement of the leave, is allowed to take up to twelve weeks of unpaid leave in any twelve-month period for the birth of a child; the adoption of a child; to care for a child, a dependent son or daughter over the age of eighteen, a spouse, or a parent with a serious health condition; or to convalesce from a serious condition that makes it impossible for the employee to work.

The twelve months of employment need not have been consecutive. Additionally, some employees who require continuing medical supervision (e.g., workers with early-stage cancer or who have had major heart surgery) and must undergo frequent medical examinations or treatment but are nonetheless capable of working part-time still fit into the category of suffering from a "serious health condition" and qualify for leave time. Women who qualify are required to give thirty days' advance notice unless this is not practical, such as in a premature birth or sudden, unexpected illness.

The law applies equally to female and male employees. Thus, a father as well as a mother can take family leave, at the same time or sequentially, depending on the family's preferences and economic considerations. (If both spouses work for the same company, the law limits the total maximum amount of leave to twelve weeks for both in most situations.)

For workers who claim serious health situations, the law permits an employer to obtain medical opinions and certifications regarding the need for a leave. The certification must state the date on which the serious health condition began, its probable duration, the appropriate medical facts within the knowledge of the health care provider regarding the condition, and an estimate of the amount of time an employee needs to care for a family member or herself. If an employer has doubts about the certification, it may require a second opinion from a different health care provider chosen by the employer. If the two opinions differ, a third opinion from a provider jointly designated or approved by the employer and the employee will be final and binding.

The key element of the law allows a person taking leave to be given her old job back or assigned an equivalent position, with equivalent benefits, pay, and other terms and conditions of employment, when she returns. The burden is on the employer to give the worker back her same or an equivalent job (not a comparable job) wherever possible. Moreover, no employer may deprive an employee of benefits accrued before the date on which the leave commenced. During the time the worker is on leave, an employer is not required to pay her but is required to maintain health insurance benefits as well as life and disability insurance, pensions, educational benefits, and any annual sick leave that has accrued prior to the commencement of the family leave, at the level and under the conditions coverage would have been maintained if the employee had continued in employment. However, if the employer was legitimately about to lay off the worker just before being notified of the leave, the employee's right of reinstatement is no greater than what it was when the discharge was contemplated.

Counsel Comments: Nothing requires an employer to provide health benefits if it does not do so at the time the employee commences leave. However, if the employer was considering establishing a health plan during the employee's leave, the worker on leave is entitled to receive the same benefits other workers still on the job receive. In addition, an employer has the right to demand repayment for group health care premiums that it has paid during the leave if the employee fails to return after the period of leave to which she is entitled has expired and the reason was not caused by a recurrence or onset of a serious health condition or other circumstances beyond the employee's control.

There are numerous exceptions to be aware of. First, the FMLA prohibits a worker on leave from collecting unemployment or other government compensation. Part-time workers and those who have not worked for at least a year do not qualify. Furthermore, an eligible employee may elect, or an employer is permitted, to substitute any paid vacation leave, personal leave, or family leave accrued by the employee under preestablished policies in handbooks or employee manuals for any part of the twelve-week period of family leave. As a result, companies are required to provide both paid and unpaid leave only up to a total of twelve weeks and may count time off against paid vacation days or other accrued personal leave.

Generally, the leave requested may not be intermittent or on a reduced schedule without the employer's permission or except when medically necessary; employers are permitted to require an employee taking intermittent leave as a result of planned medical treatments to prove the medical necessity for the leave and to transfer temporarily to an equivalent alternative position. Thus, for example, employers may have the right to demand that pregnant workers take the time off in a continuous period and then return. This provision gives employers greater staffing flexibility by enabling them to transfer employees who need intermittent leave or leave on a reduced schedule to positions that are more suitable for recurring periods of leave.

If you are a top executive (defined as being in the highest 10 percent of the company's payroll), the company may refuse your request to take a leave when it would cause substantial economic harm. If you nonetheless take the leave, you are still eligible for continuation of medical benefits, but the company is *not* obligated to take you back or guarantee that an appropriate job will be available on your return. However, in such situations, no recovery of premiums may be made by the employer if the employee has chosen to take or continue leave after being denied her request for leave because she is still ill or needs to continue the care of a relative or child. (If the employee does not come back because she took a better-paying job, the company can lawfully demand repayment.)

Although many situations may be important or qualify as emergencies (e.g., having to accompany your child to an out-of-state college or take care of a sick grandparent for several weeks), they may not be covered under the law. While you are out, you must report regularly to your employer and advise when you think you will be returning.

Tip: Speak to a knowledgeable lawyer if you return from pregnancy leave or unpaid child care leave to a different position. This is advised because receiving a job of equal pay and grade may still violate the law if it is a different job.

The U.S. Secretary of Labor has the authority to investigate alleged violations of the FMLA. This includes requesting employers to submit

Joan works for a large company as a supervisor. She takes unpaid leave to care for her sick husband. When she returns ten weeks later, she is given a new job at the same rate of pay. But the new job has fewer duties (she supervises only two people instead of five), and she is required to perform clerical functions not present in her prior position. Joan advises management that she is dissatisfied with her new position and that the company has violated the FMLA by not giving her her old job or an equivalent one back. The company states that it reorganized her department while she was on leave.

Joan consults a lawyer for advice. Rather than sue her employer, she is told to first try to negotiate better benefits. Joan listens to the lawyer. She receives another week of paid vacation, an office with a window, a prime parking spot, and her employer's promise not to terminate her for at least two years. She is also promised her old job back if it becomes available. Joan is pleased with her negotiation efforts.

their books and records for inspection. Violations are punishable by injunctive and monetary relief. For employers who violate the law, monetary damages include an amount equal to the wages, salary, employment benefits, or other compensation denied or lost to an employee. In cases where no compensation or wages are lost, the law imposes other forms of damages, such as the actual amount of out-of-pocket money incurred in paying someone else to provide care. In the event a willful violation is proved, employers are liable for additional damages equal to the amount of the award. The law also imposes reasonable attorney fees, expert-witness fees, and other costs and disbursements. Employers are forbidden from discriminating against workers who attempt to utilize the act or who protest alleged violations. Similarly, it is unlawful to retaliate against any worker by discharge or reduced benefits because he or she has filed a charge or instituted a proceeding concerning the law or is about to give (or has given) testimony regarding the FMLA.

Counsel Comments: In the event your state law is more comprehensive or offers greater benefits than federal law, state law will control. State or local laws that provide greater protection, longer leave periods, or paid leave are enforceable, so check the law in your state. You may also discover, for example, that state law applies to smaller-size employers (i.e., those with twenty or more full-time employees).

Tip: The FMLA cannot rescind rights granted to employees in collective bargaining agreements, pension plans, ERISA rights, or rights granted as a result of the ADA and other discrimination laws. If you believe you have been discriminated or retaliated against by asserting your rights, speak to a lawyer. You have the option of commencing a private lawsuit and seeking money to pay for a caregiver's bills (for up to twelve weeks) if you were denied leave, provided you bring the action within two years of the date of the violation or three years if the violation is willful. You can also sue for job reinstatement and resulting damages if you are illegally denied a leave, take it anyway, and are not given your old job back when you want to return. An employer may appeal negative results of an investigation by the Department of Labor. All your options and rights should be explained to you by your lawyer to map out an effective action plan.

FINAL WORDS ABOUT PREGNANCY

Employers cannot treat pregnancy-related disability or maternity leave differently from the way they treat other forms of disability or leaves of absence. To do so violates both federal and state discrimination laws. The law requires employers to review their health, disability, insurance, sick leave, benefit, job reinstatement, and seniority policies to ensure that they treat pregnancy-related disability and maternity leaves of absence the same as other temporary absences for physical disabilities.

What Employers May and May Not Do

The following general rules illustrate what employers may and may not do in this area:

- Employees who are on maternity leave (defined as the child care period commencing after disability from the pregnancy and birth has

Employees at one company were granted basic hospital, surgical, and major medical benefits under the company's health insurance plan. Employees and their dependents were reimbursed 100 percent of the charges for basic medical care with the exception that wives of male employees were reimbursed for pregnancy-related charges at the rate of only 80 percent of the actual charges. Benefits for dependents terminated at the same time as those for employees except for pregnancy benefits for dependent spouses. A spouse of a male employee was covered for maternity expenses throughout her pregnancy, even if it extended for more than three months after her husband's termination.

Marsha, terminated because of a business slowdown, learns she is pregnant a few weeks after her dismissal. She participates in the three-month continuation of the medical plan and then requests medical benefits for her pregnancy equal to those provided to the wives of male employees under the company's health insurance plan. The company rejects her claim.

Marsha hires a lawyer and commences a lawsuit charging sex discrimination. In court, the company argues that benefits to a female employee could be different from those granted to the spouse of a male employee and that her claim confused discrimination between employees (which the law forbids) with discrimination between an employee and a nonemployee spouse (which the law allows).

The court rules in Marsha's favor. It states that it is an unlawful employment practice for an employer to make available benefits for the wives and families of male employees where the same benefits are not made available for the husbands and families of female employees, or to make available benefits for the wives of male employees that are not made available for female employees.

ended) are entitled to accrue seniority, automatic pay increases, and vacation time on the same basis as other employees on medical leave.
• Employers may not require pregnant workers to exhaust vacation benefits before receiving sick pay or disability benefits unless all temporarily disabled workers are required to do the same.

- Employers may require a physical examination and doctor's certification of ability to return to work only if this is required of all temporarily disabled workers.
- Although employers may require workers to give notice of a pregnancy, such a requirement must serve a legitimate business purpose and must not be used to restrict the employee's job opportunities.
- Employers are prohibited from discriminating in hiring, promotion, and firing decisions on the basis of pregnancy or because of an abortion.
- After the birth, an employer cannot prohibit a woman from returning to work sooner than company policy dictates.
- Employers are barred from forcing pregnant workers to take mandatory maternity leaves (i.e., forcing a woman to leave work against her wishes in anticipation of giving birth) as long as the employee is able to do her job.
- The decision as to whether payment for pregnancy disability leave will be given must be in accord with policies governing other forms of disability leave; if paid leave is provided for workers with other disabilities, the employer must provide pregnant workers with paid leave for their actual disability due to pregnancy and related childbirth.
- Time restrictions placed on pregnancy-related leaves (e.g., that pregnancy leaves not exceed four months) must be reasonable and job-related; if not, they may be illegal. In addition, employers are generally required to provide disability benefits for as long as a pregnant woman is unable to work for medical reasons.
- It is illegal to place pregnant workers on involuntary sick leave if the company has no policy of placing workers with other forms of disabilities on involuntary leave; if a worker is physically able to work, the company cannot force her to leave merely because she is pregnant.
- An employer cannot refuse to hire a pregnant worker because it does not want to find a replacement when the employee takes a leave to give birth if her skills and qualifications meet or exceed those of other applicants.
- Women who take maternity leave must be reinstated under the same conditions as employees who return from leaves for other disabilities. For example, if an employer reinstates a worker who was absent from work due to a case of chronic bronchitis, the employer must reinstate a worker after childbirth to avoid violating Title VII.

- If an employer accommodates partially disabled workers who cannot perform certain job assignments (such as lifting heavy objects because of a strained back), the employer is obligated to make similar arrangements for a pregnant worker.
- Employers cannot limit pregnancy disability benefits to married employees. Federal law states it is illegal to fire female workers who get married if the employer does not fire male workers who get married. Many state laws have gone even further to protect women; statutes have been enacted that prohibit employers from making any adverse decisions on the basis of a person's marital status even if the employer applies its policies equally to males and females.
- At the hiring interview, you cannot be asked questions about childbearing plans or pregnancy.
- Employers are not allowed to ask a pregnant employee to choose between a lower-level job and resignation.

Tip: The above rules may or may not apply depending on the law and the particular facts and circumstances of your case. Know your rights regarding pregnancy and when you want to return to work after giving birth. Time and time again, women are fired after returning from maternity leave. Typically, firms will cite a poor attitude, tough economic times, or declining work quality to support their decision. You should point to excellent work reviews and argue that the employer has invented or magnified the criticisms (and possibly prepared phony documentation for your personnel file) from the moment you announced your pregnancy. Always consult an experienced employment lawyer for advice and guidance.

CHAPTER 4

Fired Because of Your Handicap, Race, Religious Beliefs, or in Retaliation for Filing a Charge of Discrimination

Mary worked in a small office with five other employees. Often she did not get along with her coworkers. During one heated argument, a coworker told her that she was acting "like a bitch in heat" and that he was not happy working with her.

Mary reported the incident to a supervisor. Later that day, she was called to the human relations department. Instead of being asked about the incident, she was reprimanded about her performance and the operations at her office. One week later, she was fired.

Mary filed a retaliation lawsuit in state court. She claimed that her former employer fired her for complaining about working in a hostile environment and suffering the vulgar comments of coworkers. The employer argued that she was fired because she wasn't a team player and for poor performance.

A jury returned a verdict in Mary's favor and awarded her $60,000 in back pay as lost wages and benefits, $5,000 in compensatory damages for emotional pain and suffering, seven weeks' front pay, attorney fees, and interest. Mary's verdict was sustained on appeal.

In this chapter, you will learn how to recognize if you have been fired illegally as a result of a disability, your race, or your religion or in retaliation for complaining about discrimination to management. You will learn how to file a claim effectively and increase your chances of a successful outcome if discrimination has occurred.

HANDICAP DISCRIMINATION

The federal Americans with Disabilities Act (ADA) was enacted in 1990 to widen the scope of protection available to disabled workers. Employers with more than fifteen workers must avoid disability discrimination in all phases of the job. In many states, people who work in small firms (i.e., those having five or more employees) are also protected against disability discrimination under more stringent state laws, so it is important to be familiar with your state's law as well.

Employers are required to eliminate any inquiries on medical examinations and forms designed to identify an applicant's disabilities. Employers cannot deny employment opportunities to an employee because of the need to make reasonable accommodation for a disability, and persons with disabilities cannot be fired because of the inability to perform nonessential or marginal functions of the job.

The main object of the ADA is to protect any person with a physical or mental impairment that substantially limits one or more life activities. This covers a broad range of disabilities, including deafness, AIDS, cancer, and learning disabilities. It does not include compulsive gambling or pregnancy. (State law may be more inclusive as to what constitutes a covered disability, so speak to a lawyer for more details.)

Every aspect of the employment relationship is protected, from employee compensation, terms, and privileges to job classifications, fringe benefits, promotions, training opportunities, and discharge. Although the ADA does not require an employer to give preferential consideration to persons with disabilities, such persons cannot be excluded for consideration for a raise, a promotion, or an on-the-job opportunity because of an inability to perform a marginal function. The law also states that persons associated with those who have a disability, such as an individual who does volunteer work with AIDS patients, cannot be fired because of that relationship or association.

The law does *not* cover workers who cannot work because of a total disability; the law protects only workers with disabilities who are capable of *continuing* working if the employer provides reasonable accommodation. On-the-job accommodations that must be provided to handicapped employees include:

- Restructuring or modifying work schedules
- Offering part-time work
- Permitting the employee to work at home
- Reassigning an individual to a vacant position
- Providing readers or interpreters for blind or deaf persons
- Acquiring or altering equipment or devices
- Making existing facilities readily accessible to the disabled
- Adjusting marginal job requirements
- Allowing flexibility in arrival and departure times for people who require special vehicles for transportation or who are confined to wheelchairs

Employers are required to make such accommodations only if the disability is known, if the accommodation requested is reasonable, and if the employee is truly partially disabled. An employer is relieved of responsibility to accommodate a disabled employee when to do so would impose an undue hardship. Factors considered in determining whether undue hardship exists include the nature and the costs of the accommodation to the employer, the overall financial resources of the employer (i.e., number of employees, overall size of the business, etc.), and other related factors. Courts will look at the type of operation, overall size, budget, profitability of the employer, and the financial impact of the suggested accommodation in determining whether undue hardship exists. The facts concerning what constitutes undue hardship vary from case to case; however, if the employer can afford to accommodate, it must generally do so.

As a result of the ADA and various state laws, employers now have enhanced obligations to current employees who develop disabilities while working. In particular, wrongful discharge of workers who contract the AIDS virus, develop alcohol problems affecting their attendance or performance, or even become obese can result in severe penalties. (Under the ADA, while you cannot be refused a job or be fired because of past drug addiction, there is no protection for current drug use. You can be legally terminated for using drugs on the job or working in an impaired state because of current drug use.)

You can be legally terminated for taking an excessive amount of time off due to illness. In one recent case, an employee called in sick over two dozen times in an eighteen-month period. According to *Personnel Legal Alert*, the newsletter that reported the case, each time her sick leave was approved she was warned that her excessive absenteeism could lead to discipline or termination.

The woman was eventually fired because of her chronic absences. She sued the company in court and argued that the firing was illegal because each legitimate absence had been approved as sick leave. But the court ruled against her. It said that in order to prevail, she would have to prove that the employer acted in retaliation against her for using sick leave benefits. But it was her absences, not her use of sick leave, that got her fired.

Although employers are generally permitted to terminate workers who become completely disabled, they must give handicapped workers the opportunity to work at less demanding jobs or offer other accommodations. Employers must also provide such workers with existing short- or long-term disability benefits and other medical coverage (as well as an enhanced severance package if the worker can negotiate it) before they leave. Thus, always try to obtain the best post-termination benefits if you are fired and possess a disability.

Counsel Comments: I have represented many clients who were considered an important asset of the firm until they announced a disabling medical condition, such as skin cancer. I have noticed that employers then often began treating such individuals differently—for example, not inviting them to frequent lunches, not giving them periodic raises, or leaving them out of the loop. This kind of unfair treatment is subtle, but its victims are probably not imagining it. If you feel you were treated differently or were fired after becoming disabled, contact a lawyer immediately to discuss your rights and options.

For example, in a boost to the rights of cancer patients undergoing chemotherapy, the New York State Division of Human Rights recently awarded $70,000 to a legal secretary who was fired after her treatment for breast cancer began. In this case, the woman missed three days of work following a mastectomy. After three days of half-time work, she resumed working full days. A few weeks later, she took one day off because she felt weak from chemotherapy. She returned and worked full-time the rest of the week but was fired a week later.

She sued her former law firm employer in state court because the five-attorney firm was too small to be covered under the federal ADA. She was awarded $20,000 in lost pay for the year following her dismissal and $50,000 for mental anguish. The state human rights agency noted that she lost her job even though she had enough sick days to cover the time projected to be lost due to ongoing treatments. The agency also noted that while someone suffering from an illness must still be able to perform his or her job in a reasonable manner (which is not defined as flawlessly or with perfect attendance), employers have an affirmative duty to reasonably accommodate a disabled employee.

Counsel Comments: This state case is important because some federal ADA cases involving cancer patients are not successful or do not result in large verdicts. However, it appears that this kind of harsh treatment may be common on the part of small employers, so always consult an employment lawyer.

Although it is permissible to fire workers who use illegal drugs, alcoholism is considered a protected disability. Generally, workers *cannot* be fired for drinking excessively off-premises if they are participating in an alcohol rehabilitation program. An employer may prohibit the use of illegal drugs and alcohol at the workplace and require that employees not be under the influence of alcohol while at work (since they may be considered a direct threat to the health or safety of other workers or customers). However, employers must understand that since alcoholism is considered a disability and protected under the ADA, every effort must be made to avoid making an adverse decision.

For example, some lawyers recommend that companies offer counseling before discharge. If the employee refuses counseling, the employer should offer a choice of alcohol-related treatment or discipline and should not take any adverse action during the period of a rehabilitation program. In case of relapse, employers may consider some additional discipline short of discharge to adequately protect themselves in this area.

Recently, the EEOC issued guidelines for applying the ADA in psychiatric disability cases. The EEOC has determined that workers suffering from mental or psychological disorders, including schizophrenia, major depression, and stress disorders, must be treated the same as workers with physical disabilities, requiring employers to provide reasonable accommodations. The guidelines state that some medications for psychiatric disabilities cause extreme grogginess and lack of concentration (especially in the morning) and employers may be required to allow an employee with such a condition to start work later in the day or provide extra unpaid time off. Other options include providing a temporary job coach or modifying workplace procedures, such as providing employees with written instructions if they have trouble following oral instructions.

Counsel Comments: You can still be fired (for gross misconduct, for example) even if your mental disability was the cause of the act (e.g., stealing). But some experts suggest that these guidelines will unfairly help a person who doesn't get along with coworkers to hire a doctor to say that he or she has a mental disability, thus making it much more difficult legally to be fired. The benefit to employees is that the EEOC regulations now significantly expand protections for mental disabilities as a recent case demonstrates.

In that case, after one employee started receiving medical treatment for manic-depression, he asked his employer of fourteen years to adjust his work schedule to the day shift only, rather than nights and sometimes days. This was based on a doctor's advice that he needed a regular sleeping pattern. Shortly after making the request, he was fired. He sued the company under the ADA and obtained a six-figure settlement.

Tip: Always seek the advice of a knowledgeable employment lawyer if you believe you were fired or treated unfairly because of a bona fide physical or mental disability.

RACE DISCRIMINATION

Title VII of the Civil Rights Act and various other federal and state laws prohibit intentional discrimination based on ancestry or ethnicity. Some employers practice blatant forms of minority discrimination by paying lower salaries and other compensation to blacks and Hispanics. Others engage in quota systems by denying promotions and jobs to individuals on the basis of race or color. Federal laws prohibit employers of fifteen or more employees from discriminating on the basis of race or color. Virtually all states have even stronger antidiscrimination laws directed toward fighting job-related race and minority discrimination. In some states, companies with fewer than fifteen employees can be found guilty of discrimination.

Both federal and state laws generally forbid private employers, labor unions, and state and local government agencies from:

- Denying an applicant a job on the basis of race or color
- Denying promotions, transfers, or assignments on the basis of race or color
- Penalizing workers with reduced privileges, reduced employment opportunities, and reduced compensation on the basis of race or color
- Firing a worker on the basis of race or color

Typically, the EEOC or related state agency will investigate charges of race discrimination or race-related retaliation. The EEOC has broad power to secure information and company records via subpoena, field investigations, audits, and interviewing witnesses, both employees and outsiders. Statistical data may be presented to demonstrate a pattern or practice of discriminatory conduct. As in other forms of discrimination, the contents of an individual's personnel file and the files of others in similar situations are often examined. Data on workplace composition may reveal a pattern or practice of exclusion. Regional or national data may shed light on whether a decision locally made was, in fact, racially discriminatory.

In cases where circumstantial evidence is presented to prove race discrimination, the burden is on the plaintiff to raise an inference of discrimination. This is often done through the use of statistics and payroll records.

Tip: Proving you were individually excluded from a job or fired based on your race or color may be difficult. It is often helpful to obtain statistical data to show that the employer's practices are illegal. For example, if ten positions for an engineering job were filled and none of the jobs was offered to a minority (or a woman), that may be sufficient to infer that the company violated the law. You would need assistance from a competent lawyer or discrimination specialist to prove

this, because the rules necessary to prove statistical disparitie
plex.

You may have an easier time of demonstrating race discrimination
when you are directly treated unfairly on the job. For example, if you
are repeatedly harassed and called names on the job, or are treated differently from nonminorities and then fired (e.g., you are absent several days from work and are suspended or placed on formal probation,
while white workers with the same or a greater number of absences
are given an informal warning), it is best to gather this factual information for discussion with an executive or officer in your company's
personnel department.

In light of the Supreme Court decision *Wards Cove v. Antonio,* you
may have an easier time proving race discrimination on an individual
basis as opposed to relying on statistical disparities. This is because in
certain cases employers now have to offer only a business justification
for actions that are shown by statistics to have an unfair impact on minorities. The burden then shifts to the complainant to demonstrate
that the alleged business justification is not legitimate.

RELIGIOUS DISCRIMINATION

The Civil Rights Act of 1964 prohibits religious discrimination and
requires employers to reasonably accommodate the religious practices
of employees and prospective employees. Various state laws also prohibit discrimination because of a person's observance of the Sabbath or
other holy day. In many states, employers may not require attendance
at work on such a day except in emergencies or situations in which
the employee's presence is indispensable. Absences for these obser-
vances must be made up at some mutually agreeable time or can be
charged against accumulated leave time.

A U.S. Supreme Court decision illustrates just how costly a lack of
knowledge in this area can be for an employer. A terminated worker
sued after she was fired for refusing to work overtime on Saturdays
due to her religious beliefs. In this particular case, an auto manufacturer hired the woman to work on an assembly line. The job did not
initially conflict with her religious beliefs (which required that she not
work from sunset Friday to sunset Saturday) because the assembly line
operated only from Monday through Friday. However, when the

company began requiring mandatory overtime on Saturdays, the worker refused on religious grounds, and she was fired after missing a series of Saturday work shifts.

The woman brought suit in federal court, alleging that the company violated Title VII of the Civil Rights Act, which makes it unlawful to fire or discriminate against an employee on the basis of race, color, religion, gender, or national origin, and that a 1972 amendment to the law requires employers to prove they are unable to accommodate an employee's religious practice without "undue hardship."

The primary issue before the trial court was whether the company had made a bona fide attempt to meet the needs of the employee. The court ruled that the woman's absence did not injure the company and that her request was not unreasonable. She was awarded $73,911 in back pay and benefits, despite the employer's argument that the proper running of the business would be affected by high absenteeism rates on Saturday, complaints from coworkers that she not receive special privileges (i.e., it was unfair to require them to work on Saturday while allowing the woman to take time off), and waiting lists of more senior employees requesting transfers to departments with no Saturday work.

The Supreme Court let the lower ruling stand, commenting that the company could have acted on the employee's request without undue hardship through the use of people employed specifically for absentee relief.

The following points summarize what companies are obligated to do to avoid lawsuits:

1. Employers have an obligation to make reasonable accommodations to the religious needs of employees.
2. Employers must give time off for the Sabbath or holy days except in an emergency.
3. If employees don't come to work, employers may give them leave without pay, may require equivalent time to be made up, or may allow employees to charge the time against any other leave with pay, except sick pay.

Employers may not be required to give time off to employees who work in key health and safety occupations or to those whose presence is critical to the company on any given day. Employers are not required to take steps inconsistent with a valid seniority system to accommodate an employee's religious practices. They are not required to incur overtime costs to replace an employee who will not work on Saturday. Employers have no responsibility to appease fellow employees who complain they are suffering undue hardship when a coworker is allowed not to work on a Saturday or Sabbath due to a religious belief while they are required to do so. Finally, employers are generally not required to choose the option the employee prefers as long as the accommodation offered is reasonable. However, penalizing an employee for refusing to work on Christmas or Good Friday most likely constitutes religious discrimination, depending on the facts.

Counsel Comments: The definition of a "religious belief" is quite liberal under the law. If your belief is demonstrably sincere, the belief can be considered religious even though it is not an essential tenet of the religion of which you are a member. The applicant's or employee's knowledge that a position will involve a conflict does not relieve the employer of its duty to reasonably accommodate, absent undue hardship.

In most cases, the court weighs the facts to determine whether the employer offered a reasonable accommodation or that undue hardship existed; the plaintiff will attempt to show that the hardship was not severe or that the accommodation offered was not reasonable. What constitutes undue hardship varies on a case-by-case basis. Generally, undue hardship results when more than a *de minimis* cost (i.e., overtime premium pay or a collective bargaining agreement is breached) is imposed on the employer.

Tip: The "undue hardship" defense is an exception that companies try to assert to successfully circumvent current law in this area. When you request time off for religious practices, document the date and nature of the request and the reasons given by the employer (or the alternatives it considers) in meeting or denying that request. If your request is denied, insist on an explanation. Speak to counsel to fully explore your options, such as filing a charge of religious discrimination with the EEOC or a state agency or suing the employer in either state or federal court, whichever is applicable. You have certain rights if you are a true religious observer whose beliefs conflict with your work schedule and you are fired as a result.

Recognize, however, that you probably cannot practice your faith to the detriment of other coworkers or customers. For example, a flight attendant was fired for allegedly reading her Bible and professing her beliefs to passengers while flying. The case is currently pending in a federal district court in Texas. The airline justified the termination by stating that she was proselytizing on the job and violated company policy by reading while on duty. A jury will be selected to decide whom to believe.

In another case, a worker claimed he was fired merely because he kept a Bible in his drawer, displayed religious plaques in his office, and had his secretary type his Bible study notes after hours. The employer argued he was fired for poor performance, but an Iowa jury awarded him $325,540 for back pay, front pay, and consequential damages for his emotional pain and suffering.

Experts suggest that "religious harassment" cases are on the rise, and the number of religious discrimination cases generally filed with the EEOC has gone up almost 50 percent between 1991 and 1995. Another related key issue that is often involved concerns freedom of expression in the workplace. For example, can employers bar employees from wearing any sort of religious symbols or garb at work or from discussing religion at work? Lawyers representing employees who are fired from their jobs as a result claim that people are free to discuss their religious beliefs while working. However, reported case decisions generally indicate that you cannot do so if it intrudes on another person's ability to work or you are asked to stop but persist.

RETALIATION DISCRIMINATION

Perhaps the most common form of illegal treatment that employees suffer is retaliation discrimination. Employees who legitimately assert discrimination rights by filing charges in federal or state court, with the EEOC, or through state agencies, complain to the employer before taking action, testify on behalf of another party, assist another party in administrative or judicial proceedings, or advise fellow employees of their rights under the discrimination laws are protected from adverse retaliation by an employer. If you reasonably believe that a Title VII violation was committed, an employer cannot take any action adverse to such rights, such as failing to promote, discharging, or unduly criticizing you as a direct result of that action.

Acts taken by an employer as a direct result of your filing charges or threatening to go to the EEOC or bring a lawsuit are viewed by the courts as retaliatory. Many employers who are accused of discrimination have valid defenses and can overcome the charges. However, they foolishly take steps deemed to be in retaliation against an individual's freedom to pursue such claims and eventually suffer damages resulting from their retaliatory actions, not the alleged discrimination.

The following list identifies common areas where retaliation often occurs, depending on the facts:

- Transfer or reassignment that is undesired (even with no loss in pay or benefits)
- Transfer out of the country
- Threats, when repeatedly made and when disruptive to your job performance
- Giving unfavorable references to a prospective employer, threatening to do so, interfering with your efforts to obtain a new job, or wrongfully refusing to write a recommendation on your behalf
- Firing you or forcing retirement by eliminating the position and offering only lesser alternative positions
- Denying or suspending severance payments
- Retroactively downgrading your performance appraisals and placing derogatory memos in your personnel file
- Refusing to promote or reassign you or adding preconditions for a requested reassignment
- Transferring you to a job with fewer amenities, such as no office, phone, or business cards
- Increasing your workload without good reason
- Adversely changing or decreasing your wages, vacation time, or benefits
- Delaying the distribution of tax and Social Security forms
- Interfering with an employment contract

Robin has been sexually harassed on the job. Before being harassed, she was given a poor work evaluation and told she was being placed on probation. Although she disagreed with the company's position, she is trying her best to demonstrate satisfactory work to remove herself from probation status.

Robin is concerned that if she complains to management about the sexual harassment, she will be fired. She consults an employment lawyer. Robin learns that by sending a letter to her company documenting and complaining about the illegal incidents, she may be *protecting* her job, because if she is then accused of poor work performance and fired, she can assert that the employer's adverse action was in retaliation for her filing a valid discrimination charge.

The U.S. Supreme Court recently ruled that the antiretaliation provision of Title VII is not limited to current employees but also extends to former employees. In the case, an employee of Shell Oil who was fired filed a charge with the EEOC alleging that Shell unlawfully discharged him because of his race. While the case was proceeding, he applied for a job with another company, which contacted Shell for an employment reference. The man claimed that Shell gave him a negative reference in retaliation for his filing with the EEOC. He won the case when the U.S. Supreme Court determined that the term "employee" as used in Title VII's antiretaliation provision applies to both employees and former employees. Experts suggest the case is significant because it may make ex-employers less likely to give spiteful false references on behalf of former employees who file discrimination charges after a firing.

Recognizing what constitutes retaliation is not always clear. In one case, for example, a New York court ruled that the loss of an office and phone previously provided to an employee who was informed of a termination decision and is waiting out his numbered days on the payroll searching for a new job does not, in and of itself, amount to adverse employment action. Nor does preparing a poor performance review in the absence of evidence that the employer gave the negative evaluation in bad faith. Thus, you may not be able to sue over every action that causes you dismay. The acts must be serious and provable—that is, there must be a causal connection between the protected activity and the adverse employment action.

Counsel Comments: Never falsely accuse an employer of a wrongful act in an attempt to obtain leverage, because you may not be legally protected if you then suffer harmful retaliation. However, you are protected against retaliation in a variety of nondiscriminatory areas, such as complaining about overtime policies, safety (OSHA) violations, and filing a workers' compensation claim. Most federal laws, such as the Civil Rights Act of 1964, the Family and Medical Leave Act, and the Americans with Disabilities Act, prohibit retaliation against anyone filing a charge. So do many federal and state whistle-blower statutes.

Tip: Do not stand idly by when an employer fires or demotes you, gives you an unfair or harsh evaluation, or singles you out in a negative way. This also includes giving a bad reference after you leave.

Constructive discharge, defined as conduct forcing you to resign, is an indirect violation of the same laws, and the employer cannot mistreat you to the extent that you suffer intolerable working conditions and are forced to resign. If you prevail in such a case, damages you may receive include reinstatement, back pay, attorney fees, punitive damages, and front pay with interest.

Often a supervisor will say to a worker, "If you don't like it, quit." Reconstruct such statements (e.g., note down the time and place it was said and who overheard the remarks). Speak to those witnesses and prepare a diary to document what was said. If you state in court that you quit because this is what your supervisor told you to do, your case can be strengthened, depending on the facts.

Always view suspiciously an employer's actions if you are transferred or demoted after complaining about alleged discrimination. Demand specific factual reasons for any company action if this occurs. If you believe the reasons are false, or you were treated unfairly as a result of complaining about an employer's illegal acts, speak to an employment lawyer immediately for advice and guidance.

Recognizing discrimination is only part of the battle; you must take the proper steps to enforce your rights. As I stated previously, the law entitles victims of discrimination to recover a variety of damages. These may include reinstatement or job hiring; receiving wage adjustments, back pay, and double back pay; receiving promotions and future pay; recovering legal fees, filing costs, and fees paid for expert witnesses; receiving punitive damages and compensatory damages up to $300,000 depending on the size of the employer; and other damages depending on the facts of your case. Even if you work in a right-to-work state and can be fired easily, it is illegal to be fired because you belong to a protected class, such as being a woman, over forty, a minority, handicapped, or a religious believer.

In seeking to enforce your rights, you will not be alone. More than 100,000 formal complaints are filed each year with the EEOC, and approximately 10,000 private discrimination lawsuits are tried in court annually. This does not include the many hundreds of thousands of complaints brought to state and local agencies and other institutions.

If you believe you have been victimized by employment discrimination, consider filing a charge with the Equal Employment Opportunity Commission and/or your state agency. The EEOC is a federal agency responsible for investigating claims of discrimination under various federal laws, including the Americans with Disabilities Act, Title VII of the Civil Rights Act, and the Age Discrimination in Employment Act. The headquarters of the EEOC are in Washington, D.C., and there are numerous regional and local offices throughout the United States.

At the end of Chapter 13 is a list of the addresses and telephone numbers of EEOC and state human rights agency field offices. (Note that certain addresses or telephone numbers may have changed since the publication of this book.) Consult your telephone directory under United States Government or call 800-669-4000 or 800-669-3362 (Spanish bilingual) to discover the EEOC office closest to you. You can locate state agencies by calling your state's department of labor or an EEOC office in your area.

In some states, filing a charge with either the EEOC or a state agency will be treated as a filing with both. Although some state agencies permit a longer period (e.g., up to 300 days depending on state law), to be timely you must file a charge with the EEOC within 180 days of the date the last incident occurred. You should also know that the EEOC is authorized to contract with state agencies to handle some of its cases, so it is possible your case will automatically be turned over to a state agency.

Tip: Before deciding whether to file with the EEOC or a state agency, speak to an employment lawyer for advice, because some state discrimination statutes provide greater protection and some state agencies have more powers than the EEOC. For example, although the EEOC cannot investigate charges of discrimination with companies that have fewer than fifteen full-time employees, most state agencies can.

You must also first decide whether to commence a private discrimination lawsuit in state court or file a charge with the EEOC or a state agency. The advantage of commencing a private lawsuit may be the more liberal statute of limitations if you are concerned that the time to file may soon expire. It is also possible to recover more damages under some state laws. You may also be able to receive a judgment quicker, since the EEOC has more than 100,000 cases pending and is understaffed. Cases often take years to be decided, and obtaining a favorable decision (i.e., a letter stating your case has probable cause) does not automatically mean you will receive big bucks. The employer may appeal an EEOC or state agency decision and force you to sue it in federal court or have the case remanded to a state administrative hearing. This could effectively stall any financial recovery for many more years. If you decide to file a private lawsuit, however, you will probably need to hire a lawyer to represent you in court, and this can be expensive.

The advantage of initially commencing a claim through the EEOC or a state agency is that it costs you nothing. Once a claim is accepted by the EEOC or a state agency, an investigator in charge of your case will attempt to eliminate the alleged discrimination through investigation and conciliation. The agency may render a nonbinding decision only when an informal settlement cannot be reached.

The EEOC performs the following general functions in any discrimination charge for free:

1. It will conduct interviews with you to obtain as much information as possible about the alleged discrimination and to explain the investigative procedure.
2. It will notify the company about the charge that has been filed.

3. It will investigate the charge. This includes interviewing witnesses and reviewing all pertinent records, documentation, and other written materials.
4. It will attempt to resolve the matter amicably between the parties.
5. It will drop your case if it determines that it does not have merit.
6. It may conduct a fact-finding conference with all parties present in one room.
7. It will decide whether discrimination took place (i.e., issue a formal decision of probable or no probable cause).

Counsel Comments: In an effort to eliminate an estimated 97,000-case backlog, the EEOC recently dismissed more than 18,000 cases it believed were without merit in order to free up staff. Moreover, Dominic Bencivenga reported in the *New York Law Journal* (February 29, 1996) that the EEOC has abandoned its decade-long policy of investigating every complaint that comes its way, in favor of a new, more selective procedure.

Mr. Bencivenga states that unlike the old system, where the EEOC accepted every complaint presented, the new rules allow agency staff to rate cases to determine if an investigation should be conducted. Cases will be classified as A or B if they have a strong likelihood of success, affect a large class, advance antidiscrimination law, or involve conflicts within the federal circuit courts. Complainants whose matters fall into the weakest C category will be eligible for an EEOC "right to sue" letter and can take their chances in court without an agency investigation.

According to Spencer H. Lewis, Jr., director of the EEOC's New York district office, this will enable the EEOC to encourage settlements earlier in the administrative process because employers will know that when a case is accepted by the EEOC it is considered serious. It will also free up the EEOC to handle more legitimate cases and process them more quickly. Speak to a knowledgeable employment lawyer for more details concerning this new policy and the consequences to your case.

Once you file a charge with the EEOC, you cannot litigate the matter privately until the EEOC dismisses your case (finds no probable cause), rules in your favor, or permits you to do so (i.e., issues a "right to sue letter"). In these situations, you then have 90 days to file a private lawsuit to be timely after receiving a final disposition notice right-to-sue letter from the EEOC.

Typically, you must give your name if you want an investigation to proceed, but you cannot be retaliated against for filing a charge.

Information and strategies on how to successfully maximize the chances of winning a discrimination case are included in Chapter 13.

CHAPTER 5

Fired to Deprive You of Benefits, for Attending Jury Duty, for Whistle-Blowing, and for Other Employment-at-Will Exceptions

Jim has worked as a company salesperson for close to thirty years and receives a salary plus commission. He diligently works to make the sale of a lifetime, but right before a major customer agrees to sign a $5-million contract, he is suddenly fired.

Jim learns that the customer eventually signs the contract several months later. He sues the company for damages, arguing that although he was an at-will employee, it was unfair to deprive him of the commission otherwise due, especially since he was primarily responsible for the deal taking place.

In court, the employer argues it has a policy of paying commissions only to employees still on the payroll when the sale occurs. It also argues that Jim was not responsible for the sale because others worked hard after he was fired to make the deal and that he was fired for poor performance.

The court believes Jim and awards him commission for the sale, notwithstanding the firing.

Historically, employees had few options when they received a pink slip because a legal principle called the employment-at-will doctrine was generally applied throughout the United States. Under this rule of law, employers were free to hire workers at will and fire them at any time with or without cause or notice. However, beginning in the 1960s, courts and legislatures started handing down rulings and enacting legislation to safeguard the rights of workers. Commentators suggest that this has occurred primarily to offset the harsh treatment of the employment-at-will doctrine. In addition to the antidiscrimination laws discussed in Chapters 2, 3, and 4, other forms of terminations are illegal even if you were hired at will without a written contract.

Although the law varies from state to state, and each case warrants attention based on its particular facts, the categories discussed in this chapter may help you recover greater benefits or damages when you are fired. These categories often serve as exceptions to the traditional employment-at-will rule in certain circumstances.

When a discharged employee consults me, I carefully analyze the following subjects to determine if they apply in the state where the client lives and/or works.

FIRED TO DENY ACCRUED BENEFITS

In some states, the law obligates employers to deal in good faith with longtime employees, and you can recover damages for breach of contract if you can prove your dismissal was motivated by malice or bad faith. If you have been at your job for a considerable length of time and are fired just before you are supposed to receive anticipated benefits (e.g., an earned bonus, vested stock option rights, accrued pension, profit sharing, commissions due, or additional wages), demand that the employer pay you those benefits or consult a lawyer immediately. But if an employer fires you for a lawful reason—that is, for cause—the fact that you are about to become eligible for a substantial benefit may not make the firing illegal.

The duty of employers to act in good faith and deal fairly applies generally to cases where an employee has been working for the company for many years or where an employee is fired just before becoming eligible to receive anticipated financial benefits. In one case, I represented a fired analyst who had worked on Wall Street. He was discharged on December 23 of a particular year. For the past seven years, he had consistently received sizable year-end bonuses. Although the amount of bonus paid was discretionary, he expected to receive a bonus of between $50,000 and $75,000 for the year in which he was fired.

At a National Association of Securities Dealers arbitration, the company stated it was not legally obligated to pay my client anything because bonuses were paid on March 1 of the following year and it had a long-standing written policy of not paying bonuses to people not on the payroll on the payment date. I argued that since my client had worked well during the whole year, it was obvious he was fired out of greed. I pointed out that he had not received any formal written warnings or poor performance reviews and was never advised his job was in jeopardy before the ax fell. The arbitrators agreed and awarded him $37,500.

In another case, an employee was fired after working fourteen years without a written contract or job security. The court ruled that the main reason for the sudden discharge was to deprive her of the vesting of valuable pension benefits commencing several months into her fifteenth year of service, and awarded her significant damages.

The Employee Retirement Income Security Act of 1974 (ERISA) prohibits the discharge of any employee who is prevented from attaining immediate vested pension benefits or who is exercising rights under ERISA and is fired as a result. In an important case, the Supreme Court recently ruled that employers cannot dismiss workers and contract out their jobs in an effort to reduce the workers' health insurance and other benefits. Under federal ERISA law, an employer can reduce benefits as part of a legitimate business decision, especially when a written plan contains language permitting the employer to modify benefits at any time at its discretion. But the Supreme Court stated that employers cannot fire or otherwise discriminate against workers for the purpose of interfering with their rights under an employee pension or benefits plan and denying them the right to collect benefits.

Tip: This case has been viewed as a major victory for workers. If you are fired at the end of the year and are denied a year-end bonus or other benefits about to vest in the following year, consult a lawyer immediately in the attempt to enforce your rights. Based on my experience, you may possibly have a valid claim in certain circumstances when you are fired and are denied pension or stock option benefits that would have vested within six months to a year after the firing.

A competent employment lawyer may be able to successfully recover those benefits for you. In the case of a bonus, a strong argument can often be made if you are fired within three months of the expected payment date. Sometimes a company will agree to keep you on unpaid leave status during the appropriate period as a way of qualifying. Speak to your lawyer about this negotiating strategy for more details.

If you cannot get your job back using a violation of good faith and fair dealing argument, you or a lawyer may be able to negotiate for you to obtain benefits you were expecting and would have received but for the firing. As the recent Supreme Court decision indicates, you should also consider asserting a claim for benefits based on a violation of your ERISA rights or other equitable claims, such as unjust enrichment (also referred to as *quantum meruit*), especially in commission cases.

FIRED DUE TO PUBLIC POLICY EXCEPTIONS

The most widely applied exception to the employment-at-will rule has been the public policy exception, under which claims for wrongful discharge can be brought in a contract or tort action (where punitive damages may be awarded in special circumstances). More and more state courts are recognizing the validity of this legal category, and it is essential to know the law in your state to improve the chances of success.

Public policy exceptions are generally divided into three basic categories:

1. Being fired for performing an important public obligation (e.g., whistle-blowing, attending jury duty or serving in the military)
2. Being fired for refusing to commit an unlawful act (e.g., refusing to give false testimony at a hearing)
3. Being fired for exercising a statutory right or privilege (e.g., filing a workers' compensation)

FIRED FOR VOTING OR SERVING ON JURY DUTY

Federal and state statutes generally prohibit employers from firing workers who take an hour or so off to vote or who are selected for jury duty. The Jury System Improvement Act of 1978 forbids employers from firing employees who are impaneled to serve on federal grand juries or petit juries, and many states have enacted similar laws. You cannot be disciplined, discharged, or threatened with unfair action for responding to a summons to serve on a jury in state court (or even being summoned to court as a witness). Generally, you can't be forced to use vacation days for jury time, either.

Counsel Comments: My brother Jonathan Sack, Esq., also an employment lawyer, once represented a client who was fired after serving on a lengthy twelve-week murder trial jury. The day the trial was finally over, the client was ordered to report back to work. Exhausted, he requested the day off before returning. The company refused and fired him. The client received a six-figure settlement after Jonathan filed a lawsuit on his behalf.

In another case, a Tennessee company was ordered to pay $575,000 in damages for demoting and subsequently firing an employee for a thirteen-week absence for jury duty.

Tip: In most cases, employers are not obligated to pay the difference between your salary and what you receive while serving as a juror (usually $40 per day for serving in federal courts and less in state courts). Only a few states, including Alabama, Nebraska, and Tennessee, require employers to pay their employees' wages for the entire time they serve on a jury. A few other states, including Colorado, Connecticut, Massachusetts, New Jersey, and New York, require employers to pay their employees' wages for a specified number of days (e.g., up to three). Since the law in your state may have changed by the time you read this book, speak to a lawyer or a representative from the nearest state department of labor office for more details. Also, in a few states, you may be legally fired if you don't return to work within a few weeks while serving on jury duty. Thus, get advice where warranted.

FIRED FOR WHISTLE-BLOWING

Various federal statutes protect federal workers who complain about safety or environmental hazards. Many of these laws, including the Clean Air Act, Toxic Substances and Control Act, Atomic Energy Act, Solid Waste Act, Safe Drinking Water Act, and Comprehensive Environmental Response, Compensation, and Liability Act, protect employees who expose public health and safety violations. The False Claims Act prohibits retaliation against employees who sue their employers alleging wrongdoing in the execution of government contracts.

More than forty states have whistle-blower protection acts that shield workers who reveal abuses of authority. These statutes penalize employers who discharge or discriminate or retaliate against workers who report suspected health, safety, or financial violations and provide specific remedies, including reinstatement with back pay, restoration of seniority and lost fringe benefits, litigation costs, attorney fees, and large fines.

For an employee's conduct to constitute protected activity, the majority of whistle blower statutes require that the employee have a reasonable belief that the employer's conduct violated a law, regulation, or ordinance. Most statutes also require some proof that the employee intended to, or did, report the violation.

The following true cases illustrate examples of firings found to be illegal due to whistle-blower statute protection:

- A nurse was dismissed after reporting abuses of patients at a Veterans' Administration Medical Center.
- A quality-control director was fired for his efforts to correct false and misleading food labeling by his employer.
- A bank discharged a consumer credit manager who notified his supervisors that the employer's loan practices violated state law.
- A financial vice-president was fired after reporting his suspicions to the company president regarding an embezzlement of corporate funds.

Counsel Comments: Generally, the same standard of proof is required to prevail in whistle-blowing cases as in discrimination claims;

the employee must make out a *prima facie* case that he or she was un-lawfully discharged in retaliation for reporting the employer's unlaw-ful conduct. If the employee establishes a *prima facie* case, the burden shifts to the employer, who must prove that the discharge was for a le-gitimate business reason. The employee may then show that the em-ployer's reason was a pretext for the unlawful discrimination.

Many employment lawyers believe that whistle-blower cases focus-ing on severe egregious actions are likely candidates for large settle-ments early on, because many companies do not want even to be accused of alleged harmful events that can become public. In addition, certain federal and state laws may give incentive to employees to tat-tle on management, especially when an employee senses he will not be employable after speaking out. For example, under the federal False Claims Act, a bounty is paid when the government recovers money on the tip of an employee. One whistle-blower allegedly received $22.5 million after the government collected $150 million from United Technologies on his tip.

Employees claiming retaliation for whistle-blowing can sue their employers under several theories, including wrongful discharge, defamation, and sometimes even wrongful imprisonment when workers are interrogated in a room and cannot leave. Attorney Stan-ley S. Arkin, in an article in the *New York Law Journal* (December 12, 1996), states that jury verdicts in favor of employees alleging wrong-ful discharge or retaliation from their whistle-blowing activities are often generous, with juries decidedly sympathetic to the "plight" of discharged employees. He reports a California case where one whistle-blowing employee was awarded $45 million in punitive damages in a wrongful-discharge action and another whistle-blower employee who was awarded $17.5 million.

To find out if your state has such a law and the elements and pe-culiarities of a whistle-blower statute, contact a knowledgeable em-ployment lawyer, legal referral service, or an American Civil Liberties Union office near you.

Tip: The law is often complicated in this area. For example, the Michigan and New York statutes would not protect you if you cor-rectly reported that a vice-president was embezzling funds or that an employer was in violation of internal rules, regulations, or policies. These statutes only protect employees reporting safety, health, and environmental violations that have actually occurred and have affected the community at large. Assuming these facts, you could be legally fired under New York or Michigan law by the company president even if your allegation was true!

Always research applicable state law or speak to a knowledgeable lawyer to understand your rights before reporting alleged violations. Some companies have successfully fired workers who blew the whistle without properly investigating the facts, bypassed management, or tattled in bad faith. In some states, employers must be given a reasonable period of time to remedy any violation before the employee has the right to report the violation to a public body. Generally, however, the employee is not required first to report the violation to his employer when the report would obviously not result in the prompt resolution of the problem.

A company may also defeat a claim by demonstrating you were fired for a legitimate business reason, such as for poor work performance or a reorganization.

Only an experienced employment lawyer in your state can analyze potential damages and determine the best course of conduct either after or even before you are considering coming forward. For the best result, speak to a lawyer before making the decision to engage in whistle-blowing activity.

FIRED FOR COMPLAINING ABOUT HEALTH OR SAFETY VIOLATIONS

The 1970 Occupational Safety and Health Act requires employers to provide a safe and healthful workplace, and the Occupational Safety and Health Administration (OSHA) is the federal agency created to enforce the law in this area. The law protects employees who band together to safeguard wages, hours, or working conditions. Under this law, workers are allowed to refuse to perform in a dangerous environment (e.g., in the presence of toxic substances, fumes, or radioactive materials) and to strike to protest unsafe conditions. Employees may also initiate an OSHA inspection of alleged dangerous working conditions by filing a safety complaint and cannot be retaliated against by taking such action when justified. While it may not necessarily be a good idea to walk off the job suddenly when you believe you are working in a dangerous or unhealthful environment (unless it is likely that the work is placing you in imminent danger of serious injury), always discuss such conditions with a supervisor, union delegate, management, or OSHA representative. This will make your demands seem more reasonable and minimize potential conflict.

Tip: Employers cannot fire, demote, or transfer workers who assert their health and safety rights to any federal, state, or local agency empowered to investigate or regulate such conditions. Contact your union, regional labor relations board, OSHA representative, lawyer, or state department of labor if you believe your rights have been violated.

In one case, for example, seven machine shop workers walked off their jobs, claiming it was too cold to work. The company fired them, stating they violated company rules by stopping work without notifying the supervisor. The workers filed a complaint alleging this was an unfair labor practice. The U.S. Supreme Court ruled that the employees had a constitutional right to strike over health and safety conditions and that the firing violated the law. The workers were awarded back pay and job reinstatement as a result.

FIRED FOR FILING A WORKERS' COMPENSATION CLAIM

Each state has enacted its own peculiar rules with respect to workers' compensation, which provides aid for employees who suffer job-related injuries. Under state compensation laws, the amount of money paid in benefits is linked to the worker's rate of pay prior to the injury and the kind and extent of injuries suffered. Workers' compensation is a substitute for other remedies workers may have against an employer, such as bringing a private lawsuit for negligence. In many cases, the issue becomes one of determining whether the injuries suffered were job-related and whether the worker is legally considered an independent contractor (not subject to workers' compensation laws) or an employee. The reason is that people typically prefer to sue the employer privately and obtain greater damages than are awarded under workers' compensation statutes.

Tip: Since the outcome of each workers' compensation case varies depending on the particular facts and unique state law, always seek the advice of a lawyer specializing in workers' compensation law. Issues such as how long you may delay before filing a claim, whether coverage is available for stress-related injuries, and what kinds of injuries are covered, together with strategies to help maximize the benefits received, can be complicated.

Do not be afraid to notify your employer when you are injured while working. This is your right, and you cannot be retaliated against in any way for taking such action. If you prove that the employer fired you because you filed a workers' compensation claim, you are entitled to recover a multitude of damages, including back pay, restoration of employee benefits, possible job reinstatement, attorney fees, related costs, and other damages. Consult a lawyer immediately if you were fired for filing a workers' compensation claim or if your claim is contested.

FIRED FOR REPORTING ACCIDENTS

The Federal Railroad Safety Act prohibits companies from firing workers who file complaints or testify about railroad accidents, and the Federal Employer's Liability Act makes it a crime to fire an employee who furnishes facts regarding a railroad accident.

FIRED FOR ATTEMPTING TO UNIONIZE

The National Labor Relations Act prohibits the firing of any employee because of involvement in union activity, filing charges, or testifying pursuant to the act. Contact the closest regional office of the National Labor Relations Board if you believe you were fired for any of these reasons.

FIRED FOR SERVING IN THE MILITARY

Several federal laws, including the Veterans' Re-employment Rights Act and the Military Selective Service Act, protect the rights of veterans and military personnel. These laws provide that employees who are in military service be regarded as being on an unpaid leave of absence from their civilian employment. For example, if you are on extended duty merely to serve in a motor pool across town, you must be offered a job with the same pay, rank, and seniority on your return. An employer is prohibited from forcing employees to use vacation time for military training. Employers are obligated to assist employees who return from military service and cannot deny promotions, seniority, or other benefits because of military obligations. Thus, if an employee was promoted or promised a raise right before call-up, he must receive a job in line with the promised promotion and raise on his return, together with reinstatement of all benefits and any benefits (e.g., additional pay) that would have been earned if he had continued to work.

Tip: Companies that receive job applications from military personnel and reservists relating to work after termination of active duty status and don't hire them must fully document the reasons for denial. Any employer not following these rules is subject to investigation and action by the local U.S. Attorney's Office or a private lawsuit filed by the claimant in the federal district court sitting in any county where the employer maintains a place of business. Charges can also be brought under the Veterans' Benefits Improvement and Health Care Authorization Act. These laws prohibit discrimination in all aspects of employment, including discharge, on the basis of military membership.

Employers have to allow employees leave of absence during work hours to attend required military reserve or National Guard meetings, training sessions, and drills. But if you are called to active duty, you must give the employer sufficient advance written or oral notice. Not giving advance notice may jeopardize your reemployment rights.

FIRED FOR REFUSING TO TAKE A POLYGRAPH, DRUG, OR ALCOHOL TEST

The Federal Polygraph Protection Act of 1988 sets minimum standards for private employers to follow. Generally, employers are prohibited from directly or indirectly requiring, requesting, suggesting, or causing an employee to take any lie detector test. This federal law prohibits employers from firing workers who refuse to take a polygraph exam. Only in rare cases where employers have a reasonable basis to investigate serious workplace improprieties (e.g., a series of thefts) can such tests be ordered as part of an ongoing investigation, but many procedural safeguards must be carefully followed.

For example, the law requires that you have an opportunity to obtain and consult with a lawyer of your choosing before each phase of the test; you must be provided at least forty-eight hours' notice of the time and place of the test and notified of the evidentiary basis for the test (i.e., given a written statement outlining the employer's suspicions and the reasons for asking you to take the exam); be advised of the nature and instruments involved (e.g., that two-way mirrors or recording devices will be used); be provided an opportunity to review all questions to be asked at the examination; and be given a copy of the law, which mentions your rights and remedies and allows you to stop the test at any time.

Federal law forbids companies from asking you to volunteer for a test to "clear your name." If you submit to a polygraph test voluntarily (which I never recommend), you must be given a copy of the results along with the questions asked. The test cannot run longer than ninety minutes. All persons who administer the test must be licensed and bonded with at least $50,000 of coverage, and they are forbidden from recommending action regarding test results. All exam results and action taken on them must be guarded against careless dissemination to nonessential third parties to avoid charges of defamation.

Tip: An employer's decision to terminate you for refusing to take a test will be barred unless it can prove at trial that your failure to take the test played no part in the decision to fire or suspend you. This is often difficult for the employer to prove. Additionally, unless you are notified regarding the reasons why you are linked to an alleged crime, you cannot be forced to take the test. For example, in one recent case, a judge ruled that a former Citibank employee who was fired for refusing to take a lie detector test was allowed to sue for damages because bank officials did not properly inform him of their suspicions that he was involved in a fraudulent wire transfer.

Speak to a lawyer immediately if it is proposed that you submit to a test. A competent lawyer may be able to recover huge fines and penalties, including back pay, job reinstatement and related damages, attorney fees, and costs to successful litigants, plus civil penalties of up to $10,000 and injunctive relief for actions brought by the U.S. Secretary of Labor within three years from the wrongful act.

All forms of employee testing raise significant issues of potential violations of an employee's privacy rights. Federal law also prohibits employers from administering "deceptographs, stress analyzers, psychological stress evaluators or any other similar device" and restricts employers from taking action against employees who refuse to submit to such tests.

Due to the enactment of the Americans with Disabilities Act, many forms of tests are closely scrutinized. With respect to HIV testing, such tests are permitted in certain states only in limited circumstances where the job involves the public health and safety, such as for food handlers and hospital workers. It is also permitted for people in the military. Most genetic testing is prohibited.

With respect to drug and alcohol testing, some experts prohibit such tests, but state law varies dramatically. For example, some states permit employee testing with required procedural safeguards to ensure the testing is done in a reasonable and reliable manner with concern for an employee's rights of privacy. Thus, intrusive monitoring of blood and urine testing through the use of closed-circuit cameras is not permitted. Other states permit individual tests where a particular employee is suspected of being under the influence of drugs or alcohol and in an impaired state that adversely affects job performance. In some states, employees who test positive may not be fired if they consent to participate in and successfully complete a rehabilitation program.

Since the law varies so much from state to state, is constantly changing, and may even be more stringent as a result of the ADA, speak to a lawyer or representative from the Department of Labor or the EEOC for advice in this area to determine relevant state law. In approximately two-thirds of the states in this country, private employers may implement and conduct drug and alcohol tests provided certain procedural safeguards are followed that minimize potential offensiveness. This typically includes adopting a comprehensive testing policy and putting it in writing, periodically reminding employees of the stated drug or alcohol testing policy, reducing the incidence of errors, treating test results carefully (i.e., confidentially) to avoid improper dissemination, and following local, state, and federal laws and decisions.

Counsel Comments: Generally, the decision to test is basically a voluntary choice for private employers.

Tip: If you work for a private employer and are not a member of a union, what concerns should you have when advised that the employer intends to test you for drugs and alcohol? First, it is preferred that you receive advance notice in work rules and policy manuals. For example, the manual should outline the steps management will take when it suspects that an employee is impaired on the job, such as immediate testing, with a description of how the test will be administered and the consequences flowing from a positive result (such as suspension without pay or discharge for cause). If no such notice was received before a test was administered, you may have a valid claim that your privacy rights were violated, especially when there was no rational reason for asking you to submit to the test (e.g., you were randomly selected).

Even if your privacy rights are not violated, all tests must be administered in a consistent, evenhanded manner. For example, if female employees are being tested and fired as a result of such tests in far greater numbers than other classifications, a charge of sex discrimination may be valid under certain circumstances.

How the employer handles the test results is another important consideration. Results must be treated in the same manner as other confidential personnel information. Unwarranted disclosure of this information (even within your company) when made with reckless disregard for the truthfulness of the disclosure, or excessive publication, can allow you to sue for damages. One employee was awarded $200,000 for defamation after her employer internally and externally published written statements regarding drug screening results incorrectly showing a trace of methadone.

Additionally, a firing based on a positive test finding that later proves inaccurate may lead to a multitude of legal causes of action, including wrongful discharge, slander, and invasion of privacy. Thus, if the employer fails to hire a reputable testing company or the test results are inaccurate, you can challenge the test on this basis.

Recognize that there may be ways to challenge the test results in the event you are fired or treated unfairly. Speak to an experienced lawyer immediately when:

- A test was not administered fairly (i.e., no advance warnings were given or there was inconsistent enforcement)
- The penalty for violations was too severe (e.g., an employee was fired for possessing a minuscule amount of marijuana in her locker but proved she did not smoke the drug on company time)
- The reliability of test procedures and/or results is suspect
- The employer cannot prove the identity of the illegal drug allegedly found in the test
- The specimen was not properly identified as belonging to the accused worker
- No confirmatory tests were made following positive preliminary screening
- The company engaged in discriminatory practices relating to its testing procedures

Be aware that federal workers, employees engaged in security-conscious industries (e.g., those who are required to carry firearms), and employees who handle money or engage in transporting members of the public (bus drivers and train engineers) have fewer legal rights to oppose drug and alcohol tests because of the nature of their jobs. However, even when testing is legal, employers must follow proper procedures to be sure that results are accurate and are not disseminated carelessly. Results should be handled on a strict need-to-know basis, employees should be given an opportunity to explain any result, and the test results should be reconfirmed if possible.

Finally, since former drug users (and current alcoholics) may be characterized as individuals with a former or current disability that does not prevent them from performing the duties of their job, any adverse action taken (such as discharge) may be fought under federal and state disability discrimination laws, even in the presence of positive test results.

FIRED AFTER A CREDIT CHECK

Employers routinely use credit checks to evaluate the credentials of a potential or current employee. When credit checks are conducted improperly, legal causes of action ensue. Most state and federal laws limit an employer's ability to take adverse action on a negative finding regarding a person's credit background. For example, according to the federal Bankruptcy Code, no private employer may terminate the employment of an individual who is or has been a debtor or bankrupt solely because such debtor or bankrupt had or has financial problems.

Under the federal Fair Debt Credit Reporting Act, employers are generally forbidden to use credit reports for firing decisions unless the job is security-conscious or the financial integrity of the employee (e.g., someone in a bookkeeper or comptroller position) is essential to continued successful job performance. Even when such a report is made, you must be told the report is being ordered and provided with the name and address of the credit agency that is supplying it. If you are fired as a result of the information supplied, you have the right to go to the credit agency and investigate the accuracy of the report or allege discrimination in a lawsuit against the ex-employer when appropriate. Speak to an employment lawyer for advice.

FIRED FOR NONPAYMENT OF A DEBT

In the majority of states and pursuant to the federal Consumer Credit Protection Act, it is illegal for a company to fire a person being sued for nonpayment of a debt or to fire an employee when asked to cooperate in the collection of a portion of the person's wages through garnishment proceedings arising from a single debt. This is so regardless of how many times your employer has to withhold money from your paycheck to satisfy the court order. Enforcement of this federal law is tough; violations are punishable by a fine of up to $1,000 and imprisonment for up to one year. (Note: Getting fired as a result of the garnishment of more than one debt is not illegal, but such a policy may be restricted by Title VII of the Civil Rights Act of 1964 when it has a disproportionate effect on minority workers.)

Tip: Some states have even stricter laws on the books in this area and prohibit the garnishment of your wages or your being fired as a result of one garnishment order or a number of wage attachments. Always research the law in your state or speak to a lawyer for more advice.

If you believe you were fired as a result of having your wages attached pursuant to one court order, federal law may have been violated and you should consider contacting the EEOC for help. If you believe state law was violated, consider going to your state human rights commission to file charges. Damages for successful litigants typically include making you whole, such as being awarded back pay, interest, attorney fees, related costs, and possible job reinstatement.

FIRED BECAUSE OF PERSONAL APPEARANCE

Some employers prescribe standards in dress and personal appearance. Although such codes have been attacked at times, they are legal provided the policies do not unfairly impact a group of workers such as females. If a different rule is imposed for female employees than for male employees (such as requiring women waitresses to wear skimpy clothes while male counterparts wear whatever they wish), the policy may be discriminatory and a violation of Title VII for an adverse (disparate) impact based on gender.

Appearance-based discrimination may be actionable if it has a nexus to gender, race, age, religion, disability, or some other protected category. For example, a motel was found to have unlawfully fired a pregnant desk clerk who refused her supervisor's directive to wear makeup when her complexion had broken out. A grooming code that severely impacts women (e.g., requiring all female employees to have short haircuts), thus having an adverse impact under Title VII, may also violate the law unless the employer can demonstrate a legitimate business necessity (such as safety considerations) to enforce the rule.

When employers prove that a dress code is reasonable and job-related, it will probably be enforceable and employers may fire workers who refuse to follow it. In many situations, arbitrators and judges will uphold a company's personal appearance policy when it is justifiable. Good grooming regulations are often imposed in an attempt to reflect a company's image in a highly competitive business environment. Reasonable requirements in furtherance of that policy may not constitute an invasion of privacy if challenged, particularly if the company disseminated written rules advising workers of the consequences flowing from violations of such policies.

However, the law varies by state and depends on each set of facts. In one case, for example, a worker dyed her hair purple. She was given one week to change her hair color. When she rejected the boss's order, she was fired. The company was so incensed that it opposed her claim for unemployment compensation. It stated at a hearing that her job involved dealing with customers, many of whom were revolted by her unconventional hair coloring, and keeping her aboard would have resulted in loss of business. The company also believed it was misconduct and insubordination for the worker to refuse a reasonable request to change her eccentric hairstyle.

The worker defended her position by stating that the company had no right to dictate her personal appearance and that there was no evidence that customers complained about her purple hair. She stated that since several customers had complimented her new appearance, she was unjustifiably terminated in a manner that should not have precluded her from receiving unemployment benefits.

The court found there was no evidence that the color of the worker's hair significantly affected the employer's business or caused customer complaints. Although it stated that the company had the right to fire her as an at-will employee, it was unlawful to deny her unemployment benefits for her actions. It wrote: "We do not question the employer's right to establish a grooming code for its employees, to revise its rules in response to unanticipated situations, and to make its hiring and firing decisions in conformity with this policy. However, it is possible for an employee to have been properly discharged without having acted in a manner as would justify a denial of unemployment benefits."

FIRED BECAUSE OF AN OFFICE ROMANCE

Does management have the right to actively enforce a nonfraternization rule aimed at curbing office romances? This varies, depending on the facts. One supervisor who was fired commenced a lawsuit against a former employer. The supervisor had allegedly given his live-in lover a promotion that placed her above several employees with more seniority even though the company had an unwritten, traditional rule forbidding social relationships between management and lower-echelon employees. When questioned by the home office, the supervisor admitted that he and the coworker were lovers; citing the nonfraternization rule, the company abruptly terminated him.

The supervisor took the company to court and argued that his employment contract brought with it the company's implied covenant of good faith and fair dealing, which the company violated when he was fired. He also stated that the nonfraternization rule was unfair, unreasonable, and selectively enforced.

The company responded that its nonfraternization rule became reasonable and necessary after the company discovered that attachments between supervisory employees and their subordinates led to accusations and favoritism, which had a negative impact on morale. The company also argued that since the employee had no written contract guaranteeing job security, he could be fired at any time for any or no reason.

The court found that the company was legitimately concerned with appearances of favoritism and employee dissension caused by romantic relationships. Given his actions, the terminated supervisor did not make a strong case that the company failed to act in good faith toward him.

Counsel Comments: Other courts have similarly upheld the dismissal of employees romantically involved with coworkers. A Wisconsin court ruled that there were no constitutional or statutory rights barring such a dismissal. In another case, termination because of marriage to the employee of a competitor was found not to violate the law, and the worker's lawsuit for unfair discharge was rejected. Other employees have been fired for violating company fraternization rules by having extramarital affairs or taking a girlfriend to an out-of-state convention. In some cases, an employer's rule prohibiting workers from dating employees of a competitor was found to be illegal. Since the law is unsettled in this area and each case is decided on its own set of facts and circumstances, never assume that a company's actions are legal in this area. Consult an employment lawyer for advice.

Tip: Although it may be legal to forbid employees from fraternizing, all employees must be treated similarly to avoid violations. For example, if an employer reprimands a male employee for dating a coworker but fires a female employee for a similar infraction, the employer may be committing illegal sex discrimination.

For off-the-job illegal conduct, a company typically has the right to fire a worker if the illegal conduct harms the employer's reputation or has a negative impact on job performance. The law is not so clear regarding attempts to regulate *legal off-the-job behavior.*

FIRED FOR LEGAL ACTIVITIES OFF-PREMISES

Beginning in the late 1960s, the U.S. Supreme Court ruled that government employees could not be fired in retaliation for the exercise of free speech. The notion of free speech, privacy, and related constitutional protections has now been expanded to private employees in certain instances, particularly in states that have enacted broad civil rights laws.

For example, in some states, a private employer cannot discipline, fail to promote, or fire an employee because the company does not agree with the employee's comments on matters of public concern. A majority of states have laws that prohibit employers from influencing how their employees vote.

Most states have laws making it illegal for companies to fire workers who participate in legally permissible political activities, recreational activities, or the legal use of consumable products before and after working hours. Political activities include running for public office, campaigning for a candidate, and participating in fund-raising activities for a candidate or political party. Those activities may be protected if they are legal and occur on the employee's own time, off company premises, and without the use of employer property or equipment.

Recreational activities are defined as any lawful leisure-time activities for which the employee receives no compensation. The definition of consumable products includes cigarettes and alcohol when used before and after working hours and off the company's premises.

The right not to be demoted, retaliated against, or fired for engaging in these legally permitted activities generally depends on state law.

To date, many states have passed laws making it illegal to be fired from a job because you are a smoker and smoke off the premises; the trend is for more states to follow. In New York, for example, employers cannot discriminate against or fire workers due to off-duty activities in four specific categories: political activities, use of a consumable product, recreational activities (i.e., participating in sports, games, hobbies, exercise, reading, and watching television), and union membership or exercise of any rights granted under federal or state law (such as voting).

However, a female employee was recently fired by a New York company for dating a coworker after hours. She sued the employer and argued that her discharge violated this law. The judge, however, ruled that having a sexual relationship was *not* included in the definition of a "recreational activity" as defined by the statute (skydiving, scuba diving, bungee jumping, and overeating were included) and ruled against her.

But in another case, a federal district court ruled that cohabitation with a former coworker *was* a protected off-work "recreational activity" under New York state law and could not be grounds for discharge. In that case, a woman employed by a radio station had worked her way up from an entry-level position to administrative assistant for the company vice-president. She had been living with the vice-president for several years, and this was generally known to everyone at the company.

Two days after her lover was fired, she was told her job would be eliminated under a company reorganization; in the interim, she was demoted. Yet the company eventually ran advertisements for her job and then replaced her with a man of fewer qualifications.

The court ruled that cohabitation that occurs off the employer's premises without the use of the employer's equipment and not on the employer's time is a protected activity for which the employer may not discriminate unless the employer can prove it involves a material conflict of interest with the employer's business—for example, relating to possible theft of its trade secrets or confidential information.

Counsel Comments: In the vast majority of states with such laws, it is illegal to refuse to hire or fire smokers. It may also be illegal to discriminate against smokers by charging higher insurance premiums unless the company can demonstrate a valid business reason, such as higher costs. However, people who smoke off-duty must still comply with existing laws and ordinances regulating smoking on-premises (e.g., only in designated areas). And just because it may be legal to drink alcohol off-premises late into the night does not give you the right to stagger into work drunk the next morning.

Employers who violate state law in this area are generally subject to a lawsuit by their state's attorney general seeking to restrain or enjoin the continuance of the alleged unlawful conduct. Significant penalties are provided in most of these laws. Additionally, individuals may commence their own lawsuits and recover monetary damages and other forms of relief, including attorney fees, under the laws of many states.

Tip: Contact a representative at the American Civil Liberties Union in New York City for advice and guidance if you are being pressured to stop asserting legal political activities, affiliations, or political action. This includes organizing with other workers to protest poor working conditions. In one recent California case, a group of individuals organized to promote equal rights of homosexuals at a large company via a class-action lawsuit. The court ruled that such activity was protected by state law.

Since some states do not have specific laws protecting employees who engage in political activity and other activities, and the laws vary so much, always consult with counsel and review applicable state law *before* engaging in questionable activities or taking action to protect such activities.

In addition to public policy exceptions to the employment-at-will rule, there may be several other areas where you can legally fight a firing. These include being fired in a manner inconsistent with company handbooks, manuals, and disciplinary rules or oral promises, fired as part of a large layoff and not given proper notice, and fired in a manner inconsistent with your written contract.

FIRED IN VIOLATION OF A COMPANY RULE

Some employers have written progressive disciplinary programs for employees that are supposed to be followed before a firing. Failure to follow these rules, such as not giving a formal warning or not placing an employee on ninety days' probation before a firing, may give rise to a lawsuit based on violation of an implied contract in some states.

In some states, courts are ruling that company manuals and handbooks can create contractual rights between employers and employees and that companies who fail to follow policies presented in their manuals may be found liable for breach of contract. The following true case is a good example.

A man worked as a copywriter for a major publishing company. He did not sign an employment contract when he was hired. However, during negotiations, he was assured that the job was secure because the company never terminated employees without just cause, and his employment application stated that employment was subject to the provisions of the company manual on personnel policies and procedures. The manual stipulated that "employees will be fired for just and sufficient cause only" after internal steps toward rehabilitation had been taken and had failed.

For eight years, the employee received periodic raises and job promotions, and turned down a number of offers from other companies. Despite that, he was suddenly fired without warning. He sued the company, claiming that he had been wrongfully discharged.

The company argued that he was an at-will employee and could be fired legally at any time, with or without notice, warning, or cause.

The court ruled in the employee's favor, stating that the facts created a company obligation not to deviate from termination procedures as stated in its policy manual.

Counsel Comments: To successfully assert this claim, it is essential to have previously received a copy of the company's manual and read it carefully. If you can prove that promises are clearly contained in a manual, and you relied on them to your detriment, you may be able to assert a valid lawsuit. Remember, if a company fails to act in accord with published work rules or handbooks, it may be construed as violating an important contract obligation in some states.

Types of promises to look for (which may give you additional rights during and after a firing) include:

• Allowing you to appeal or mediate the decision through an internal nonbinding grievance procedure

- Requiring an employer to give reasonable notice before any firing
- Stating that you can be fired for cause only after internal steps toward rehabilitation have been taken and have failed
- Guaranteeing the right to be presented with specific, factual reasons for the discharge before the firing can be effective

Note, however, that employers may be able to prevent the creation of employment contracts by drafting effective disclaimers and prominently displaying them in the handbook and requiring employees to sign an acknowledgment that they have received a copy of the manual, have read it, and agree that no promises of job security have been made to them orally or in the manual.

Tip: Try to obtain a copy of any handbook or manual given to employees at your company before you are fired. Review it carefully. If you think you were fired in a manner inconsistent with language in a manual, contact an employment lawyer immediately to discuss your rights and options. You may be pleasantly surprised to learn that the company is contractually bound by the provisions in its handbook, especially when you can prove that you affirmatively relied on such statements (e.g., rejected other offers of employment) to your detriment.

FIRED INCONSISTENT WITH A VERBAL PROMISE

In some states, it is illegal to be fired or treated differently when you receive a verbal promise of job security or other rights that the company fails to fulfill. When promises of job security are offered at the hiring interview, they may be enforceable provided they can be proved. This is another exception to the employment-at-will doctrine. For example, if a company president tells you at the hiring interview, "Don't worry, Gwen, we never fire anyone around here except for a good reason," a legitimate case may be made to fight the firing provided you can prove that the words were spoken and that it was reasonable to rely on them (i.e., that they were spoken seriously and not in jest).

More and more courts throughout the United States are ruling that employees have the right to rely on representations made to them before hiring and during the working relationship regarding job security. As a result, some discharged employees are suing and winning "truth in hiring" and fraudulent inducement cases against ex-employers for breach of oral agreements promising secure employment and even jobs for life. While many courts have generally recognized that employers may be bound by written assurances and statements in employee manuals, handbooks, and work rules, some are now increasingly willing to consider oral contracts extended by management and company officials having the apparent authority to make such promises.

This occurred in a case decided in Alaska. At the hiring, an employer stated that an applicant could have the job until reaching retirement age so long as she performed her duties properly. When the employee was suddenly fired, she argued that her job performance was excellent and that she had relied on the promise of job security in deciding to accept the job. She won the case after proving the words were spoken. Several witnesses had overheard the promises at the job interview and testified to this fact at the trial.

In another case, a New Jersey employee complained that, relying on an employer's oral promise that he could be fired only for cause, he turned down a position offered by a competitor. Several months later he was summarily fired. The court, noting that promises were made inducing him to remain in the company's employ, ruled that the employer had made specific factual representations that transformed the employment-at-will relationship into employment with termination for cause only. After finding that the employee's decision not to accept the competitor's offer was significant, binding the employer, the court ruled in the employee's favor.

A Michigan jury awarded $1.1 million to a worker based on a claim of an oral promise of lifetime employment. In that case, the jury found the existence of a valid, oral contract and ruled that the company unjustifiably breached that contract when the worker was terminated. In another case, a Connecticut executive was awarded $10.1 million in compensatory and punitive damages after he left a company to join a competitor who promised a large bonus and profit-sharing plan that never materialized.

Counsel Comments: Not all oral promises are enforceable against a company, particularly when an employee is promised "a job for life."

Promises of lifetime employment are infrequently upheld due to a legal principle referred to as the statute of frauds. Under this law (recognized in many states), all contracts with a job term exceeding one year must be in writing to be enforceable. As a result, courts are generally reluctant to view oral contracts as creating permanent or lifetime employment. Often, depending on the facts, such contracts are viewed as being terminable at will by either party.

Tip: Some states have laws that limit the duration of an employment contract to a specified maximum number of years (e.g., seven). Thus, if you anticipate obtaining and enforcing a lengthy agreement, consult a lawyer and have a formal, comprehensive, unambiguous document prepared and signed by all significant parties (such as the company president) to reduce problems.

FIRED IN BREACH OF CONTRACT RIGHTS

If you are fired in a manner inconsistent with or different from rights in a written contract or collective bargaining agreement (if you belong to a union), you may be entitled to damages. If a contract exists, examine it upon termination. The failure to give timely notice as required by a contract, or failure to follow the requirements set forth in a contract, may expose a company to a breach of contract claim. In some instances, it can even cause the agreement to be extended for an additional period.

Tip: All the preceding topics are areas for you to contemplate if you think you have been fired illegally. Armed with this knowledge, you can be in a better position to recognize when you are being treated unfairly and know when to speak to an employment lawyer. Since the topics are merely a summary of key areas the law protects, seek advice from a professional to explore all your rights and options whenever you have been fired from an important job.

RIGHT TO BE WARNED BEFORE A MASSIVE LAYOFF

Employees are entitled to be warned of large layoffs under the federal Worker Adjustment and Retraining Notification Act (WARN). Em-

Judith is a fashion designer who works for a small company. Several years ago, desiring job security, she negotiated and received a one-year written contract before beginning work. The benefit of having a one-year agreement was that Judith could not be fired prior to the expiration of the one-year term unless she was fired for cause (which Judith knew was hard to prove).

Judith's contract stated that if timely notice of termination was not sent by either party at least sixty days prior to the expiration of the original one-year term, the contract would be automatically renewed, under the same terms and conditions, year to year. Her company apparently forgot about the contract's existence and notified her two weeks prior to the expiration date that the agreement would not be renewed.

Judith immediately advised the company of the existence of the written agreement. She consulted and hired a lawyer to protect her rights. The lawyer told Judith that the company had breached the agreement, but if Judith found another job during the following year, her damages would be reduced by the amount of compensation she received from the new job plus any unemployment benefits she obtained.

Judith felt confident she would find another job quickly. Thus, rather than sue, she authorized her lawyer to accept a settlement immediately equal to four months of her salary to resolve the matter. The experience taught her that a few favorable words on a piece of paper can mean thousands of dollars in additional benefits when an employer fails to act according to the terms of a written contract.

ployers with more than one hundred workers are required to give employees and their communities at least sixty days' notice or comparable financial benefits (sixty days' notice pay) of plant closings and large layoffs that affect fifty or more workers at a job site unless the employer was forced to shut down operations for business circumstances not reasonably foreseeable or unless it is a distressed company trying to find a buyer or fresh capital. Speak to an experienced employment lawyer or contact your nearest regional office of the Department of

Labor for more information. Companies must be careful when contemplating a substantial reduction of their workforce, and a representative from the Department of Labor can advise you if your WARN rights are being violated.

This claim applies not only to union employees working at plants. It can be asserted when a private employer lays off hundreds of workers at one time or when a company discharges large numbers of secretaries or dismantles an accounting, business, or financial department due to a reorganization.

For example, a federal judge in New York found that a major law firm violated the federal plant closure law when the 125-partner firm failed to give its 250 former staff attorneys and clerical help the required sixty days' notice. To avoid damages, it was reported that the law firm offered former employees one week's salary in return for their promise to opt out of the case, and about 150 accepted the offer. The others remained in the case and will receive significantly more compensation (i.e., one day's back pay for each day of violation up to sixty days; the value of medical expenses and other benefits paid directly to the affected employee; and the value of actual payments made to third parties on behalf of the affected employee). Employers are also subject to fines exceeding $500 per day to the appropriate unit of local government where the closing or layoff occurs.

Tip: Consider filing a lawsuit alleging WARN violations if you are terminated due to a large reorganization or downsizing (e.g., your whole department is suddenly axed) and are not given reasonable warning or a decent severance package. Thus, if you are fired suddenly and are part of a massive layoff, consult a lawyer immediately to discuss your rights and options under WARN.

There are some exceptions to the law that do not help you. For example, the layoffs of workers employed by the same company but located at different sites cannot be combined to meet the threshold minimum. However, you may be entitled to recover damages under the law if you are a traveling salesperson working for the company like others all over the country and the field sales staff is fired en masse.

PART II

Negotiating the Best Severance Package After You Are Fired

CHAPTER 6

Preparing for the Inevitable

Sharon is a fifty-four-year-old frustrated executive. Despite twelve loyal years with her company, she senses her job is no longer secure. Her boss rarely invites her to important meetings and she is excluded from strategic planning sessions. She is angered by her annual performance review rating, which over several years went from "exceeds expectations" to "satisfactory."

Sharon does not want to be fired without a fight. She has invested too much of herself in the job. She doesn't know what she is entitled to or how to negotiate a better severance package. She is also interested in learning what materials she should accumulate before being terminated to help her case.

Sharon makes an appointment with a knowledgeable employment lawyer. At the interview, she learns that proper planning is essential to protecting her rights and maximizing severance and other benefits.

The lawyer advises her to accumulate and save all favorable correspondence, copies of records, and other documents (like company handbooks and kudos letters). She should notify the employer immediately when she discovers errors in her bonus, commissions, or compensation, and she should not accept reductions in salary or other benefits, particularly if she has a written contract prohibiting oral modifications of important terms. She is also advised to write a letter protesting any illegal actions, such as sexual harassment or health and safety violations, when they happen so that she will not be deemed to have consented to such treatment by a lack of action.

If she has not been fired by the date of her next performance review, Sharon is advised to write a rebuttal to any subjective or incorrect comments and explain why the review is inaccurate. She is told to find out if other workers are being fired; their ages, salary, gender, and race; and what the company is paying in severance. The lawyer also advises her about the proper way to act when the ax falls to set the stage for a more effective negotiating session.

No one should go into a job expecting the worst, but there are steps you can take while you are employed that, later on, will increase your severance package and negotiating leverage in the event you are fired.

In Chapters 2 through 5, you learned how to recognize if you are being treated illegally and unfairly. Chapters 6 through 10 will tell how to get more benefits when you are fired. This chapter will provide you with my thinking and strategies.

Do not panic if you think you will be fired. Before being laid off is the best time to take control and implement as many of the following legal and nonlegal strategies as possible.

RECOGNIZE THE WARNING SIGNS

Experts suggest that it takes roughly one month for every $10,000 of salary to find a comparable job after a termination. Thus, for example, if you make $50,000 a year, chances are you may not be reemployed within five months after being fired. While unemployment benefits will provide you with several hundred dollars of weekly income up to a maximum of twenty-six weeks in most states, anticipate that you may have problems paying a mortgage or rent and other regular expenses if you do not have substantial savings.

That is why it is essential to heed the warning signs as soon as possible. The time to make the right moves, such as trying to establish a line of credit (which is always easier to get while you are employed) or selling a large house to avoid a potentially devastating cash drain (which takes at least several months after the decision to sell is made), is *before* a firing whenever possible. It is also easier to get copies of important information and documentation from your files while you are still on the payroll.

Being aware can help you detect early signs of an impending discharge. If you are left out of important meetings, hear whispers when you walk down the hall, your boss doesn't look you squarely in the eye anymore, you are not promoted, do not receive an expected raise or promotion, are given unfavorable performance reviews or final warnings, or aren't paid an expected year-end bonus, the employer may be telling you that you are headed for the door. If your senses tell you something negative is going on, it is time to swing into action.

Even if your concerns are unfounded, the following strategies will not harm you in any way but may help prioritize your efforts to protect the current job or enable you to look more effectively for a new one.

REVIEW YOUR CONTRACT

If you signed a written contract, reread it. Review what it says about termination. For example, can you be fired at any time without cause, or must the employer send you written notice before the effective termination date? (Most independent sales agents, brokers, or reps receive written contracts from their principals requiring either party to give thirty to sixty days' notice before the contract can be effectively terminated.) Remember that the failure to give you timely notice, or any notice at all, may place the company in breach of contract if notification is required. To map out an effective action plan, be sure you know exactly what the contract says.

If you signed an employment contract with a definite term, you may have more protection than you thought. For example, if your contract states that it is effective for a period of one year commencing on X date and expiring on Y date, you can be legally terminated prior to Y date only for cause. The following are examples of cause that justify premature contract terminations:

- Theft or dishonesty
- Falsifying records or information
- Punching another employee's time card
- Leaving the job or company premises without prior approval from a supervisor
- Insubordination or disrespect for company work rules and policies
- Willful refusal to follow the directions of a supervisor (unless doing so would endanger health or safety)
- Assault, unprovoked attack, or threats of bodily harm against others
- Use of drugs or possession of alcoholic beverages on company premises or during company-paid time while away from the premises
- Reporting to work under the influence of drugs or alcohol
- Disclosing confidential and proprietary information to unauthorized third parties
- Unauthorized possession of weapons and firearms on company property
- Intentionally making errors in work, negligently performing duties, or willfully hindering or limiting production
- Sleeping on the job
- Excessive lateness or irregular attendance at work
- Failing to report absences
- Sexually harassing or abusing others
- Making secret profits
- Misusing trade secrets, customer lists, and other confidential information

Counsel Comments: You are increasing your chances of recovering damages in a lawsuit when you are hired for a fixed term of employment. This is because the burden of proof falls on the employer to demonstrate the specific actions constituting a legitimate reason to fire before the expiration of the fixed term. Often it is difficult to do this. Thus, where possible, always try to negotiate for a fixed term of employment before being hired.

Review if the contract prohibits additional benefits on termination. Some agreements specify that employees have no additional claims for damages after discharge. Others place a limit on benefits (e.g., "Upon termination for any reason, the employee will be limited to receiving severance equivalent to two weeks' pay for each full year of service"). By signing a written contract containing such a clause, you may be minimizing your post-termination negotiating power.

Does the contract restrict you from working for a competitor or establishing a competing business after termination? This is referred to as a restrictive covenant or covenant not to compete, which may or may not be enforceable depending on the particular facts and circumstances. (Restrictive covenants are discussed in detail in Chapter 12.)

Remember that your rights may be enhanced or diminished depending on the type of contract in existence. That is why it is important always to negotiate a fair agreement before accepting a job.

Tip: If you remember signing a formal employment contract but do not have a copy, discreetly ask the human resources department to make you a copy of the original. If you are asked why, just say that you misplaced or accidentally destroyed your copy recently and you need it for your records.

ACCUMULATE AND SAVE COPIES OF ALL PERTINENT DOCUMENTS AND RECORDS

Now is the time to collect all correspondence, records, and documents that may confirm your deals, the company's actions or promises (e.g., you have been told, "You are doing a great job here, so we would never fire you without adequate notice except for cause"), or show that you are doing a great job (e.g., a recent letter from the company president thanking you for a job well done or recommending you for a raise or promotion). Accumulating such evidence can help your case immeasurably in the event you are fired unfairly and decide to take legal action down the road.

Hopefully, you have taken steps right along to indicate your dissatisfaction with unfair company actions so that a court will not conclude that you accepted such actions by your conduct. As an example, many employees refuse to sign unfair and subjective employee evaluations. This is not recommended. Rather, it is better to sign the review with a notation that you are attaching a rebuttal as part of the evaluation. This is the way to properly document your dissatisfaction, and the rebuttal can protect you against subsequent illegal action by the company.

Firing and/or disciplining workers is not as simple as it used to be. Because many terminated individuals are now consulting lawyers, companies are being instructed to "set you up" (i.e., document problems in your personnel file). The reason is that when employers have failed to note performance problems on appraisals and lack sufficient documentation to prove inadequate job performance, they may not have a legal basis for firing an employee (since a poor performance excuse may then be viewed as a pretext) and may be leaving the company open to a ready-made claim of gender, race, or age discrimination if the employee fits into one of these protected categories. Thus, it is a good idea to protest (always in writing preferably) company actions you do not agree with.

Counsel Comments: If you believe that a future lawsuit with your employer is inevitable, get the edge by planning ahead. It is easier to obtain pertinent documents, including a copy of your employment contract, employee handbook, performance reviews, and favorable recommendations contained in your file from coworkers and management while you are still working at the company.

I once represented a man who worked for a prestigious financial institution. He was part of a four-member team responsible for devising and selling tax shelters on behalf of the employer.

The man had worked about nine and a half years for the company and was earning an annual base salary of $125,000. Each year he had consistently received large year-end bonuses (the previous year's bonus had been $50,000).

The man was suddenly fired in late November. The company claimed that his work performance was not satisfactory and that he did "not fit the image of an investment banker." The client hired me because he believed his job performance was excellent. He also felt cheated because the company offered no severance benefits, would not allow him to receive a pension that was due to vest within six months, and refused to pay him a bonus for the substantial portion of the current year he had worked.

After thoroughly investigating the matter, I asked the client if he had collected copies of pertinent information from his personnel file. Fortunately, he produced a number of excellent performance reviews. In addition, he was able to locate a memo that had been circulated throughout the company and delivered to the company's president. The memo congratulated each member of his group by name for placing a large tax shelter that year, and each member (including my client) was cited for outstanding work.

During negotiations, I informed management of the existence of this memo. I argued that in view of my client's history of receiving large raises and year-end bonuses, excellent performance evaluations, and the favorable memo, his firing was unjustified and was probably done to save the company a large sum of money. I also advised the company that a jury would probably take a dim view of what had transpired.

After many meetings, I was able to obtain an out-of-court settlement that included a year-end bonus, severance pay representing one month's salary for every year of employment, the company's agreement to qualify my client for a substantial pension, continuation of employer-paid medical insurance for six months, substantial payment for an outplacement employment search (up to $7,500) by a reputable firm, and a favorable recommendation in writing.

It is highly doubtful that I would have been able to negotiate such a favorable settlement without a copy of the "kudos" memo collected by my client. Thus, never underestimate the importance of collecting *all* favorable documents while working for a company.

Even if you did not keep copies of such material, don't despair entirely. Employees may have access to their personnel files as part of the discovery process during a lawsuit even in those states that do not ordinarily allow access.

Some states have passed laws allowing employees access to their personnel records. If your state permits this, it is a good idea to view information in your file and correct incomplete or inaccurate information before you are terminated. In some of these states, you may not be allowed to copy any of the documents in the file except those you previously signed (e.g., an employment application or a performance review), but you are allowed to make notes. And in other states, you may *not* even have the right to review your records, so check the law in your state. (The Federal Privacy Act, which deals mainly with access to employee records, forbids federal government employers from disclosing any information contained in employee files without the written consent of the employee in question. Discuss the ramifications of this federal law with your lawyer.)

Even in states where access to records is not permitted, employers are generally prohibited from distributing confidential information, such as medical records, to nonessential third parties and prospective employers, and you are generally permitted to inspect all your files containing confidential medical and credit information. Some union employees covered under collective bargaining agreements have the right to examine their own records and to be informed of what information is used in making decisions relevant to their employment.

Tip: Since it is often difficult to review the contents of your personnel file, make and save copies of all documents the minute you receive them so you don't have to retrieve them later.

In most arbitrations and lawsuits, employers are prohibited from introducing "memos in the file" that were never read or signed by you. This means that the company cannot attempt to prove an issue at a trial, such as your alleged misconduct, by submitting to a judge or jury a warning memo that was never given to you or that you never saw. During litigation, a few employers advise supervisors to prepare harmful documents after the fact, so be aware and advise your lawyer about this.

Some states permit workers to place a rebuttal statement in their personnel file if incorrect information is discovered. Other states allow employees to do this when the employer will not delete such comments. A few states (notably Connecticut) have laws that require employers to send copies of rebuttal statements to prospective employers or other parties when information pertaining to workers or their employment history is conveyed. Since each state treats the subject differently, review your state's law.

Counsel Comments: Some states require employers to seek workers' approval before employee records can be collected, distributed, or destroyed, and it may be illegal to distribute personal information without your consent. With respect to medical records and investigations, the law generally recognizes that a duty of confidentiality can arise to protect this information and avoid dissemination to nonessential third parties. Under emerging state laws and case decisions, employers who request medical information may be liable for the tort of intrusion and for the tort of public disclosure of private data. Several states have recognized a claim for negligent maintenance of personnel files when files containing inaccurate medical information are made available to third parties. For example, Connecticut has enacted a statute requiring employers to maintain medical records separately from personnel files and permitting employees to review all medical and insurance information in their individual files.

Thus, know your rights and review your state's law.

MAINTAIN A DIARY

It is easier to remember important incidents while they are happening instead of trying to remember and writing them down later. Your main focus in any diary is to reconstruct harmful events, workplace discrimination, oral promises of job security, or statements to show you are being treated unfairly by a supervisor or manager. Keeping a regular record of promises made and not kept concerning your job can assist you if you decide later to pursue legal action. A diary will also help construct a time frame and chronology of important events and ensure that your memories are accurate. Thus, wherever possible, if you sense your job is in jeopardy, start making daily entries such as the date, time, place, and comments you heard, noting exactly what was said and the names of witnesses who overheard the statements.

Interviewers, recruiters, and officers make oral statements that can be construed as promises of job security. They sometimes use words like "permanent employment" or "job for life," make broad statements concerning job longevity, and give assurances of continued employment or specific promises about career opportunities. When such statements are sufficient to be characterized as promises of job security, when you can prove the actual words were spoken, and when you can demonstrate that you relied on such statements to your detriment, you may be able to contest a firing. The following true case illustrates this.

An executive who worked for a company for thirty-two years without a written contract was suddenly fired. The man sued the company and argued that he had done nothing wrong to justify the firing. At the trial, he proved that the company's president told him several times that he would continue to be employed if he did a good job. He also proved that the company had a policy of not firing executives except for cause and that he was never criticized or warned that his job was in jeopardy. He also proved that he had a commendable track record, his employment history was excellent, and he had received periodic merit bonuses, raises, and promotions. He won the case because the facts created an implied promise that the company could not arbitrarily terminate him.

Tip: Try to document what was said, when, where, who said it, and the names of witnesses who were present whenever promises were made. This may help your case at a later date if you are fired in a manner inconsistent with such promises and your state recognizes this exception to the employment-at-will rule. Maintaining a contemporaneous diary will help you prove that such statements were actually made because you will be able to remember them in court and your recollection may be viewed as being more reliable because you could refer to a diary.

CONSIDER MEETING WITH A LAWYER BEFORE YOU RESIGN OR ARE FIRED

Show the lawyer the documentation you have accumulated. If you perceive problems that are valid, your lawyer may be able to recommend additional strategies, such as sending a final letter of protest or requesting a meeting to discuss and attempt to resolve the difficulties. These options may not be available after your firing and can enhance your case if litigation proves necessary.

The lawyer can give you a better evaluation of the possibility of success with your case when he or she has viewed all pertinent records and documents. That is why it is important to collect key evidence for presentation to your lawyer before a case is litigated. Be aware of this and act accordingly.

Marcia is an executive who has worked eight years for a company. She previously received excellent performance reviews, merit raises, and promotions. Her performance was never criticized until a new supervisor with less experience replaced her boss, who retired.

The new supervisor and Marcia clash on petty matters. Soon they disagree on what is expected and demanded of Marcia. Although she tries her best, it is apparent that their personalities clash and her work is not appreciated. Marcia then receives a neutral-to-negative annual review, which she believes is subjective, biased, and unfair. She senses the company is setting her up to be fired. She is so unhappy that she is considering resigning just to get away from the stress her supervisor is causing.

Marcia consults a skilled lawyer for advice and guidance. The lawyer recommends that she not, under any circumstances, resign from her job because she will forfeit valuable stock options, retirement benefits, and severance pay. He drafts a respectful but accurate rebuttal on her behalf, which Marcia retypes and submits. The lawyer reviews her employee manual and notices that the company maintains an informal internal grievance procedure to handle employee complaints. He recommends that she discreetly contact the president of the company (whom Marcia likes and has known for many years) for a private informal meeting.

Marcia meets with the president and explains her dissatisfaction and problems. She shows the president her review and rebuttal. The president was unaware of the problems she was having. He advises her that she is an important part of the company and that her work and dedication have always been appreciated. Marcia's next review is excellent. Her job is saved and the supervisor is eventually reassigned.

START LOOKING FOR NEW EMPLOYMENT

The best time to seek reemployment is while you are still working. There is less pressure to find a replacement job when a steady paycheck is still coming in. You also have the luxury of not appearing as hungry, since the prospective employer knows you are currently employed. This means you may have more clout and be able to command a higher salary or more benefits during negotiations.

People often ask me if it is legal to look for a job while they are still employed. The answer is yes, provided you do so discreetly and not on company time. Thus, schedule your telephone calls and interviews during lunch hours or after work. If you have to prepare for and attend an important interview, take a vacation day.

If you are employed full-time but also work for a competitor or hold another job, that is probably illegal without your employer's knowledge and consent. For instance, one salesperson was accused of violating his duty of loyalty by distributing a competitor's catalog to his customers while still working for his company.

In preparation for quitting a job, you are generally allowed to look for another job without advising your employer. You can quietly advise customers and friends of your intention to leave and even take minor steps to compete and organize a new company while still working (e.g., prepare stationery and business cards or arrange for a new telephone number if you are going into business for yourself).

What you cannot do is take active steps, such as solicit business for the new entity, while on your present employer's payroll, hurt its reputation by talking poorly about your employer, or lie down on the job by not taking orders or working as diligently as before.

Start calling business contacts for leads. Prepare long and short lists of all the people you would call if you did lose a job and start calling them regularly. It is essential to maintain an active network of business associates, and now is the time to start. You may want to make a personal copy of your Rolodex for this purpose.

Update your résumé. Schedule an appointment with a career counselor or an employment agency for advice and guidance.

REMOVE PERSONAL DOCUMENTS FROM YOUR OFFICE

After being fired, you may have difficulty removing personal effects and business materials from your office. In fact, many employers, after suddenly notifying you that you are fired, will escort you back to your office and stay there to approve the materials you want to pack up and take home. Plan ahead to avoid this potential problem.

I recently represented a female employee who resigned from a job. She returned the next morning to retrieve the personal contents from her office. However, many of these items were not given to her. The company claimed that boxes of expensive items (including textbooks, course materials, and technical manuals) were purchased with company funds and remained the property of the company. The woman hired me to retrieve these valuable materials.

Tip: You can avoid this kind of aggravation by being discreet and removing valuable items now. But be sure not to take clearly designated company property to avoid being accused of theft or conversion.

TALK TO FELLOW EMPLOYEES

It is easier to learn about a company's termination and severance policies while you are still on the premises. Find out all you can about what was paid to other employees when they were fired. This information can be quite useful to your lawyer during severance negotiations. For example, if you belong to a protected class (e.g., are a woman, over forty, a minority, or handicapped), your lawyer can argue that the company violated its policy or engaged in discrimination by not paying you the same rate of severance as other nonprotected employees.

ANALYZE YOUR FINANCIAL SITUATION

How much cash do you currently have on hand to pay your bills? If you do not have at least a six-month cushion, you should consider planning for the termination by reducing your overhead, bills, and lifestyle. Of course you will be reluctant to do this, but it makes sense to consider an austerity budget before the ax falls.

Speak to your accountant or financial planner for guidance. Experts suggest it is a good idea to pay off large credit card bills with high interest rates while you are still receiving a regular paycheck. Look into refinancing your mortgage and consolidating all your debts for this purpose. Worse, if you live above your means and the chances of being reemployed at your current level of salary may not materialize for

Sylvia thinks she is going to be fired. She is friendly with Beth, an assistant in her company's human relations department. In response to Sylvia's question, Beth quietly informs Sylvia at lunch one day that when Jim, a coworker in Sylvia's department, was let go several months ago, he received a two-month severance package after working two years.

Sylvia is terminated. Although she worked for the company for eight years, she is initially offered the same two-month severance package. She consults a lawyer, who advises that the offer may violate sex discrimination laws.

Sylvia contacts the employer and demands an additional six months' severance, for a total of eight months. She argues that she should receive the same pro rata package (i.e., one month of severance for every year worked) that similarly situated males received. The company argues that every employee, regardless of gender or amount of tenure, receives two months' severance as standard policy. From information she learned, Sylvia knows this is untrue.

Sylvia sticks to her guns and continues to negotiate. She finally agrees to accept an additional four months' severance (for a total of six months' severance pay) from the employer to compromise and settle the matter amicably.

many months, you may be forced to sell your house to lower your debt. But selling can take many months, so plan ahead if this is a viable option.

Find Sources of Cash

In his excellent article "Prepare Before the Pink Slip Comes" (*Newsday*, August 23, 1996), Lloyd Chrein writes that it is critical to locate areas where you will be able to receive a cash infusion until you find a new job. He recommends trying to establish a line of credit or taking out a home equity loan. The trick is to act before being laid off, because banks generally don't lend to the unemployed.

Another source of funds is bank accounts. Where possible, liquidate long-term accounts like CDs and place ample funds into checking accounts so that you can use the money immediately without paying a penalty. Although you may get less interest, availability should be your concern and you don't want the money tied up.

Mr. Chrein suggests that you check your company's 401(k) plan if applicable, because you may have the option of borrowing from it. If you are in the process of buying a home, you may want to postpone the decision if you can get out of the transaction. If you can't, Mr. Chrein advises putting down as little cash as possible so you don't have all that money tied up. Avoid adjustable mortgages. These can be costly if rates go up and you are out of a job, so he recommends fixed or fixed/adjustable hybrids instead. Finally, if you own a vacation property, Mr. Chrein advises that you not stay in it; rent it out or sell it to get cash.

Tip: If all else fails and you have no other possible sources of funds, speak to family members or friends about short-term loans. Consult your accountant to get advice about whether the interest payments on such loans are tax-deductible and how to structure them in your best interest. If you can take out a personal loan from a bank, so much the better.

Suspend Payments on Loans if Possible

Some lending institutions will let you suspend payments on school loans and other loans without penalty when you are unemployed. Inquire if this is feasible and whether your future credit will be impaired.

Start a Part-time Business or Freelance Job Now

Such a business has the potential of keeping you going after you are laid off and may even expand into your next career.

Review Your Pension Plans and Rules

Confirm that the amounts you will receive on termination are accurate. By asking for a current statement, you can ascertain that your years of service are properly credited and that your income is properly reported in the final computation. Now is the time to check for mistakes so you can receive the money immediately after a termination if you need it. Check to see that there is no break in service or that the benefits have not been reduced for technical reasons (e.g., because the company you work for was acquired by another). Ask for copies of pertinent company plans and review what they say. If someone asks why you want this, just say "because I have the right to this information by law." Write a letter to the plan administrator if you cannot obtain a copy or do not agree with the numbers. (More information about this subject and how to protect your rights is given in Chapter 8.)

After reviewing and approving the amount, you can compute what your monthly income will be after counting expected pension or profit-sharing monies plus unemployment payments for the first twenty-six weeks after you are unemployed (and possibly for another twenty-six weeks depending on your state or federal law at the time you receive such benefits).

Consider Your Eligibility for Bonuses, Stock Options, Profit-Sharing Monies, or Commissions About to Become Due

Be aware of the date when the money will be vested or when it is supposed to be paid. Do not allow the company to fire you to deprive you of these expected benefits.

Review Your Health Benefits to Be Sure You Are Properly Covered

Your entitlement to continued health and medical benefits under federal COBRA law is discussed in Chapter 8. But if you anticipate special needs for yourself or your family, or are worried that company-supplied benefits may be too costly, it may be wise to shop around for a more attractive policy before you are laid off.

CONSIDER SENDING DEMAND LETTERS

Sending demand letters to confirm all actions or complain about illegal treatment may strengthen a legal claim. The time to demonstrate your nonacceptance of a company's act is *before* you are fired, not after. Complaining in writing after a firing may not mean as much and be viewed merely as sour grapes.

If you complain about illegal treatment before a firing, your employer may be advised by its legal counsel not to fire you (since the action may be viewed as illegal retaliation). In some cases, you can save your job or forestall the firing by complaining in writing. This action may also enable you to recover additional damages if you are fired. However, it is best to do this only after speaking with an employment lawyer.

AVOID RESIGNING

Never resign from a job just because you suspect you are about to be fired. By resigning you may forfeit valuable benefits. I repeat: Do not resign for this and many other reasons (to be discussed in Chapter 10). Seek legal guidance to avoid acting incorrectly or irrationally.

PRACTICE WHAT YOU WILL SAY AND HOW YOU WILL ACT

Acting properly after being advised of a termination can go a long way toward obtaining more severance pay and other benefits. The key is not to panic, lose your temper, or passively accept the package offered. This will be explained in detail in Chapters 7 and 8 and is another reason why it is best to consult an employment lawyer when you think you may be fired. The lawyer can prioritize the issues and advise you on what you should attempt to accomplish, regardless of a group termination or a one-on-one firing.

Tip: I frequently role-play a mock termination session with my clients and tell them what to say and how to respond after hearing the news. Most employers prefer to fire people suddenly without warning, to keep them off guard. Being prepared can greatly diminish stress and anxiety and help you even the playing field.

CHAPTER 7

Facing the Music and Taking Charge

Robert is called into his boss's office and told things aren't working out. He is told he will receive two weeks' severance pay and is given fifteen minutes to leave the premises. After being escorted back to his office, his replacement stands over him while he packs. He is not allowed to take his Rolodex or other business items. He hardly has time to say good-bye to his coworkers.

Arriving home embarrassed, stunned, and exhausted, Robert ponders what he did wrong and why he was treated in such an arbitrary and capricious manner. He calls an employment lawyer he knows and schedules an appointment to learn about his rights and how to get a better severance package. Rather than stay mad, he decides to get even and assert himself.

Being notified that you are fired can come as a shock even when you are prepared for it. Most people experience strong feelings of panic because they suddenly have no control of how they will maintain their present lifestyle, pay debts, become reemployed, and tell their friends and loved ones. Some become physically sick. Others feel deeply embarrassed. Many feel used and resent the years of loyal and dedicated service they gave without being more fully appreciated. Yet some clients tell me that being fired is a relief.

In my daily law practice over the past nineteen years, I have observed that terminated workers basically share one common denominator: they all feel cheated and want to even the score.

Whether you are fired for a valid reason (such as for poor performance, misconduct, dishonesty, or being accused of sexual harassment) or due to a downsizing or reorganization, you expect that your employer will treat you with respect and dignity. This means, for example, that you will not suddenly be fired before a vacation, during an office Christmas party, or in the presence of a large group of your colleagues. The firing should be discreet and professional. All precautions should be taken to avoid embarrassing you in front of coworkers. No information about the dismissal should be revealed to nonessential third parties.

Marshall Loeb, in his comprehensive article "What to Do if You Get Fired" (*Fortune*, January 15, 1996), writes that if you're ever fired (as 415,000 employees were, he says, in 1995), remember these three rules for negotiating your exit: "(1) Never quit; make the company fire you; (2) He who acts first, loses; and (3) Your pride is the company's best weapon. Don't get proud, get even."

This chapter will answer many questions you'll have if you are fired. Helpful strategies will enable you to begin the process of getting the most out of your separation package with or without a lawyer, protect and enhance your reputation, and help you feel you did everything possible to rectify a situation that may have been caused through no fault of your own. More important than trying to get your job back or discovering the true reasons for your discharge is getting the most money possible in your situation. In this chapter and in Chapter 8, I'll explain how by telling you how to negotiate the best severance package.

LEARNING WHY YOU WERE FIRED

An initial inquiry should be to ascertain whether the employer had a valid reason to fire you. This is important because it can impact your severance package and whether you are entitled to receive severance and other benefits in the first place. Many employers will not offer you post-termination benefits if you are fired for misconduct (i.e., cause) unless you are an important officer or executive. Chapter 6 lists many examples of "for cause" firings. Briefly, the following are common examples of acts that justify "for cause" job terminations: habitual lateness or unexcused prolonged absence; current drug abuse; disrespect or fighting on the job; disobedience of company work rules, regulations, and policies; gross negligence or neglect of duty; and dishonesty or unfaithfulness.

Although these reasons may appear to be fairly straightforward, it is often difficult to prove that they occurred with sufficient intensity to justify a firing. For example, in union firing cases, arbitrators look first to see whether a legitimate company rule was violated and whether or not that rule was justified. Other times, an act or behavior cited as the reason for termination may not even fit in a "for cause" category. For example, most labor contracts do *not* specifically define drug or alcohol abuse as unacceptable workplace conduct.

I once obtained a copy of the manual that arbitrators use to assist them in rendering employment decisions. The manual lists standards for "just cause" firings, which are given here in modified form for their importance and instruction. Every company official entrusted with hiring and firing employees should be familiar with the following guidelines:

1. Did the company have a clear rule against the kind of employee behavior for which discipline was administered?
2. Is the rule reasonably related to the orderly, efficient, and safe operation of the company's business?
3. Has the company provided employees reasonable opportunity to learn the company's rules?
4. Has the company provided employees reasonable opportunity to learn the possible consequences of disregarding the rules?
5. Has the company administered and enforced the rules evenhandedly and without discrimination among the employees?
6. Did the company investigate fairly the circumstances involved in an alleged offense?
7. Did the company, through its investigation, obtain substantial evidence of guilt?
8. Was the degree of penalty imposed for a fairly investigated, fact-supported offense reasonably related to (a) the seriousness of the

proven offense and/or (b) the nature of the guilty employee's past record?

The burden of proving these points rests with the company. That burden is usually one of "clear and convincing" proof rather than the "preponderance" standard that is typically required in other kinds of lawsuits.

Counsel Comments: If you are fired for cause, you may not be able to collect unemployment insurance and your COBRA health benefits may be impaired. The employer may also decide to give you a poor reference. Thus, consult an employment lawyer if you are terminated for cause, because the lawyer may be able to help you regain benefits.

To illustrate this point, I once represented a young man who, due to an innocent lapse of judgment, faced many obstacles. The twenty-nine-year-old client managed a Broadway theater and was doing a terrific job. He worked eighty-hour weeks, had received a raise, and was in line for a Christmas bonus.

Someone who worked for the company staging the current production at the theater told my client she was leaving to get married and asked if he could give her a T-shirt souvenir. These souvenirs were handed out regularly to customers attending the show as a free Christmas promotion gift.

My client went upstairs to the main star's dressing room and removed a T-shirt from his locked cabinet. He was spotted by an assistant, who alerted management. My client was suddenly fired for stealing. Devastated, the man came to me for help. He related how he had keys to every office, door, and locked closet in the theater and didn't feel he was required to ask anyone's permission just to remove a T-shirt. Besides, he said, the company gave away thousands of garments that week after every performance.

I conveyed this to management and pleaded that my client's firing was unjustified due to his record of loyalty and hard work. I argued that he was being used as a scapegoat. I stated that there was no malicious motivation behind the act because he was taking the item for a friend, not himself (this was confirmed in a letter I prepared, which the woman signed to support my client's story), and it was not taken for resale. As a last resort I offered that he be briefly suspended without pay for his actions.

Although the ex-employer refused to give him back his job or pay him severance, I did manage to recover a small year-end bonus. The company agreed it would not contest his application for unemployment insurance and he was allowed to collect benefits. I also received a letter confirming that no record of the true reason for the discharge would be revealed to third parties in the future. Hopefully, my client is managing another theater these days, which was his passion.

In order to learn if the employer's reason for firing you was valid, you must first discover the reason. If you are terminated illegally, there are up to thirty-five causes of action that can be asserted in court before a jury. According to Jury Verdict Research, the median compensatory award returned by juries in wrongful-termination cases in 1995 rose by 56 percent over a year earlier, to $204,300 and since 1992, such awards have increased by 94 percent.

The best way to discover the reason for your discharge is to ask. Inquire why you are being let go. If the employer refuses to answer, an effective method of getting the employer to talk is to state that you need to know what happened so you don't act the same way in your next job. Although the law in most states does not obligate employers to spill the beans, a jury may well believe that decency and compassion require, at a minimum, that the employer provide you with an honest explanation.

Counsel Comments: Although you may not be able to get your job back, a lawyer may be able to use the following reasons as leverage in the attempt to get you more severance and other benefits. When a terminated worker consults with me regarding his or her discharge, I consider the following factors to determine whether the firing was justified and/or legal:

- Are there mitigating factors that excuse or explain the employee's poor performance or misconduct?
- Was the employee victimized by a supervisor's bias or subjective evaluations rather than objective criteria?
- How long has the employee worked for the company? What kind of overall record does the employee have?
- Is termination appropriate under all the circumstances? Does the punishment fit the crime?

- Has the employer followed a consistent policy of terminating workers with similar infractions?
- Is the employer retaliating against the employee because of a refusal to commit illegal or unethical acts (such as falsifying records), for obeying a subpoena (in a legal case involving the employer), or for serving on extended jury duty or in the military rather than due to a bona fide business reason, disciplinary problem, or poor performance?
- Has the employee been fired because she filed a sexual harassment complaint, is pregnant, or refused to submit to demands for sexual favors?
- Is the fired employee being deprived of severance or other financial benefits that are due? Is this contrary to the employee's contract, letter agreement, company handbook, or employee manual?
- Is the firing contrary to a written contract?

If any of the above considerations apply to you, consult an employment lawyer immediately.

HOW TO PROPERLY HANDLE THE NEWS

Typically, you will be called into a supervisor's, manager's, or executive's office when being informed of the firing. Decisions such as who should tell you, where, and when have already been made. The employer should decide these matters with an eye to minimizing your discomfort and embarrassment, and increasing the chances you will have an opportunity to regain your composure and begin taking steps to find employment elsewhere. People who quickly find satisfactory replacement jobs are less likely to sue ex-employers. Smart employers know this and should be willing to do everything possible to help you in this pursuit.

Some companies will fire you at the end of the week (so they don't have to pay you for any remaining days that week) and order you to leave the premises immediately. For example, the *Wall Street Journal* reported that computer maker Hewlett-Packard usually escorts fired employees out of the building, sometimes shipping their belongings to their homes.

If you are requested to leave the premises, do so quietly. The decision to fire you has already been made. Typically, it is final and not appealable in most cases. However difficult it may be, the trick is to *stay calm* when you are told the news. Raising your voice and arguing will get you nowhere and burn bridges.

Asking the person to reconsider is generally a waste of time unless he or she is a trusted friend and your request has a good chance of paying off or the employer has a stated policy of allowing workers to grieve and/or appeal a termination decision. If you are aware of such a policy, consider taking appropriate steps immediately, since you have nothing to lose. Thus, if the policy requires you to appeal the decision in writing no more than X (e.g., three) days after being fired, do so to avoid a claim that your appeal was not filed timely or properly. Just don't get your hopes up, because requests for reconsideration rarely work.

Counsel Comments: Although I disagree, some experts advise against asking the employer to reconsider under any circumstances. This minority view is that your acquiescence may be viewed positively (as a relief) and the company may reward you for "not rocking the boat" by giving you a generous severance package. Since each situation depends on the unique facts and personalities of the players involved, it is always recommended you seek the advice of an experienced employment lawyer before embarking on a particular course of action.

There are situations, however, where the employer may have a confirmed progressive discipline system in place. To combat the trend toward awarding fired workers large verdicts in discrimination and breach of contract cases and to avoid looking foolish or biased to a jury, most employers are being advised by their lawyers to enact a progressive discipline system before firing workers (especially those over forty, women, or minorities). They are advised to structure the discipline so that it appears rational and proportional. This includes first giving employees notice that their performance is unsatisfactory and extending an opportunity to improve. If they do not meet expectations, workers then receive a written warning that sets deadlines for improvement. When there is no improvement after a final warning, termination follows, with the decision to terminate being reviewed and independently approved by several people (such as a supervisor,

the president, and an executive from the human resources department) before it occurs.

Tip: If you believe the company has a policy of giving written
warnings before a firing but you were not given the same opportunity to improve as other coworkers, ask the employer to reconsider, or
consult a lawyer for advice. Many employers violate the law when they
fail to apply a system of progressive discipline consistently, properly, or
fairly.

When companies decide to terminate workers in a large layoff or
restructuring, the same executives typically review the ages and personal characteristics of all those chosen to be fired to be sure the layoffs are not skewed and predominantly affect one protected class of
workers (such as older workers). Again, if you are part of a protected
class and believe that a predominant number of women, older workers, or minority workers were fired en masse along with you, speak to
an employment lawyer for guidance.

Tip: A request to reconsider, however, if presented in a calm and
professional manner, may cause the owner or president to gain sym-
pathy for your predicament. This can translate into more severance
and post-termination benefits if you play your cards right. (More on
this later.)

There may also be occasions when it is wise to request that the decision be postponed. These include if you are close to earning a vested
pension or profit-sharing benefit, commission, bonus, or stock option
grant and need the additional time to "bridge the gap." Request this
when applicable, because you have nothing to lose. If you feel the decision was financially driven and you need to stall the effective termination date, consider telling the employer you might take a cut in pay
in return for a higher bonus or commission. If you are told you were
fired for poor performance, ask to be placed on final warning or probation and given one last chance. And if you must stay on the payroll
a little longer because you desperately need the money that a regular
paycheck will bring (e.g., to pay for your child's large tuition bill that
is due in a few weeks), tell the employer you are willing to work different or part-time hours, or will accept a transfer or even a temporary demotion if this is applicable.

Tip: This is a very important concept to think about and act on. Too often, employees accept a firing very close to the vesting of a significant financial benefit without a fight.

You may also have grounds for a valid lawsuit in the event you have a vested pension but are fired just weeks short of becoming entitled to greater severance, larger monthly pension payments, and improved medical and insurance benefits. This happened to an executive who sued his former employer in federal court.

The case involved the termination of a former vice-president of a large manufacturing company after thirty-two years of service. At the time of the firing, the man earned $132,500. Although the executive was fully vested before he was terminated, he was approximately one month short of becoming entitled to substantially higher pension payments and additional severance. He sued his former employer under Section 510 of ERISA, which makes it illegal for employers to discharge anyone for the purpose of cutting off their employee benefits or stopping them from collecting vested pension rights.

After the employee persuaded the jury that the reasons advanced for his discharge were unworthy of credence and were motivated by a discriminatory purpose—to deny him additional benefits (which the employer could not rebut)—he won the case and recovered damages of $650,000, representing additional pension and severance payments.

Cases such as this demonstrate the responsibility of employers to comply with all pension laws and ERISA provisions regarding severance when a business is sold or when company policy has created an expectation that the purchasing company will continue an established severance policy crediting employees with prior years of service from the selling company.

STAY CALM

Your goal when being informed of the termination decision is to increase the chances of getting more severance and other post-termination benefits. Don't panic, lose your temper, or passively accept the package offered. Yelling will not help your cause. I frequently advise my clients to act composed, surprised, and hurt, even if this is out of character. You want the employer to feel sorry for you. Representing thousands of terminated workers from all walks of life and job levels has taught me that sympathetic employers are more amenable to offering a generous severance package than irritated or angry ones. Sending obnoxious letters, screaming, fighting, making threats, or otherwise acting improperly will only reaffirm the employer's decision to fire you and may cause the employer to refuse to negotiate a severance package with you or your lawyer in the future.

Stay calm and collected, even if it kills you, since you don't want to be labeled a troublemaker due to an angry outburst. Employers are quite familiar these days with stories of angry ex-employees who resort to violence to even the score. Never even remotely create the impression that this is possible.

Do not let the employer know what you are thinking when you initially hear the news. Be reserved. Listen to what the employer says (especially what the initial severance package comprises). When presented with an initial package, act noncommittal. Marshall Loeb states that the best way of getting even is to keep your cool during that most stressful moment when the boss calls you in and wields his terrible swift sword. He recommends that you should say almost nothing— you don't want to start negotiating now. Instead, carefully write down what your boss is saying. This may make him or her be more conciliatory. It also sends a signal that you're not about to surrender, and so the company had better prepare to deal with you.

Counsel Comments: Taking notes during the meeting conveys the message that you're compiling information that someone else, like a lawyer, will review. It also signals that you may be documenting the substance of the conversation for possible use in a future lawsuit. Stephen M. Pollan and Mark Levine, in their article "How to Survive Getting Fired" (*New York* magazine, September 7, 1992), agree that it is important to write down everything you hear. They recommend that, if the supervisor asks why you are taking notes, you state, "It's very important for me to understand everything you're saying." They also advise you to take notes even if you are told that a formal severance package in writing will be coming shortly, and not to act positive or negative once you hear the company's initial offer but simply repeat the terms as you've written them down, saying, "I just want to make sure I have this right."

STALL FOR TIME

Try to stall for time when you are fired. Stalling for time can help you learn more important facts. This includes many of the points discussed in Chapter 6 (e.g., requesting to see your personnel file to review and collect favorable documents; learning who made the decision to fire you to see if there is a possibility of appealing that decision or whether that person had proper authority to terminate you; reconstructing promises of security that were made; reviewing employment manuals). This information can help you in negotiations for additional severance and other benefits.

Do not accept the company's first offer of severance if possible. Always request a negotiating session to obtain more benefits. As Messrs. Pollan and Levine explain in their fine article, "If you're pressed to accept the package offered or to sign any type of form, refuse. Tell the employer that you need time to consider without specifying whom you'll be discussing it with. Make an appointment for another meeting several days later. This will give you time to speak to your lawyer or advisor and formulate a response to the initial severance offer."

Marshall Loeb says, "If you cave in, the company will say thanks a lot and figure you're a wimp. On the other hand, if you bargain hard, the company will almost certainly not retaliate."

Counsel Comments: I have contacted thousands of employers to negotiate more generous severance packages on behalf of fired workers, and not once has an employer revoked the initial offer made to my client. In a minority of instances, they will say, "Mr. Sack, it's the best we can do, take it or leave it (by X date)." But employers or their counsel have *never* insulted me and revoked the offer in spite because I contacted them. This is probably due to the fact that since there is generally no legal obligation to offer severance, the fact that an offer was made can be viewed as an employer's attempt to buy peace and avoid litigation.

ALWAYS ASK FOR MORE

Although there is generally no legal obligation to pay severance monies, employers in the United States do offer such payments when a firing is due to a group layoff, business conditions outside the employee's control (such as a reorganization, downsizing, job elimination, or other "neutral" factors), or for reasons other than employee misconduct.

However, there may be a legal obligation to pay severance when:

- You have a written contract stating that severance will be paid
- Oral promises are given regarding severance pay
- The employer voluntarily promises to pay severance
- The employer has a policy of paying severance, and this is documented in a company manual or employee handbook
- The employer has paid severance to other employees in similar firings and has thereby created a precedent

If you are fired and are not offered severance, it is advisable to request a meeting with a qualified representative of the employer to discuss clarification regarding severance and available wage equivalents. As you will learn, there is generally nothing to lose and plenty to gain.

The amount of severance pay offered is typically derived from a formula based on a person's length of service (e.g., two weeks for every year of work), but each company and industry is different. For example, I have observed that people who work in publicity-conscious industries, such as advertising, will receive greater severance packages than those working for heavy-manufacturing concerns, especially when they worked many years or made significant achievements or revenue for the company.

The ability to request a better severance package is greatest when you alone have been singled out for firing. When a job elimination affects a large group of workers, each will have a tougher time getting a better package. In such a case, a company's standard response is often: "We would like to offer you more, but then we have to offer the same benefits to everyone fired in your department to be fair and consistent, and we can't afford it."

Tip: Even if you are fired as part of a group, you should still request an appointment to ask for a better package. Go for it, since you have nothing to lose. The goal is to try to demonstrate that you are different from the pack, that your special achievements warrant a better package, or that your personal situation (e.g., caring for an infirm parent) requires that you be treated differently. Your efforts can work if the company believes giving you more is fair or decent and you will keep your mouth shut and not reveal the more favorable terms to others. If applicable, tell the company that you will sign a gag order clause in a separation agreement, with hefty penalties if you ever reveal the terms of the settlement to anyone other than your lawyers, accountant, or spouse. The company may be willing to accommodate you provided you sign a release, especially if you are over forty, a female, a minority, or in a protected class. It may view giving you additional benefits worth it when you sign a release agreeing not to sue and agreeing to keep quiet.

Counsel Comments: As I have said many times, it pays to ask for more severance and other perks when you are fired, regardless of the circumstances. This is so even when you are told the company never deviates from its established policy. I have observed that the bosses who do the actual firing are not typically the ones who negotiate the package. This is done by someone from human resources or a company lawyer. If your proposal is presented early and professionally, it may be viewed as an honest attempt to reach an agreement, regardless of how much more you're asking for and even if you were fired along with others in your department. You've already been terminated: what more harm can an employer do to you?

APPEAL TO DECENCY AND FAIR PLAY

In my experience, this is the most effective way of getting a better package. Most employers are fearful of the increasing amount of employee-related litigation and are flexible in easing the departure of terminated individuals, especially those who can sue for discrimination (i.e., people over forty, women, minorities, and others in a protected class). After you are granted an appointment, you should begin the negotiating session by appealing to corporate decency and fair play. For example, you may state that severance pay is needed to carry you over while you look for a new job or that more severance is needed because you anticipate it will take longer to find a suitable job than the amount of severance currently offered will cover. Tell the employer that experts state it takes an average of one month for each $10,000 of salary to find a replacement job.

Rather than state, "If you don't give me more money, I'll sue," it is more effective to say, "I have two children in college, an expensive home with a hefty mortgage that I can barely afford, and I recently lost a parent (or spouse) (or have just gone through a nasty divorce). If I don't receive more severance pay, I may have to foreclose my home, file for bankruptcy, and tell my kids they'll have to drop out of school. By not offering more money, I'm afraid you're putting me on the road to financial ruin."

Employers are often sympathetic to this approach. Be polite; being vindictive or making threats won't solve anything. But acting in a polite way doesn't mean that you can't be demanding and forceful during the presentation. Recognize that most companies want you to feel you've "won" something from them. So they may be inclined to offer you at least some of the extras they have quietly granted to others in your situation. That way, you'll be less likely to bad-mouth your ex-employer to customers or the press, hire a lawyer (which companies want to avoid whenever possible), or file a lawsuit, which can cost the company valuable time and expense even if it wins. This is why you should not believe a company's claim that it cannot afford to pay you more because word may get out to others and create a precedent.

Tip: If your efforts are unsuccessful with the HR person or bureaucrat, go back to your boss and explain that you are being treated unfairly. Marshall Loeb comments that by then guilt may have sunk in and the ex-boss wants to get it over with. That's when exceptions are made.

Most important, you must know what you want out of the negotiations before you begin. The material in Chapter 8 explains in detail each of the major elements you should be discussing and fallback strategies to employ if you don't initially get what you want. This is the same information I give to my clients to help them obtain a better severance package. Recognize that this information can help you obtain more money and benefits, whatever your situation.

Tips in Chapter 9 will tell you how to confirm the agreement you reach in writing, plus steps to take, such as bringing in a lawyer, if you are unable to obtain an adequate package on your own. I also provide a host of actual demand letters that you can draft and send when you fail to get expected commissions, bonus, vacation pay, and medical and retirement benefits after being fired.

CHAPTER 8

Getting the Best Package

Jim is suddenly fired without cause. He worked fourteen years for a company and is shocked when he hears the news. The company initially offers him a meager severance package of two weeks' pay.

Jim does his homework. He requests a meeting with the senior vice-president to discuss the offer and how he feels about the company and his discharge. Jim chose to speak with the senior VP because he respects him and has always considered him to be a friend. In fact, the senior VP attended the wedding of Jim's daughter.

Jim states that he may not be able to find a comparable job in the near future. He discusses the effect the discharge will have on his marriage and finances. He offers to work for the company as a consultant or sales rep. The senior VP is moved by Jim's candor and professionalism. He recommends to the company president that additional severance be given to Jim. In the end, Jim receives three months' severance, outplacement assistance, and a favorable reference. Although Jim is not thrilled with the offer, he is satisfied knowing he made the best of a bad situation.

After you have been fired and decide not to accept the company's initial offer, it is critical to prepare a proper battle plan to maximize your severance package. Understand what you want to ask for, whom you will talk to, and what you want to achieve before you attend the negotiation session. Prioritize the critical elements of the package and try to obtain them in order of importance. This chapter will help you decide what to ask for and how to request it.

WAGES

The longer you've worked at a company and the better your job reviews have been, the more leverage you may have. Most employers have different policies regarding severance wages depending on the industry, company, and your title, job status, and achievements. Although you may initially be offered between one and two weeks of pay for each year worked, ask for more. Avoid accepting the employer's first offer; negotiate, negotiate, negotiate. I recommend that you attempt to receive *one month* of severance for each year worked as a starting point. Ask for an additional month of pay for every dependent you claim on your tax return. If this can be achieved, you can leave the company knowing that you have received a fair severance offer.

Stall for time while you are negotiating the package. Delaying the start date before the package kicks in means that you will receive more money in the aggregate. You are in good shape while your regular salary and benefits continue, since you are still being paid. Most terminated employees forget to negotiate this simple point.

Avoid arrangements where you are offered severance for a specified period (e.g., six months) that automatically ceases when you obtain a new job. Rather, make the offer noncontingent on new employment, or arrange that differential severance will be paid in a lump sum when you obtain a new job prior to the expiration of the severance period. For example, arrange that three months' worth of severance will be paid in a lump sum if a new job is obtained three months before the six months of salary continuation expires.

Tip: Here's an effective negotiating strategy to receive more severance. If the company offers you three months' severance, for example, and you want more, tell the company you will accept this provided you receive an additional month of severance (up to three months) for every month you continue to remain unemployed after the initial three-month period from the date of your discharge. Many employers will agree to this because they believe the goal of severance is to help you survive while you are out of work.

If severance pay is to be paid in a lump sum, ask for it immediately, not in installments over time (e.g., 20 percent now and 20 percent every month for the next four months). Some employers insist on structuring severance this way as a guarantee that you will not violate the terms of a restrictive covenant or reveal the terms of the settlement to others, knowing that if you do, all payments will stop. Avoid this arrangement whenever possible.

Tip: Since severance pay is taxable, it may be advantageous to defer a portion of the income into the next tax year, when you may pay less in taxes. Speak to your accountant or financial adviser for more details.

If you are being paid severance regularly over time, negotiate for the employer to continue to provide paid medical, dental, and hospitalization coverage for you and your family while you are receiving severance wages. Some of my clients also successfully negotiate to receive regular 401(k), pension, and profit-sharing contributions from the employer during the severance continuation period. This can add up to plenty of extra compensation.

Counsel Comments: In some states, if you receive salary continuation with benefits, you may be ineligible for unemployment compensation. But if you receive salary without benefits or are paid in a lump sum, you may be able to file for and receive unemployment benefits immediately. The rules are often tricky, and it is important to understand your state's regulations before you begin severance negotiations.

If you are offered a choice between a lump sum and salary continuation, discuss the advantages and disadvantages of each arrangement with your lawyer, accountant, or financial adviser. Call your local unemployment insurance department for details. Find out under what conditions you qualify. If you learn you may not qualify, weigh if it is advantageous to receive benefits instead of unemployment compensation before making your decision. Compute the economic effect of receiving paid medical and pension contributions and whether this outweighs the maximum $300+ per week of taxable money you will receive from unemployment compensation. If you elect to defer un-employment benefits or do not presently qualify, you are still entitled to receive unemployment benefits if you are out of work when your salary continuation expires.

In addition to receiving immediate unemployment benefits, there are other advantages to being paid severance in a lump sum. One ben-efit is that all contact with the former employer ceases. You don't have to worry that you were overpaid or that periodic payments may stop. Getting a lump sum also gives you the ability to invest the funds im-mediately or pay bills. But once you accept a lump sum package, your fringe benefits (if any) will stop and you will not receive any more as-sistance from your ex-employer.

Tip: The key advantage of being paid salary continuation is that valuable fringe benefits may continue.

If money is your main concern, there are strategies to receive more cash in lieu of benefits. If the company offers to provide you with paid outplacement assistance, job-hunting, or relocation expenses, negoti-ate to trade off these benefits for cash if you don't need them. For ex-ample, many of my clients receive outplacement assistance that may cost a former employer up to $10,000. You may be able to substantially increase a severance package by accepting a lesser amount (say $3,500) in lieu of this benefit. This is a good idea if you know you will find another job quickly and don't need outplacement assistance.

The same is true with respect to medical benefits. If your spouse works and you can be covered under the spouse's plan at no additional or nominal cost, why not thank the company for its offer of paying continued premiums for your medical coverage and receive, say, 50 percent of that cost in cash?

OTHER COMPENSATION

If you have relocated recently at the request of the employer, try to obtain additional relocation allowances. This can amount to a large sum if you recently sold your house at a loss in order to move per the ex-employer's demands, or must return to a distant state to be with your family and look for work there. Additional expenses to ask for where applicable include expenses incurred to transport your personal possessions back to another state or travel and lodging expenses incurred to find a replacement job in a distant locale.

Discuss accrued salary, vacation pay, overtime, and unused sick pay. Be sure you are paid for these items. In most states, there is no legal obligation for a company to pay you *unused* vacation or sick time. Check your company handbook to determine what rules, if any, apply. Hopefully, there was no company policy stating that vacation or sick days are forfeited if they are not used in a given year.

If you worked for a sufficient time (e.g., more than six months) during the year, you may have accrued vacation time. It is illegal in most states for employers to withhold accrued vacation money even if you are fired for cause. Although each company is free to implement its own rules governing vacation pay, employers must apply such policies consistently to avoid charges of discrimination and breach of contract.

Inquire and demand to be paid for all earned, accrued vacation, sick leave, and overtime pay at the final negotiating interview. Chapter 9 contains various letters that you can send to enforce your rights if the company refuses to pay you accrued benefits.

Tip: Some employers are not inclined to pay more (or any) money unless you sign a release. But it is generally illegal for the company to refuse to pay your salary, wages, overtime and accrued vacation pay earned through the termination date at the time of discharge. There can be no strings attached; you are entitled to receive the money immediately regardless of whether you decide to sign a release or not. If you do not receive such monies immediately after a firing, contact a lawyer or your nearest department of labor office for advice.

Counsel Comments: Overtime is not generally available for salaried workers who work in executive, administrative, or professional jobs (called exempt employees). But if you are a salaried worker, your company is not generally allowed to deduct a few hours off your weekly paycheck for time off for any reason, including personal time. If it does, you may be determined to be an hourly worker, capable of receiving overtime for up to three years.

If you are an hourly worker, kept proper records, and took authorized overtime, discuss the amount of money due you (at time-and-a-half rates) with your company. Tell the ex-employer you may contact a representative at your state's department of labor or the Wage and Hour Division of the U.S. Department of Labor for help if the ex-employer fails to respond to your request.

Tip: If you were fired without notice, ask for two additional weeks of salary in lieu of the employer's lack of notice. This is an effective strategy to help get more severance. Even if the employer is not willing to pay you more severance, this is the one area where your request has a good chance of being accepted.

If commissions are due or are about to become due, insist that you be paid immediately; do not waive these expected benefits.

Salespeople who earn commissions are now receiving additional statutory protections in this area. Many states now require that companies promptly pay commissions to their independent sales representatives (or agents) who are fired. When prompt payment is not made, companies may be liable for penalties up to *three times the commission amount* plus reasonable attorney fees and court costs if the case is eventually litigated. Some of the states that have enacted laws protecting sales representatives and their commissions are Alabama, Arizona, California, Florida, Georgia, Illinois, Indiana, Iowa, Kansas, Kentucky, Louisiana, Maryland, Massachusetts, Minnesota, Mississippi, Missouri, New Hampshire, New Jersey, New York, North Carolina, Ohio, Oklahoma, South Carolina, Tennessee, Texas, and Washington, and more states are bound to enact similar legislation.

Check your state's sales rep law or speak to a knowledgeable employment lawyer for more details.

Bonus

Understand how your bonus is computed. If you were entitled to receive a bonus at the end of the year, ask for it now. If you were fired close to the end of the year, and the company says it has no legal obligation to pay you a bonus because you didn't work the full year or are not on the payroll the day the bonus is paid per company policy, argue that the firing deprived you of the right to receive the bonus, especially if you were terminated through no fault of your own (not for cause). If this request is rejected, insist that your bonus be prorated according to the amount of time you worked during the year. If this request is denied, ask for your full bonus but settle for less (e.g., half).

Retirement and Savings Plans

Understand if you are a participant in any retirement or savings plan and be aware of all plans, funds, and programs that may have been established on your behalf. This may consist of:

1. Defined contribution plans include profit-sharing plans, thrift plans, money purchase pension plans, and cash or deferred profit-sharing plans. All these plans are characterized by the fact that each participant has an individual bookkeeping account under the plan that records the participant's total interest in the plan assets. Monies are typically contributed by the employer and are credited in accordance with the rules of the plan contained in the plan summary. The amount of money due you in such accounts often changes depending on investment gains and losses and other contributions (i.e., interest and dividend payments). Information concerning the lump sum amount due is contained in a benefit statement given to you periodically or on your discharge.

2. Defined benefit plans are characterized as pension plans that compute the benefits payable to participants on a formula contained in the plan (typically based on a person's age and length of service). Such funds are typically funded on a group basis, and everyone is entitled to the same benefits (e.g., $600 per month) on retirement.

3. Employee welfare benefit plans are often funded through insurance and typically provide participants with medical, health, accident, disability, death, unemployment, or vacation benefits.

4. ERISA (Employee Retirement Income Security Act) plans may not be as definite as the above. Rather, if the employer has communicated that certain benefits are available, who the intended beneficiaries are, and how the plan is funded, the employer may be liable to pay such benefits even in the absence of a formal, written plan.

Tip: You are not legally entitled to define benefit plan monies until you become vested. Once vested, your money becomes nonforfeitable. Each pension plan has rules to determine when vesting occurs. If you are fired just before the vesting of a pension (e.g., two months before your fifty-fifth birthday or the vesting date), argue that the timing of the firing is suspect and that public policy requires the employer to grant you your pension.

Although federal law states that employers generally do not have to change their pension rules to accommodate individual cases, I have represented many employees who were terminated close to a vesting date. I have negotiated for the employee to be placed on unpaid leave status or to receive a small monthly check for several months and stay on the payroll as a way of qualifying for the pension. This is called *pension bridging* and can be done in special circumstances. If you are fired just before qualifying for a long-awaited pension and the employer refuses this request, consult an experienced employment lawyer immediately.

The fact that you are fired before receiving full pension benefits (because you did not reach the age of sixty-five, work twenty or more years, or some other requirement) may not preclude you from receiving a monthly pension, albeit a smaller one. Where applicable, evaluate whether it pays for you not to start receiving your pension immediately after a termination, especially if the few additional years of postponement will mean more hefty vested monthly benefits later. Speak to your accountant or financial adviser for more details, and ask the employer if you can agree to defer your benefits for more money later.

Counsel Comments: In some states, if you begin receiving pension benefits, the amount of unemployment compensation you will receive weekly will be reduced accordingly. Always take this into account.

Tip: Some plans permit early retirement with a smaller monthly pension. If you are terminated, you may, depending on your age and length of service, still be eligible to receive reduced benefits. Be sure you understand your rights with respect to smaller vested benefits.

Negotiate to receive full enhanced pension benefits as consideration for accepting early retirement. If this cannot be done, think twice before accepting early retirement. Investigate the amount of pension reduction or penalty for early withdrawal. Lesley Alderman, in her article "Walk Out the Door with All the Money You Deserve" (*Money*, August 1996), states that, where applicable, you should ask if the employer will add a few years of service to your employment record so you will be able to qualify for an early pension.

Although your pension and other contributions from the employer may stop on termination, ask the employer to continue to contribute these benefits while you are receiving salary continuation. Getting the employer to agree to this can mean thousands of additional dollars to you.

Ask for a copy of pertinent plan summaries and statements of benefits when you learn of your firing. Carefully review these and other documents. Talk to a benefits officer or someone in the personnel department if you do not understand something. Do not rely on oral promises; ask for all explanations in writing. If there is any doubt concerning your rights, write to the plan administrator for a written explanation.

Employer-sponsored health, pension, and profit-sharing plans are governed by ERISA, which sets minimum standards for benefit plans, the vesting of benefits, and communication to plan participants and their beneficiaries. This includes all plans, funds, or programs that provide medical, surgical, or hospital care benefits; retirement income or the deferral of income after retirement or termination (such as severance); or deferred compensation plans such as stock bonus and money purchase pension plans. The act covers six basic areas:

- Communications: what must be disclosed to employees, how it must be disclosed, and what reports must be filed with the federal government
- Eligibility: which employees may participate in a benefit plan
- Vesting: rules regarding when and to what extent benefits must be paid
- Funding: what employers must pay into a plan to meet its normal costs and to amortize past service liabilities
- Fiduciary responsibilities: how the investment of funds must be handled and the responsibilities of the plan administrators to oversee the plan and plan benefits
- Plan termination insurance: the availability of insurance to protect the payment of vested benefits

The law does not require employers to establish pension or profit-sharing plans. Once they do, however, virtually all private employers are regulated by ERISA in one form or another.

To safeguard benefits, ERISA mandates that assets in a beneficiary's pension be virtually "untouchable." This is accomplished by requiring that plan administrators file numerous reports with the U.S. Department of Labor, the Internal Revenue Service, and the Pension Benefit Guaranty Corporation (a federal agency located in Washington, D.C.), including plan descriptions, summary plan descriptions, material changes in the plan, description of modifications of the terms of the plan, an annual report (Form 5500), an annual registration statement listing employees separated from services during the plan year, and numerous other reports for defined benefit plans covered by the termination insurance provisions with the Pension Benefit Guaranty Corporation.

Demand a copy of the employer's pension and/or profit-sharing plans from the plan administrator if the employer refuses to furnish you with accurate details. (You may have to pay for the cost of photocopying said plans when requesting them.) ERISA provides that plan participants are entitled to examine without charge all plan documents filed with the U.S. Department of Labor, including detailed annual reports and plan descriptions. If you request materials and do not receive them within thirty days, you may file suit in federal court. In such a case, the court may require the plan administrator to provide the materials and pay up to $100 a day until you receive the materials, unless the materials are not sent for reasons beyond the control of the administrator.

Contact the plan administrator immediately to protect your rights if your claim is denied or if you suspect there are problems with your plan. Under federal law, every employee, participant, or beneficiary with a benefit plan covered by ERISA has the right to receive written notification stating specific reasons for the denial of a claim. You have the right to a full and fair review by the plan administrator if you are denied benefits.

If you suspect the company has not acted properly with respect to your benefits, inquire about your account with the plan administrator. Determine whether the amount of each payment corresponds with the amount that was deducted from your paycheck and reflects any promised matching contributions. If you are not satisfied with the answers, contact your nearest Department of Labor office to discuss the matter with a representative. Request an investigation on behalf of you and your coworkers where warranted.

If you have a claim for benefits that is denied or ignored in whole or in part after making a request to a plan administrator, speak to a lawyer and consider filing a lawsuit in either state or federal court. If it should happen that plan fiduciaries misuse a plan's money, or if you are retaliated against for asserting your rights (such as being demoted, reassigned, or fired), seek assistance from the U.S. Department of Labor or file suit in federal court. The court will decide who should pay court costs and legal fees. If you are successful, the court may order the employer or person you have sued to pay these costs and fees.

Tip: If your company goes out of business, files for bankruptcy, or has no assets, many states require the owners (i.e., stockholders) and officers to be personally liable to repay pension and other retirement benefits. Thus, all may not be lost if you discover your benefits were diverted and the company goes out of business. Speak to a lawyer about this point.

The Pension Benefit Guaranty Corporation has created an office to help workers trace their pensions. By law, a pension plan that terminates is required to make only one attempt to get in touch with workers. The Pension Benefit Guaranty Corporation can assist you by making repeated attempts to find the plans of employers that have gone out of business. Contact this agency in Washington, D.C., and supply it with copies of any plan summaries and plan identification numbers, which are often printed on such papers. Permanently save all plan documents and summaries because you never know when the information will come in handy to document and enforce a claim.

Speak to a benefits lawyer if your company orally modifies any plan benefits, if a summary description does not accurately depict essential elements of the plan, or if a division of the company you are working for is sold and the new company offers far less severance and other benefits than previously promised. When companies merge and workers are laid off or denied promised benefits they previously enjoyed, issues of severance and other post-termination and on-the-job violations arise that should be addressed.

Final Tips: If you are satisfied that all monies due you have been accounted for, you will have to decide whether to keep the funds in their present accounts, withdraw the funds for your personal needs, or transfer the funds into other investments. The questions of where to put the money and whether you will suffer harmful tax consequences should be answered by a competent accountant and/or financial adviser. Some company plans allow participants to roll benefits over so you do not get hit with hefty early-withdrawal penalties. I strongly recommend that my clients seek professional tax and financial advice when retirement and savings plan monies are involved at the time of a termination. It is also a good idea to speak with the person in charge of the company's benefits or investments before making an informed decision in this area.

Stock Options

Your right to continued stock options will either vanish or be substantially impaired once you are fired. This is especially true if the employer claims you were fired for misconduct. But if you were fired through no fault of your own (e.g., due to a downsizing or job elimination), try to negotiate an arrangement that accelerates the vesting of stock options. If you cannot obtain this, discuss taking less severance pay if the company will vest your options now or stretch out the deadline for exercising them. Tell the company this is a win–win for both parties because it will cost the employer less money in the short term and you can get more money in the future if the value of the company stock appreciates. Review these strategies with your employment lawyer.

Medical, Dental, and Hospitalization Benefits

Have your benefits explained to you at the negotiation session so you'll understand them. For example, does coverage stop the day you are fired or is there a grace period? Ask for a copy of all applicable policies and review them carefully. Negotiate to extend coverage beyond the grace period, especially if you are responsible for maintaining your family's health coverage and do not expect to find a replacement job in the near future.

Tip: Ask the employer to continue paying your medical and health premiums for another six months (or a year) while you are receiving salary continuation. Many employers will grant this request if you ask for it. The advantage of this arrangement is that in addition to receiving free medical coverage for several months, you may have the right to receive COBRA health benefits at your expense up to eighteen months after the employer-paid-for benefits during the salary continuation period stop.

Some employers will concede this request in order to make a departing worker feel that he or she was treated fairly during negotiations. It is one of the most important benefits you can ask for and is often granted by an employer. Always ask for this during negotiations where appropriate.

Susan is fired from a job after working six years for a company. She is a single mother with two small children. Her monthly family medical and health coverage cost is $475.

Susan is initially offered a severance package of one month, paid biweekly. She is not offered paid medical coverage. Susan learns that under federal COBRA law she is allowed to continue the same health coverage as before but at her own expense.

Susan negotiates a more favorable severance package. Eventually, she receives another month's pay (for a total of eight weeks' severance), and the company agrees to pay her medical coverage premium for three months before COBRA kicks in. This is confirmed to her in writing.

Although most plans terminate automatically at the date of your discharge, inquire if you can assume the policy at your personal cost and find out the required time frame to implement coverage. This is referred to as a conversion policy. Such policies may also apply to long- and short-term disability insurance and life insurance plans in existence at the time of your firing.

Tip: If you are married and your spouse is working, you may be covered under your spouse's policies. If so, you may not want to continue paying for your own policies.

Be sure the employer has notified you regarding your COBRA rights. This must be done *in writing* within thirty days after you are fired and you then have several weeks to advise the company in writing if you will continue your health benefits. If you desire to continue coverage, you should promptly remit the first month's premium.

Under federal law, private employers who employ more than fifteen workers on a typical business day must continue to make group health insurance available to workers who are discharged from employment. If you work for a smaller company, you may still be protected under state law. Check your local department of labor or department of insurance for details.

Most people benefit from COBRA, since the cost of maintaining insurance is reasonable; rather than the cost of an individual policy, you pay for coverage at the employer's group rate plus a 2 percent administrative fee.

Tip: If you don't receive the initial COBRA notification letter from the ex-employer immediately after a firing, call the company and speak with the person in charge of benefits or personnel. Demand to receive a formal notice. This is your right. To ensure that your coverage will not lapse, send payments directly to the ex-employer (not the insurance carrier unless you are instructed otherwise in writing) regularly and timely.

Never ignore the notice once it is received. Send your initial check back immediately with a letter by certified mail, return receipt requested, to prove delivery. Make a copy of your check and letter and keep the canceled check as proof that payment was made and received. Contact the insurance company separately to verify that the carrier was notified that your payment was received. You can't do enough to ensure that your coverage exists and is being maintained.

Under the law, all employees who are discharged as a result of a voluntary or involuntary termination (with the exception of those who are fired for gross misconduct) may elect to continue plan benefits currently in effect *at their own cost* provided the employee or beneficiary makes an initial payment within thirty days of notification and is not covered under Medicare or any other group health plan. The law also applies to qualified beneficiaries who were covered by the employer's group health plan the day before the discharge. Thus, for example, if the employee chooses not to continue such coverage, his or her spouse and dependent children may elect continued coverage at their own expense.

The extended coverage period is eighteen months on the termination of the covered employee; on the death, divorce, or legal separation of the covered employee, the benefit coverage period is thirty-six months to spouses and dependents.

The law requires that employers or plan administrators separately notify all employees and covered spouses and dependents of their rights to continued coverage. After receiving such notification, the individual then has up to thirty days to elect to continue coverage. Additionally, employees and dependents whose insurance is protected under COBRA must also be provided with any conversion privilege otherwise available in the plan (if such coverage exists) within a six-month period preceding the date that coverage would terminate at the end of the continuation period.

In the event the employer fails to offer such coverage, the law imposes penalties ranging from $100 to $200 per day each day the employee is not covered.

Due to burdensome record-keeping requirements, it isn't surprising that many companies run afoul of the law and fail to follow properly rules regarding notification requirements, conversion privileges, excluded individuals, and time restrictions, because the law does not provide much guidance or instruction. In fact, good-faith compliance may not be sufficient to protect the employer, as a California ruling demonstrates. The employer, a mental health residential treatment facility, offered its two health care plan options to a laid-off employee. When the plan chosen by the ex-employee went bankrupt, only the second plan—an HMO—remained. All current employees of the company were in the plan's geographic area and they signed up with the HMO. Since the ex-employee lived outside the area, she was left without any health continuation coverage. She sued her former employer for the health care coverage that was her right under COBRA and prevailed. Although IRS regulations require only that COBRA coverage be the same as insurance offered "similarly situated beneficiaries"—as the employer argued—the U.S. District Court ruled that the employer had not satisfied its obligations.

Based on cases decided in this area, employers will have to assume burdens not always considered. The law is now being interpreted very broadly, and the courts are ruling regularly that COBRA coverage be provided. Because the cases typically pit a former employee or an employee's dependent with substantial medical expenses against the employer or an insurance company, many courts are willing to interpret and apply COBRA with a view toward extending coverage wherever possible.

The result of a 1992 case demonstrates the difficulty employers face when trying to comply with COBRA. Here, an employee incapacitated by a series of strokes was maintained on her employer's group health insurance policy. After about a year, the employee was taken off the company rolls. At that time, she was in a coma and the COBRA continuation notice was sent to her husband. Misunderstanding the intent of the offer, and thinking his wife was still covered under the employer's group plan without premium payments, he waived his wife's insurance continuation rights. Later, as legal guardian, the ex-employee's husband tried to regain the option of COBRA coverage, but the insurance company refused. The husband sued and won; the court ruled that the employer should have included the summary plan description with the COBRA notice sent to the husband and that without the summary he was unable to make an informed decision.

Tip: Be sure you know your rights under COBRA in the event you are fired. This is especially true if you or a spouse or dependent is sick and needs the insurance benefits to pay necessary medical bills. You are entitled to such protection even if you have worked for the employer for only a short period of time. In fact, under the law as it presently exists, most short-term employees can generally enjoy COBRA protection for periods exceeding the length of their employment. The only requirement is that you must have been included in the employer's group plan at the time of the firing.

Remember, however, that you may not be able to obtain benefits if you are fired for gross misconduct. This term is relatively ambiguous; the burden of proof is on the employer to prove that the discharge was for a compelling reason (fighting on the job, stealing, working while intoxicated, etc.). Also be aware that some employers reduce a person's working hours to a point that makes them ineligible for group health coverage.

If an employer refuses to negotiate continued health benefits as part of a severance package or fails to notify you of the existence of such benefits, contact the human resources office immediately to protect your rights. If the employer refuses to offer continued COBRA benefits after a discharge for any reason, consult an employment lawyer immediately.

Attorneys Paul H. Tobias and Susan Sauter, in their book *Job Rights & Survival Strategies: A Handbook for Terminated Employees*, comment that the recently enacted Health Insurance Portability and Accounting Act makes it easier for employees going to another job to receive coverage under the new employer's plan without being penalized for preexisting conditions. This federal law also prohibits employers from denying enrollment to an individual based on health status when the plan is available to other employees. However, although coverage may be easy to obtain, Tobias and Sauter point out it may be expensive because employers are allowed to consider your medical situation when determining the cost of premiums. Speak to a knowledgeable employment lawyer for more details.

Life Insurance Benefits

Inquire if you can convert any life insurance policies at your own cost. There may also be equity in a life insurance plan that may accrue to you upon termination. Ask about this and also obtain a copy of all policies presently in effect.

Outplacement Assistance

Many employers offer paid outplacement assistance as part of a severance package. What terminated workers do not realize is that it is usually short (e.g., no more than six months) and may consist only of simple résumé preparation, modest typing, a short seminar on proper interviewing skills, and irregular assistance. Your goal is to negotiate the best assistance possible. This should include unlimited use of a private office or cubicle space, your own personal telephone line and answering service, a secretary, and mail facilities to assist you in your job search. These services should be offered for as long as you are unemployed (or at least for a year if necessary). Many different kinds of plans are typically offered by outplacement assistance firms to employers at various costs. Since not all services are the same, try to get the company to pay for the best plan available.

Tip: Do your homework and interview various firms. If you are impressed with a particular one, ask the company to pay for the firm of your choosing. Look for a firm that designates a personal counselor to meet with you weekly. Select a firm that goes the extra mile, such as one that screens topical newspaper ads or transmits your résumé to headhunters and important employment agencies in your region.

EXTRA BENEFITS

Depending on your particular situation, there is no limit to the kinds of benefits you can request. Skilled lawyers often throw twenty darts at a wall during negotiations in the hope that five or more will stick. That is an effective way you, too, can try to obtain extra benefits.

Ask the employer to provide the same benefits you would ordinarily expect from an outplacement firm. This includes continued use of an empty office, computer or laptop, pager, secretary, mail facilities, and telephone reception to assist you while your job search continues. Ask the company to keep your voice-mail service active until you find a new job. That way, Lesley Alderman writes, you can hunt from home, without prospective employers knowing you're out of a job. Tell the company why you still need these items. Convince the company to allow you to use such property (as a courtesy) especially if it is inexpensive to the employer.

Tip: Request the continued use of your company car if you have one. Ask to buy the car or take over the lease at a reduced rate if appropriate. On numerous occasions, I have obtained favorable auto deals for my clients at substantially lower-than-market rates simply by asking for this concession. Perhaps the employer will allow you to keep the personal computer it purchased several years ago if you request it.

If appropriate, request a loan to tide you over while looking for a new job. Or, if the parting is amicable, perhaps you can convince the employer to continue paying for the degree program you started, especially if you were fired at the beginning of a semester and you have only one more semester of courses to take. Some companies may provide tuition assistance or a pay-for-retraining stipend to help you switch careers (e.g., take courses in computer training) or enhance your skills.

Ask the employer to reimburse you for job-hunting expenses. Specify the kinds of expenses you should be reimbursed for. This may include travel to and from interviews, typing, résumé preparation and printing, postage, and book purchase costs. If the employer refuses, explain why this is necessary. As a last resort, tell the employer that you will accept a modest amount with a cap.

Counsel Comments: You have nothing to lose and everything to gain by asking for these benefits. Be imaginative. Marshall Loeb reports there are executives who have successfully requested reimbursement for country club dues (or yacht slips) as an inexpensive way for the company to preserve goodwill.

The more things you ask for, the more concessions you will probably get. Even if the company refuses to provide you with many of these extra perks, you may still receive an enhanced severance package as a compromise. Prepare a detailed list of proposed benefits. Discuss these intelligently with the employer. If you're leaving on good terms, you should even consider requesting the employer to hire you as a freelancer.

COVER STORY AND JOB REFERENCES

Clarify how the news of your departure will be announced. Discuss and agree with management on the story to be told to outsiders. Consider whether you want it to be known that you resigned for personal reasons or that you were terminated due to a "business reorganization." These are neutral explanations that are preferable to firings for misconduct or poor performance.

Tip: If the company agrees to release a positive announcement, ask to review the final draft before it goes out. Ask that the memo list your major accomplishments and state a neutral reason for your departure, such as that you are leaving to "pursue new career opportunities."

THE RESIGNATION DILEMMA

Recognize that if you resign you may be forfeiting unemployment benefits. My advice is to avoid resigning wherever possible. Although you may prefer that outsiders be told you resigned for personal reasons, confirm with the employer that you will be able to apply for unemployment benefits. That way your local department of labor board will be advised that there was a termination (as opposed to a resignation, since that is what really happened) and you can still tell outsiders that you resigned.

LETTER OF RECOMMENDATION

Request that a copy of a favorable letter of recommendation be given to you *before* you leave the company. The letter should state the dates of your employment, the positions held, and that you performed all your job duties in a diligent and satisfactory fashion. If possible, the letter should be signed by a qualified officer or supervisor who worked with you and knows you well. Do not rely on promises that the employer will furnish prospective employers with a favorable recommendation, since many fail to do this after employees leave the company. Thus, *always* attempt to have such a letter *in hand* before you leave. The letter on page 166 is an example of the kind of recommendation you may find acceptable.

Tip: It is best not to include the specific reason for the parting in such a letter. This will enable you to offer whatever reasons you feel are appropriate under various circumstances.

NOTIFICATION OF DEPARTURE

Request that key members of the company be notified of your departure in writing. If possible, approve the contents of such a memo before distribution. Written memos can dispel false rumors about your termination. A positive memo may assist you in obtaining a new job. Remember, news of a firing usually spreads rapidly; you don't want to be the subject of false rumors or innuendo.

LETTER OF RECOMMENDATION

Date

To whom it may concern:

I am pleased to submit this letter of recommendation on behalf of (Name of Employee).

(Name of Employee) worked for the company from (date) through (date). During this period (Name of Employee) was promoted from (specify title) to (specify title).

During the past (specify) years, I have had the opportunity to work closely with (Name of Employee). At all times I found him/her to be diligent and dependable and (Name of Employee) rendered competent and satisfactory services on the company's behalf.

I heartily recommend (Name of Employee) as a candidate for employment of his/her choosing.

Very truly yours,
Name of Officer
Title

Such a memo (see the example on page 167) may enable you to leave in a positive manner. Additionally, it may minimize the effects of the circumstances surrounding the termination. Don't forget to ask for this when appropriate.

SEALING YOUR FILE

If you are worried that poor performance reviews and warnings in your personnel file may be leaked to third parties, ask the employer to remove all harmful documents. Some employers will seal your file and agree not to reveal its contents unless there are compelling reasons and only after notifying you first.

Try to minimize the chances that harmful information concerning your work history, performance, or alleged misconduct will be leaked to others. Many of my clients have received such assurance in writing as part of their settlement.

NOTIFICATION OF DEPARTURE MEMORANDUM

To: Employees of (Name of Company or pertinent division)
From: (Name of Officer or Supervisor)
Subject: Resignation of (Name of Employee)

I wish to inform you that (Name of Employee) has decided to pursue other interests and has elected to resign effective (specify when) from the company.

(Name of Employee) has contributed greatly to the growth of the (specify) division and he/she will indeed be missed.

We all wish (Name of Employee) the best of continued good health and success.

GOLDEN PARACHUTES

Determine if you are entitled to receive additional benefits under a severance contract or golden parachute. Generally, golden parachutes are arrangements between an executive and a corporation that are contingent on a change in control of the corporation. Typically, additional cash and other economic benefits are paid to a terminated individual following the discharge (provided the employee is not fired for cause). Although most companies cover only a limited group of key employees with golden parachutes, some companies have determined that it is appropriate to cover a much larger group.

Speak to an employment lawyer immediately to protect your rights if the employer refuses to provide all the benefits specified in your contract.

MAXIMUM TAX ADVANTAGE

During the process of negotiating a severance package or settlement, be mindful of the after-tax consequences. Try to get the employer to agree on a package that saves the company real dollars while creating greater after-tax benefits for you. For example, when settling a sex discrimination case, instead of getting $50,000 in back pay (which is completely taxable), have your lawyer or yourself try to structure the settlement in terms of money for attorney fees, interest, physical pain and suffering, and back pay. By structuring the arrangement in this fashion, you would not necessarily be required to pay tax on the money paid directly to your lawyer for legal fees, for interest, and for physical pain and suffering, and the company would avoid paying Social Security, Medicare, and FUTA taxes on these amounts.

It used to be easier to receive tax-free benefits as part of a severance package. This has changed. As a result of a Supreme Court ruling and federal legislation enacted in 1996, most payments made to you after a firing are now taxable. Severance pay and money paid to compensate you for an earned bonus, overtime, vacation pay, or commissions are taxable. So, too, are damages paid to settle an age, gender, race, handicap, retaliation, or other discrimination claim. Damages for back pay and emotional distress pursuant to discrimination, defamation, or breach of contract charges are now taxable. Even money received as punitive damages is taxable.

However, damages received for *personal* physical injury or sickness (e.g., a bleeding ulcer caused by workplace stress) pursuant to an award or settlement of a discrimination claim is excludable from gross income and is not taxable.

Counsel Comments: Get professional advice when negotiating tax-free benefits with your employer. Attorneys Paul H. Tobias and Susan Sauter suggest that you consider creative ways to avoid taxes. Payments for tuition reimbursement, outplacement services, medical insurance, pension benefits, and/or medical expenses may be treated as tax-free transactions in certain situations. The same is true for interest-free loans or the sale of company property (e.g., computers and company cars) to you.

Since money received by a judgment or settlement in a lump sum or as periodic payments as damages for personal physical injuries or sickness is not taxable, it pays to understand basic IRS rules after speaking with your accountant, financial adviser, or lawyer. The tax consequences of employee-related severance negotiations and settlements present opportunities for both parties to save money.

Tip: Be as specific as possible when drafting or reviewing the settlement document. Be sure its language complies with IRS code.

Once a tax-wise settlement based on economic realities is made, it should be adhered to by both parties. An IRS audit can be triggered when a particular allocation is agreed on but you claim a different amount on your tax return. If this happens, both you and the company could be liable for hefty penalties and interest.

CHAPTER 9

Confirming the Deal and Taking Other Steps to Protect Your Rights

Sidney does the best he can on his own to negotiate a better package. He believes he was fired as a result of his age. But the company refuses to negotiate with him in good faith. He appealed to corporate decency and fair play, stressed his accomplishments and loyalty during his twenty-two years of service, and described the sacrifices he made on the employer's behalf. All of this was done in a quiet, professional manner.

After several meetings, the company refuses to offer him a better package. He is told that he was paid everything coming to him per company policy and that the company cannot change the rules just for him. Sidney goes above the boss's head in an attempt to cut a better deal, but to no avail.

Since he is over forty and therefore a member of a protected class, Sidney believes he has legal leverage. He doesn't want to sue the employer, he just thinks he is entitled to receive more money and the company is being unreasonable. The way he figures it, the current offer requires him to sign a release before getting any money and the release states that he has the right to consult a lawyer. He doesn't understand the wording of the release and needs legal assistance to interpret it. Furthermore, the amount he stands to lose if he doesn't sign the release is quite small considering the net after-tax amount.

Sidney asks for legal recommendations from friends and business associates. He consults a skilled employment lawyer who negotiates severance packages on a daily basis. Sidney hires the lawyer. His lawyer immediately contacts the company's attorney. Interestingly enough, the lawyers have a good rapport and have dealt with each other on several matters in the past. The two professionals quickly come to terms on a better package. They iron out the details in an unemotional fashion. More money and enhanced benefits are offered to Sidney, and he agrees to settle the matter. He signs the revised severance agreement and release and goes into the workplace to look for a new job.

If you have attempted to negotiate your severance package but are not satisfied that you adequately discussed your options and benefits, if the company refuses to deal with you in good faith, or if you feel you lack the aggressiveness, inclination, knowledge, or stamina to initially negotiate the package on your own, you must decide whether to accept the company's offer or retain a lawyer in the attempt to obtain additional compensation. When there is a large amount of money at stake or the employer is acting unfairly or pressuring you, it may be a good idea to hire an employment lawyer. It is also advisable to consult a lawyer when you are told that you must sign a release and waive potentially viable claims before receiving any severance pay.

Always consider hiring an employment lawyer to negotiate your package when you believe the employer has violated the law. This is especially true if you believe you were fired for any of the following reasons: to be denied accrued benefits; due to a legitimate illness or absence; as a result of whistle-blowing; for complaining about a health or safety violation; for serving in the military; in a manner inconsistent with a company handbook, manual, or disciplinary rule; as a result of discrimination; after asserting a sexual harassment claim or in retaliation for filing a discrimination complaint; as part of a large layoff without receiving adequate notification; when the company acts inconsistent with a verbal promise; when the company is in breach of a contract right or provision in your written employment agreement; or for a host of many other illegal acts cited in this book.

Before deciding to hire a lawyer as your negotiating agent, answer some of the following questions:

- Are you prepared to lose the offer currently on the table in the remote possibility that the company will revoke it when your lawyer gets involved?
- What are the chances you will receive a better package?
- Is the additional amount to be gained worth the price of hiring the lawyer in the first place?
- Will you be satisfied if you don't get more money but receive more benefits and perks?
- Is it worth it to hire a lawyer merely to get the company to agree that it will not contest your employment benefits or that it will give you a favorable reference or outplacement assistance?
- What is the minimum amount of money and perks you will accept going into the negotiations?
- What is the minimum amount of money you will accept to sign a release and thereby be precluded from ever suing the company in the future?
- Is it advantageous for you to hire a lawyer as a coach to give you behind-the-scenes advice while you negotiate the package on your own? This can save you legal fees if you are successful.
- Can you effectively handle the negotiation yourself given the maxim "He who represents himself has a fool for a client"?
- If you can, is the lawyer agreeable to initially serving you in an advisory capacity and under what terms? At what stage should the lawyer get involved if you fail? Will your failed efforts impair the lawyer's chances of success?
- Who is the most sympathetic person you or your lawyer should initially contact in the attempt to get the best results?
- What are the strongest reasons why you are entitled to a better package?
- Are you aware of better deals other people got from the employer in the past?
- Will the company respond negatively or positively when you bring in a lawyer to negotiate? Does the company regularly back

off from confrontations, or does it have a history of sticking to its guns and fighting it out in court regardless of the cost?

• If the employer is litigation-prone, is it more advantageous for you to first deal with it directly without a lawyer so you do not jeopardize a positive relationship?

All these questions should be discussed with a lawyer before retaining him or her so that you know where each party stands in the attempt to obtain favorable results.

Before retaining a lawyer, be sure that you feel comfortable with him or her and that the lawyer will be able to render competent services on your behalf. This can be accomplished by following many of the strategies contained in Chapter 14, "How to Hire and Work Effectively with Your Employment Lawyer."

Whomever you retain, it is important that the lawyer get started on your matter immediately. Time is crucial in all termination cases; you must take action immediately to demonstrate the seriousness of your resolve. In fact, the longer a lawyer waits before contacting the employer, the weaker the case often becomes. That is why I prefer to contact the employer within several weeks after the individual has been fired.

When I am retained to represent a terminated individual, I send a letter to the employer by messenger or certified mail, return receipt requested, usually the day I am hired. This ensures that the employer is notified quickly that I have been hired to discuss and negotiate the circumstances surrounding the person's termination, the inadequacy of the severance offer, the amount of money in commissions or other benefits still due, and other considerations. The initial demand letter is usually kept brief because I do not want to tip my hand and state my case to someone I have never spoken with. Of course, it is always desired that the employer contact me as soon as possible. This helps my negotiating position.

An actual demand letter sent by my office when I represent a terminated employee seeking severance is shown on page 174.

An officer of the company or a company attorney usually contacts me after receiving such a letter. Negotiations then ensue to determine if the matter can be settled out of court. I use a variety of negotiation techniques. Typically, I stress that the employer should offer more to settle the matter amicably and avoid time-consuming and expensive legal action.

LETTER SENT ON BEHALF OF EMPLOYEE FOR SEVERANCE OWED

Sack & Sack
Attorneys-At-Law
135 East 57th Street, 12th Floor
New York, New York 10022
Phone: (212) 702-9000
Facsimile: (212) 702-9702

Steven M. Sack
Jonathan S. Sack★
★Also admitted in N.J. & D.C.

Date

Name of Company Officer
Title
Name of Company
Address

Dear (Name of Company Officer):

Please be advised that this office represents (Name of Employee), a longtime employee of your firm.

In this regard, I suggest that you or your representative contact this office immediately so that we may attempt to discuss a variety of issues regarding my client's severance and other benefits in an amicable fashion to avoid protracted and expensive litigation.

Thank you for your prompt cooperation in this matter.

Very truly yours,
Steven M. Sack

Sent certified mail, return receipt requested

Most matters are settled. I believe this is due to a number of factors. First, many employers want to avoid the poor publicity that can arise from a protracted court battle. Additionally, when companies are contacted by attorneys representing terminated employees, they must weigh whether it is wise to offer additional compensation to settle out of court versus spending thousands of dollars in legal expenses and lost work hours resulting from defending the charges in formal litigation. Furthermore, if the firing is illegal, company exposure can amount to hundreds of thousands of dollars in actual damages (which doesn't include interest, attorney fees, and costs that are sometimes awarded).

Companies often take a pragmatic approach. The employee receives additional severance and other benefits, and the employer avoids a lawsuit. Remember that the mark of a good settlement is that neither side is truly happy with the result. The employer believes too much money was paid to settle; conversely, the employee sometimes feels that he or she received too little. However, given the confines of the legal system (the long delays before the case is actually tried, the tremendous expenses involved, etc.), most terminated employees can achieve a fair out-of-court settlement.

If you or your lawyer is unsuccessful in obtaining an enhanced package, and you both believe your case is strong enough to institute a lawsuit, do so without delay to preserve your rights and avoid the action being dismissed because of untimeliness. Tips and strategies on how to win a litigation are discussed in Chapter 13.

CONFIRM THE DEAL IN WRITING

Alternatively, if you are pleased with the settlement obtained by your lawyer or if you decide that contacting a lawyer is not necessary when you have obtained a fair and equitable settlement on your own, request that the employer confirm the deal in writing. Such a letter will clarify the points that were agreed on and document the severance arrangement that has been made. Additionally, if the employer fails to abide by an important term (such as a promise of salary continuation for six months), the letter can increase your chance of success if you decide to sue for breach of contract.

The letter on pages 176–178 was given to a former client of mine

LETTER CONFIRMING SEVERANCE ARRANGEMENT

Date

Name of Employee
Address

Dear (Name of Employee):

This will confirm our agreement regarding your employment status with (Name of Employer).

We agreed as follows:

1. Your services as Vice President of (specify division) will terminate by mutual agreement effective (date).

2. Although your services as Vice President will not be required beyond (specify date), you agree to be available to (Name of Employer) through (specify termination date) to render advice, answer any questions, and provide information regarding company business.

3. Through (specify termination date) except as provided in Paragraph 4 below, you will continue to receive your regular biweekly salary of (specify) and you may continue to participate in those company benefit plans in which you are currently enrolled. In addition to your final paycheck, you will receive from the company on or about (specify termination date) or given as provided for in Paragraph 4 hereunder, the sum of (specify) less applicable deductions for local, state, and federal taxes, as a bonus for the present year.

4. If you obtain other regular, full-time employment prior to (specify termination date), then, upon commencement of such employment, your regular biweekly salary payments and your participation in company benefit plans, as described in Paragraph 3 above, shall cease; however, medical and dental coverage previously provided you shall be continued for an additional period of three months at a cost to be borne by (Name of Employer). In such event, you will receive in a lump sum (less applicable deductions for taxes) the remaining amount you would have received on a biweekly basis from the date of new employment through (specify termination date) plus the (specify sum) bonus (less taxes) payment referred to in Paragraph 3 within two weeks of your date of new employment. You agree to notify the com-

pany immediately of the date on which such regular full-time employment will commence.

5. You acknowledge that the sums referred to in Paragraphs 3 and 4 above include any and all monies due you from the company, contractual or otherwise, to which you may be entitled, except for any vested benefit you may have in the (Name of Employer) Savings and Investment Plan and the Pension Plan.

6. (Name of Employer) will provide you with available office space, telephone service, and clerical help on an as-needed basis at (address) until you obtain other regular full-time employment or (date), whichever occurs first.

7. You agree to cooperate fully with (Name of Employer) in their defense of or other participation in any administrative, judicial, or collective bargaining proceeding arising from any charge, complaint, grievance, or action which has been or may be filed.

8. You, on behalf of yourself and your heirs, representatives, and assigns, hereby release (Name of Employer), its parents, their subsidiaries and divisions, and all of their respective current and former directors, officers, shareholders, successors, agents, representatives, and employees, from any and all claims you ever had, now have, or may in the future assert regarding any matter that predates this agreement, including, without limitation, all claims regarding your employment at or termination of employment from (Name of Employer), any contract, express or implied, any tort, or any breach of a fair employment practice law, including Title VII, the Age Discrimination in Employment Act, and any other local, state, or federal equal opportunity law.

9. You acknowledge that you have had the opportunity to review this agreement with counsel of your own choosing, that you are fully aware of the agreement's contents and of its legal effects, and that you are voluntarily entering into this agreement.

10. You agree that any confidential information you acquired while an employee of the company shall not be disclosed to any other person or used in a manner detrimental to the company's interests.

11. Neither you nor anyone acting on your behalf shall publicize, disseminate, or otherwise make known the terms of this agreement to any other person, except to those rendering financial or legal advice, or unless required to do so by court order or other compulsory process of law.

12. The provisions of this agreement are severable and if any provision is held to be invalid or unenforceable it shall not affect the validity or enforceability of any other provision.

13. This agreement sets forth the entire agreement between you and the company and supersedes any and all prior oral or written agreements or understandings between you and the company concerning this subject matter. This agreement may not be altered, amended, or modified except by a further writing signed by you and (Name of Employer).

14. In the event (Name of Employer) becomes insolvent, bankrupt, is sold, or is unable in any way to pay the amounts due you under the terms of this agreement, then such obligations shall be undertaken and assumed by (specify Parent Company) and all such sums shall be guaranteed by (Name of Parent Company).

15. In the event that any monies due under this agreement are not paid for any reason, then the release referred to in Paragraph 8 shall be null and void and of no effect.

If the foregoing correctly and fully recites the substances of our agreement, please so signify by signing in the space below.

Dated: _____

>   Very truly yours,
>   Name of Employer
>   By: _____
>   Name of Officer, Title

Accepted and agreed:

_____

Name of Employee

who once negotiated, with my assistance, to receive an additional one year's severance and other benefits. Note the protections insisted on by the employer in the latter part of the agreement.

In the event the employer refuses to provide such a letter, it is advisable that you send a letter to the company by certified mail, return receipt requested, confirming the arrangement that has been made. The letter should state that if any terms are ambiguous or incorrect, a written reply should be sent to you immediately. If no response is received, you will be able to rely on the terms of the letter in most situations. The letter on page 180 is a good example.

Be sure to state everything accurately, because all ambiguities are usually construed against the person who writes such a letter. In addition, be prepared to send follow-up letters if warranted by your particular situation. Using the preceding case as an example, the ex-employee should notify the company in writing if he obtained another job prior to the severance cut-off date (in compliance with paragraph 10). This is illustrated by the follow-up letter on page 182.

BE CAUTIOUS ABOUT SIGNING RELEASES

Always be cautious if the employer asks you to sign a release. Generally, releases extinguish potential claims. Employees sometimes voluntarily sign such documents when they are fired without fully understanding the ramifications of such an act. Later they regret taking such action after consulting a lawyer and learning that they forfeited valuable rights without receiving much in return.

Since you may be out of luck if you sign such a document, consider the following strategies whenever you are asked to sign a release to be more knowledgeable in this area.

1. *Never sign a release unless you are satisfied with the company's offer.* This is reasonable because you should never relinquish a potentially valuable right without obtaining something of value in return.

2. *Read the release carefully before signing it.* Most releases are complicated documents. Many have settlement agreements, releases, waivers, and nondisclosure provisions all rolled into one document.

For example, what exactly does the release say? Are you prohibited from telling others about the terms of your settlement? This is referred to as a "gag order" provision. Many employers insert gag order clauses into releases that require all settlement monies to be forfeited and returned in the event you reveal the terms of the settlement to others. Obviously, you should question this provision and avoid signing it if possible.

Does the release prohibit you from working for a competitor or starting a competing business? Without such a clause you are free to

LETTER DOCUMENTING SEVERANCE ARRANGEMENT

Your Name
Address
Date

Name of Corporate Officer
Title
Name of Employer
Address

Re: Our Severance Agreement

Dear (Name of Corporate Officer):

This will confirm our discussion and agreement regarding my termination:

1. I will be kept on the payroll through (specify date) and will receive (specify) weeks' vacation pay, which shall be included with my last check on that date.

2. (Name of Company) shall pay me a bonus of (specify) within (specify) days from the date of this letter.

3. (Name of Company) will purchase both my nonvested and vested company stock, totaling (specify) shares at a price of (specify $) per share, or at the market rate if it is higher at the time of repurchase, on or before (specify date).

4. (Name of Company) will continue to maintain in effect all profit-sharing and retirement plans, medical, dental, hospitalization, disability and life insurance policies presently in effect through (specify date). After that date, I have been advised that I may convert said policies at my sole cost and expense and that coverage for these policies will not lapse. I will receive information concerning the conversion of my retirement plan savings within the next few weeks.

5. I will be permitted to use the company's premises at (specify location) from the hours of 9:00 a.m. until 5:00 p.m. This shall include the use of a secretary, telephone, stationery, and other amenities at the company's sole cost and expense to assist me in obtaining another position.

6. I will be permitted to continue using the automobile previously supplied to me through (specify date) under the same

terms and conditions presently in effect. On that date, I will return all sets of keys in my possession together with all other papers and documents belonging to the company.

7. (Name of Company) will reimburse me for all reasonable and necessary expenses related to the completion of company business after I submit appropriate vouchers and records within (specify) days of presentment.

8. (Name of Company) agrees to provide me with a favorable letter of recommendation and reference(s) and will announce to the trade that I am resigning for "personal reasons." I am enclosing a letter for that purpose which will be reviewed and signed by (specify person) and returned to me immediately.

9. Although unanticipated, (Name of Company) will not contest my filing for unemployment insurance benefits after (specify date), and will assist me in promptly executing all documents necessary for that purpose.

10. If a position is procured by me prior to (specify date), a lump sum payment for my remaining severance will be paid within (specify) days after my notification of same. Additionally, the stock referred to in Paragraph 3 will be purchased as of the date of my employment with another company if prior to (specify date) and will be paid to me within (specify) days of my notification.

If any of the terms of this letter are ambiguous or incorrect, please advise me immediately in writing specifying the item(s) that are incorrect. Otherwise, this letter shall set forth our entire understanding in this matter, which cannot be changed orally.

(Name of Corporate Officer), I want to personally thank you for your assistance and cooperation in this matter and wish you all the best in the future.

> Very truly yours,
> Your Name

Sent certified mail, return receipt requested

FOLLOW-UP LETTER INFORMING EMPLOYER OF ACCEPTANCE OF NEW EMPLOYMENT

Date

Name of Corporate Officer
Title
Name of Company
Address

Re: Subsequent development to our agreement dated (specify)

Dear (Name of Corporate Officer):

I hope all is well with you and yours.

As a follow-up to our letter of agreement dated (specify), I am informing you that I have accepted employment with another company effective (specify date).

Therefore, I expect to receive a lump sum payment representing all unpaid severance through (specify date) plus (specify) weeks of vacation pay on or before (specify date).

Furthermore, I believe I am entitled to compensation for my stock totaling (specify amount) within (specify date).

As of this date, I am returning all keys to the office by messenger together with keys to the company car. I have also included the last voucher for company-related expenses.

Thank you for your prompt cooperation in these matters.

Very truly yours,
Your Name

Enc. / Via Messenger

---

work for the employer of your choosing. This is a valuable right that should never be given up easily.

The cover letter and releases beginning on page 32 illustrate the kinds of documents you may be requested to sign depending on your particular circumstances.

3. *Negotiate additional clauses for your protection.* First, make sure the release will be null and void if any monies due under the agreement are

not paid. Second, include a guarantee that obligates the parent company to pay all remaining sums due under the agreement in the event a subsidiary corporation becomes bankrupt, insolvent, or fails for any reason to pay the amount due. These are examples of the kinds of points to consider and implement in your agreement.

4. *Obtain mutual releases where appropriate.* Try to get the employer to give you a release whenever you are giving one to the employer. This is because you want to be sure that the employer can never sue you at a later time for something you did.

5. *Speak to a lawyer immediately whenever the employer requests that you sign a release.* Not understanding the consequences of their actions, people often waive important rights by signing such agreements. For example, you may be waiving valuable claims based on discrimination, breach of contract, unfair discharge, or additional commissions or other monies owed. *Never* sign such a release until you are knowledgeable about all potential rights that you are giving up.

A competent lawyer can also take other practical steps for your protection, for example by insisting that the release be held in escrow until all sums due under the agreement have been paid. This means that the employer cannot rely on the signed release until it has fully performed all the obligations required by the release. Don't overlook this important point.

Counsel Comments: If you believe that you signed a release under conditions of fraud, duress, or mistake, it can be rescinded in special cases if you act promptly.

One of my clients, an African-American woman over forty, recently found herself in such a situation. She thought that she was fired illegally because of her race and age. She was told to sign a release in order to receive severance. But the release she signed was quite short (just a few sentences) and was not artfully drafted. For example, the release did not say that she had twenty-one days to review it, that she could revoke it up to seven days after signing, or that she had the right to consult a lawyer.

When she met with me, I told her that she had received very little in return for signing the document. I also advised her that she had a decent chance of fighting the release on legal technical terms because it was drafted so poorly.

The woman hired me to contact the company and negotiate a better package. Through my efforts, I was able to disallow the release and get her another $8,000 in severance. In hindsight, the company probably thought that $8,000 wasn't worth a lawsuit and the poor publicity and wasted manpower that go along with it.

Tip: Although it is generally difficult to overturn a release, always consult a lawyer immediately if you believe you were tricked into signing one.

Finally, recognize your rights with respect to releases under the federal Older Workers Benefit Protection Act (OWBPA). The act makes it clear that, in relation to a firing or a resignation of a worker over forty, a company can protect itself from potential violations of ADEA claims by utilizing waivers, provided:

1. The waiver is part of an agreement that specifically states the worker is waiving ADEA rights and is not merely a general release;
2. The agreement containing the waiver does not disclaim any rights or claims arising after the date of its execution;
3. The worker receives value (such as an extra month of severance) in exchange for signing the agreement;
4. The worker is advised in writing of the right to consult an attorney of his or her choosing before signing the agreement;
5. The worker is advised in writing of his or her right to consider the agreement for a period of twenty-one days before it is effective; and
6. The worker is given at least seven days following the execution of the agreement to revoke it.

When employers request the signing of releases or waivers in connection with mass termination programs and large-scale voluntary retirement programs, the act is even more strict. All individuals in the program must be given at least forty-five days to consider the agreement, and each employee must also be provided with numerous facts, such as the class, unit, or group of individuals covered by the program, any eligibility factors for the program, time limits applicable to the program, the job titles and ages of all individuals selected for the program, and the ages of all individuals not eligible for the program.

A benefit of the OWBPA is that all voluntary early retirement programs are now scrutinized closely to determine that there is no chance of threat, intimidation, or coercion to the worker to whom the benefit is offered. Older employees must now be given sufficient time to consider the offer and receive accurate and complete information regarding benefits.

Ask a lawyer to advise you of your rights if you are asked to sign a complicated waiver that you believe does not comply with the requirements of this law.

ACT PROMPTLY TO PROTECT YOUR RIGHTS

If you are owed earned and accrued benefits, it is strongly recommended that you send a letter or series of letters to the ex-employer immediately after being fired. You should do this before you decide to consult with or hire a lawyer, and you should do it promptly in order to document a claim. The letter(s) will help prove that a claim was made and that monies are due. If you still have trouble receiving the money, you can then contact a lawyer or a regional office of your state's department of labor for assistance. Examples of such letters, called demand letters, begin on page 186. These valuable letters can be used by anyone without the expense of hiring a lawyer. Simply fill in the blanks with the appropriate information, draft it neatly (preferably in type), and send the letter by certified mail, return receipt requested, to prove delivery. Always make and save a copy of the letter and the return receipt for your records.

Tip: Often such a letter will do the trick because the employer will know you are serious about protecting your rights and that you are knowledgeable concerning the law.

DEMAND LETTER FOR ERISA RETIREMENT BENEFITS

Your Name
Address
Telephone Number
Date

Name of Officer or Employer
Title
Name of Employer
Address

Re: My ERISA Retirement Benefits

Dear (Name of Officer):

As you know, I was terminated (or resigned) on (specify date). However, I have not received a written description of all my retirement benefits under federal ERISA law. (Or, if applicable, state: I have not received the correct computation of all benefits due me. Or: I believe I was fired shortly [i.e., two months] before the vesting of a pension, in violation of my ERISA rights.)

Your company has a legal obligation to provide me with accurate information concerning all applicable profit-sharing, pension, employee welfare, benefit, and other plans. Therefore I would like you to send me (specify what you want, such as to receive a copy of the employer's formal pension and/or profit sharing plans, recompute your benefits, or offer you a pension, if applicable).

It is imperative that I receive a response to my request immediately in writing to avoid having me take prompt legal action to enforce my rights.

Hopefully, this will not be necessary, and I thank you for your prompt attention in this matter.

If you wish to discuss this matter with me, feel free to contact me immediately.

Very truly yours,
Your Name

Sent certified mail, return receipt requested

Author's Note: Under federal ERISA law, if you request materials from a plan and do not receive them within thirty days, you may file suit in federal or state court. Contact the plan administrator for the company immediately in writing if your claim is denied or if you do not receive an adequate response shortly after a firing. If no adequate response is received, seek assistance from the U.S. Department of Labor to protect your rights.

DEMAND LETTER FOR COBRA MEDICAL BENEFITS COVERAGE

> Your Name
> Address
> Telephone Number
> Date

Name of Officer or Employer
Title
Name of Employer
Address

　　Re: My COBRA Medical Benefits

Dear (Name of Officer):

　　As you know, I was terminated on (specify date) due to a job elimination (or specify, such as business reorganization). However, more than 30 days has elapsed from the date of my discharge and I have not yet received official notification from either your company or your medical carrier that my medical benefits have been maintained and/or extended under federal COBRA law.

　　It is imperative that I receive such notification immediately in writing, specifying my cost at the group rate for such coverage.

　　I trust that such information will be forthcoming immediately so that I am not required to take prompt legal action to enforce my rights.

　　Hopefully, such additional legal action will not be necessary, and I thank you for your prompt attention to this apparent oversight.

　　If you wish to discuss this matter with me, feel free to contact me immediately.

> Very truly yours,
> Your Name

Sent certified mail, return receipt requested

Author's Note: Federal COBRA law requires that most employers offer continuation of coverage for an additional eighteen months to former employees who were discharged as a result of a voluntary or involuntary termination (with the exception of gross misconduct); all terminated employees have the option to continue medical plan benefits at their cost. You must be notified within sixty days of your right to continue such coverage. Send a similar letter whenever you do not receive such a notification shortly after a firing. A well-drafted letter should spur the company into action and protect your rights.

DEMAND LETTER FOR EARNED COMMISSIONS

> Your Name
> Address
> Telephone Number
> Date

Name of Officer or Employer
Title
Name of Employer
Address

　Re: My Commissions

Dear (Name of Officer):

It has been (specify) days from the effective termination date of our agreement. Despite our discussions and your earlier promises that all commissions presently owed would be paid immediately, I still have not received my money.

Please be advised that under this state's law, unless I am provided a final, accurate accounting, together with copies of all invoices reflecting shipment of my orders (or state if you require anything else) and payment of commissions totaling (specify $X if you know), within (specify, such as five days) from your receipt of this letter, your company will be liable for additional damages, attorney fees and costs upon my institution of a lawsuit to collect same.

Hopefully, this will not be necessary, and I thank you for your prompt attention to this apparent oversight.

If you wish to discuss this matter with me, feel free to contact me immediately.

> Very truly yours,
> Your Name

Sent certified mail, return receipt requested

Author's Note: Most states require that salespeople receive earned commissions immediately after a firing. Many of these laws provide independent reps up to three times additional damages in excess of the commission owed, plus reasonable attorney fees and costs, when monies are not promptly paid. Thus, always send a detailed written demand for unpaid commissions. This should be done by certified mail, return receipt requested, to document your claim and prove delivery. Such a demand will "start the clock" for the purpose of determining the numbers of days that commissions remain unpaid and put the employer on notice that additional damages and penalties may be owed if money is not received immediately. A written demand is essential in enforcing your rights and may get the employer to contact you and resolve the matter amicably.

DEMAND LETTER FOR EARNED BONUS

> Your Name
> Address
> Telephone Number
> Date

Name of Officer or Employer
Title
Name of Employer
Address

Re: My Bonus

Dear (Name of Officer):

Please be advised that I am currently owed a bonus of (specify $X if you know). I was fired on (specify date, such as January 15) suddenly for no valid reason and not as a result of any negative or detrimental conduct on my part. Prior to my termination, I complied with all company directives and was expecting to receive a bonus for the work I rendered in the preceding year.

This expectation was in accordance with our previous understandings and practices since I have regularly received bonuses for the past (specify) years ranging from (specify dollar amounts).

Therefore, to avoid further legal action, I request prompt payment of my earned bonus. Hopefully, additional legal action will not be necessary, and I thank you for your prompt attention to this apparent oversight.

If you wish to discuss this matter with me, feel free to contact me immediately.

Very truly yours,
Your Name

Sent certified mail, return receipt requested

Author's Note: Some employers fire workers right before they are scheduled to receive a bonus and deny such bonuses by stating a worker must be employed on the day bonus checks are issued as a condition of payment. If this happens to you, or you are denied a bonus for any reason, send a letter similar to the one above to protect your rights. Argue that you would have received the bonus but for the firing. Demand that you are entitled to receive a pro rata share of the bonus if you are fired close to but before the end of the year. For example, if you are fired on December 1, negotiate to receive eleven-twelfths of the bonus you were expecting.

DEMAND LETTER FOR ACCRUED VACATION PAY

Your Name
Address
Telephone Number
Date

Name of Officer or Employer
Title
Name of Employer
Address

Re: My Earned Vacation Pay

Dear (Name of Officer):

Please be advised that I am currently owed vacation pay totaling (specify number of days or weeks due or $X if you know). As you know, I resigned (or was fired) on (specify date). According to your company's policy specified in (state, such as a handbook or manual), I am entitled to (specify) weeks per year.

To avoid having me take legal action, including my contacting this state's department of labor and requesting a formal investigation, I expect to receive my earned, accrued vacation pay immediately.

Hopefully, additional legal action will not be necessary, and I thank you for your prompt attention to this apparent oversight.

If you wish to discuss this matter with me, feel free to contact me immediately.

Very truly yours,
Your Name

Sent certified mail, return receipt requested

Author's Note: Most states require employers to pay accrued vacation pay in all circumstances, even after resignations by employees or terminations for cause. Although each company is free to implement its own rules governing vacation pay, employers must apply such policies consistently to avoid charges of discrimination and breach of contract. To reduce problems, be sure you understand how long you must first work to qualify, whether vacation days must be taken in a given year, whether they can be carried over to the next year, and whether you can be paid in cash for unused, earned vacation days. Also, how much notice is required before being allowed to take vacation time? If the ex-employer fails to respond to your initial letter and even a second, final request, contact your state's department of labor for assistance.

DEMAND LETTER FOR ACCRUED OVERTIME PAY

Your Name
Address
Telephone Number
Date

Name of Officer or Employer
Title
Name of Employer
Address

Re: My Earned Overtime Pay

Dear (Name of Officer):

Please be advised that I am currently owed (specify hours) of overtime pay totaling (specify $X). As you know, I resigned (or was fired) on (specify date). Under federal law, since I was an hourly worker for your company, overtime at one and one half times my regular pay rate must be paid for hours worked in excess of 40 hours per workweek.

I am enclosing copies of time sheets for overtime work approved by my superior from (specify date) to (specify date). To avoid having me take prompt legal action, including my contacting this state's department of labor, and requesting a formal investigation into your company's violation of the Fair Labor Standards Act, I expect to receive my earned, overtime pay immediately.

Hopefully, additional legal action will not be necessary, and I thank you for your prompt attention to this matter.

If you wish to discuss this matter with me, feel free to contact me immediately.

Very truly yours,
Your Name

Sent certified mail, return receipt requested

Author's Note: Overtime is not generally available for salaried workers who work in executive, administrative, or professional jobs (called exempt employees). But if you are a salaried worker, your company is not generally allowed to deduct a few hours off your weekly paycheck for time off for any reason, including personal time. If they do, you may be determined to be an hourly worker, capable of receiving overtime for up to three years.

If you have kept proper records and took authorized overtime, contact a representative at your state's department of labor or the Wage and Hour Division of the U.S. Department of Labor for help if the ex-employer fails to respond to your initial letter or a second final written request.

SUMMARY OF THINGS TO KNOW IF YOUR JOB IS IN JEOPARDY

1. It may be illegal for a company to fire you to deprive you of large commissions, vested pension rights, a year-end bonus, or other expected financial benefits.
2. It may be illegal for a company to fire you after returning from an illness, pregnancy, or jury duty.
3. It may be illegal to fire you after you have complained about a safety violation or other wrongdoing.
4. It may be illegal to fire you in a manner inconsistent with company handbooks, manuals, written contracts, and disciplinary rules.
5. It may be illegal to fire you if you are over forty, belong to a protected minority, or are a female primarily because of such personal characteristics.
6. It may be illegal to fire a large number of workers and/or close a plant without giving at least sixty days' notice or sixty days' severance pay.
7. It may be illegal to fire you if you received a verbal promise of job security or other rights that the company failed to fulfill.
8. It may be illegal to fire a long-term worker when the "punishment does not fit the crime" and other workers were not similarly treated, particularly if you are over forty, belong to a protected minority, or are a female.

9. If you signed a written contract, reread it. Review what it says about termination, because if the company fails to act according to the contract, your rights may be violated.

10. Try to make copies of all pertinent documents in your personnel file while working. If you have received excellent performance reviews and appraisals and the file indicates you received merit salary increases, you may be able to use this information to successfully negotiate more severance than the company is offering.

11. Refuse the company's offer to resign whenever possible. This is because if you resign you may be waiving your claim to unemployment and other severance benefits.

12. Avoid accepting the company's first offer of severance. Stall for time and follow the negotiating strategies given in chapters 7 through 9. By doing so, you can increase the chances of obtaining more severance pay and other post-termination financial benefits than the company initially offered.

Finally, since the above twelve strategies are merely suggestions and are not intended to be legal advice per se, always seek competent legal advice where warranted.

SUMMARY OF NEGOTIATING STRATEGIES TO MAXIMIZE SEVERANCE PAY AND RETIREMENT BENEFITS

1. Generally, there is no legal obligation for a company to pay severance unless you have a written contract stating that severance will be paid, oral promises are given regarding severance pay, there is a documented policy of paying severance in a company manual or handbook, the employer voluntarily offers to pay severance, or other employees in similar positions have received severance pay in the past.

2. If you are fired, request an additional negotiating session to discuss your severance package.

3. Stall for time and try not to accept the company's first offer.

4. Appeal to corporate decency and fair play at the initial meeting. For example, it is better to say, "I am fifty-eight years old and

have to pay for two children in college right now, and your offer of just four weeks' severance will probably put me on the road to financial ruin, since it is unlikely that I can find another comparable job in four weeks," rather than, "If you don't pay me more money, I will sue."

5. Follow the negotiating strategies given in chapters 7 through 9 to maximize your chances of obtaining additional financial and other post-termination benefits. Recognize that by asking for many (e.g., fifteen) items, you may be able to get the company to settle for some (e.g., five).

6. Confirm all arrangements in writing to document the final deal of severance and post-termination benefits; do not accept the company's promise that "everything will work out."

7. Insist on receiving more money and other benefits before signing any release or waiver of age discrimination claims.

8. Do not rely on promises from the company that you will receive a favorable job reference. Rather, draft your own favorable letter of reference and get an officer or your supervisor to sign the letter of reference before you depart.

9. Do not be intimidated or forced into early retirement. Recognize that you may have rights, particularly if your early retirement causes you to lose large, expected financial benefits.

10. Be cautious when the employer asks you to sign a release, because you may be waiving valuable rights and benefits in the process.

11. Never resign from a job unless absolutely necessary. If you are given the choice between resigning or being fired, get fired.

12. Select the most favorable or sympathetic person at the company to initially negotiate the deal with.

13. Go above him or her if you don't achieve what you're seeking.

14. Never be pressured by the employer into signing a release or making a fast decision.

15. Be persistent; don't become demoralized.

16. Know your rights, ask questions, and demand answers.

17. Have a game plan in place to help you get what you want.

18. Rehearse what you will say and why it is fair for you to get a better package.

19. Consider early retirement options or other ways to keep you on the payroll such as working freelance or as a consultant where appropriate.

20. Analyze the tax aspects of any settlement.

21. Negotiate for nontaxable benefits or convert unneeded benefits (such as outplacement assistance) into more severance pay when practicable.

Finally, since the above twenty-one strategies are merely suggestions and are not intended to be legal advice per se, always seek competent legal advice where warranted.

PART III

Fighting Back

CHAPTER 10

How to Resign from a Job Properly and How to Maximize Unemployment Benefits

Sandra is called into her boss's office and told that she is being summarily discharged. However, the company states that she can resign by signing a letter of resignation, which it has prepared and presents to her.

Sandra thinks it is better to resign than to be fired, so she signs the letter of resignation and leaves the premises. When she files for unemployment benefits, she learns she is not entitled to benefits unless she can prove that she was forced to resign. The company introduces the letter of resignation as evidence that no pressure or undue influence was forced on Sandra and it was her voluntary decision; she is denied unemployment insurance benefits.

Sandra consults an employment lawyer. She learns that had she not resigned she would have received severance. She also learns that she could have made a deal with her employer (and confirmed it in writing) that although the company would agree to inform prospective employers that she resigned for personal reasons (her "cover story"), it would not contest her unemployment benefits or deny paying her other benefits she would have

received had she allowed the company to fire her. The lawyer
also explained that if she was close to earning a vesting pension,
profit-sharing benefits, or year-end bonus, her resignation would
seriously undermine a claim for those expected benefits.

As I have stated in other sections of this book, the golden rule is never
to quit a job if you can help it. Refuse an employer's offer to resign
whenever possible. This is because if you resign you may be waiving
a claim to unemployment and other severance benefits, including
earned commissions. This is a trap many employees fall into.

However, there are occasions when you may receive a better job
offer and decide to resign from your current position. Information in
this chapter will tell you how to do so properly to increase the chances
that the job at your new employer will not be short-lived. Additionally, as a separate matter, information in this chapter will tell you what
to do and how to maximize your chances of success when you file for
unemployment benefits after a discharge, termination, or layoff.

RESIGNING FROM A JOB PROPERLY

Most people do not know how to resign properly. The slightest mistake can expose you to a lawsuit or cause the forfeiture of valuable
benefits. Some people resign without receiving a firm job offer from
a new employer. Later, after learning the new job did not materialize,
they are unable to be rehired by their former employer and spend
months out of work without collecting unemployment benefits. To
avoid this and similar problems, review and implement the following
strategies where possible.

1. *Sign a written contract with a new employer before resigning.* A written
contract with a definite term of employment (for example, six months
or one year) can protect you from situations where the new employer
changes its mind and decides not to hire you, or fires you after a short
period of time. This often happens with devastating consequences but
can be avoided by insisting on a valid agreement with job security before starting work. If the new employer does not agree to this, think
twice before jumping ship.

Counsel Comments: Many of my clients wish to learn what rights they have after resigning from a job and accepting a position with a new employer. Generally, they forget (or are afraid) to get a firm commitment of job security from a new employer before they resign from a good job. On some occasions, I have observed unfortunate workers who sell their homes and relocate their family to a distant locale, only to discover they aren't happy or that the employer is not satisfied with the arrangement shortly after the move is made. They ask if they can sue the new employer for promissory estoppel, misrepresentation, and other related legal causes of action as a result of the new job going sour.

Although on some occasions I have successfully represented these people and recovered money as a result of the new employer's broken promises, this could have been avoided had they insisted on receiving an employment agreement that contained a definite promise of job security.

Tip: Remember, a job is like a romance. Companies woo applicants with promises of fulfillment and riches. Then, when the honeymoon is over, even highly qualified people find themselves being treated unfairly. This is the nature of the working world. Remember this for your own good. Never leave a good job voluntarily without a strong employment agreement from your new employer if you can help it.

2. *Review your current contract or letter of agreement.* If notice is required to be given, do this so you will not violate the contract's obligations.

Counsel Comments: This is an important concern. For example, if your contract requires you to give thirty days' notice before leaving, you must do so to avoid the company claiming you are in breach of contract. If you do not resign properly, you may be sued for damages. Damages in such cases are typically calculated at the employer's cost of training a replacement. However, if you resign prematurely at an important time (e.g., during market week if you are a salesperson, or right before a customer is consummating an important deal in which your services are required, but the deal is blown because you leave), the damages could be significant.

Tip: There are occasions where an employer will release you from your obligations immediately after you give proper notice. This is be-

cause the employer may not want you around for, say, thirty days after
it knows you will be leaving. If your contract requires notice, offer it
but anticipate, discuss, or seize the opportunity that you may leave
suddenly at the employer's request. If the employer agrees, ask to receive the wages you would have earned during the notice period as
part of a severance package. Some employers may be amenable to this.

Finally, since the employer may tell you to get out immediately after
you give notice, anticipate this may occur and plan accordingly. Consider removing valuable contents from your office *before* giving notice,
because the employer may tell you to vacate the premises and you
won't have this opportunity later. Get your affairs in order. Select the
best time to resign to suit your needs knowing this may occur.

3. *Get legal advice if you believe your current employer will reject (or rejects)
an offer to resign.* On rare occasions, an employer may be inclined to do
this, especially if you have an important job and your presence is essential to completing a major task or project. This could happen when
you have a written employment contract with a definite term (say for
a year) and you wish to resign six months into the contract period.

If you choose to leave anyway, you may be subjecting yourself to a
breach of contract lawsuit. An employment lawyer may advise that the
most obvious damages you would suffer might be the employer's costs
to train a suitable replacement. If the company was forced to hire a replacement at a higher salary or with greater benefits, the difference in
pay might also be cause for damages.

Fortunately, in many cases, the damages typically asserted by an
employer against someone breaking a contract and leaving a job prematurely are speculative and hard to prove. I have observed that the
vast majority of employers are inclined to set you free because keeping you around is dangerous (you could be sharing information with
a competitor) and bad for morale (since you will probably not be giving your best when forced to remain).

All of these factors should be considered before you decide to break
a contract. As consideration, a lawyer may recommend that you continue to work for the company as a consultant with less compensation
in return for getting the employer to "let you out" of the contract. To
minimize the risks of a lawsuit, these and other ideas should sometimes be explored before the decision to leave is made.

4. *Give notice only where necessary.* In many jobs, giving notice is not
required or necessary (contrary to the public's misconception) espe-

cially if you are hired at will. However, the employer will usually benefit when you offer notice because it may then have time to seek and train a replacement. It may also give you the opportunity to bargain for additional severance benefits before walking out the door.

Tip: Two weeks' notice is probably more than adequate; avoid giving more notice than necessary. Do not offer notice if you must start a new job immediately and believe this will jeopardize your new position. However, if you are entitled to a large bonus or commission in the near future, postpone resigning until you have received such a benefit.

Many employers often summarily reject an employee's notice and ask you to leave the minute they are notified of your intentions. The reason is that some employers believe you will copy pertinent documents or cause trouble. Don't be surprised if this occurs. Anticipate it and plan ahead.

5. *Should you resign by letter?* Only when it is used to clarify resignation benefits, request prompt payment of monies previously due, confirm unfair or illegal treatment, or put you on record that the resignation will not be effective until some later date. If these reasons are important, always resign by letter. When you do, keep the letter brief and avoid giving reasons for the resignation without having a lawyer review the letter first. The reason is that the letter may be used as evidence at a later trial or proceeding and can preclude you from offering other reasons for the resignation or tipping your hand in the event of a lawsuit.

The example on page 204 is the kind of resignation letter you may wish to draft. You should deliver it by hand or send it by certified mail, return receipt requested, in order to prove delivery.

6. *Never resign if given the choice.* Many employers have written policies that state that no severance or other post-termination benefits will be paid to workers who resign. Additionally, in many states, you are not entitled to unemployment insurance benefits after voluntarily resigning from a job. If you are a commission salesperson, it is often more difficult to argue that you are entitled to commissions due on orders shipped after a resignation (as opposed to after a firing).

Tip: Think twice if the employer gives you the option of resignation or discharge. Talk to a lawyer for advice. In general, I prefer that

LETTER OF RESIGNATION

> Your Address
> Telephone Number
> Date

Name of Officer
Title
Name of Employer
Address

   Re: My Resignation

Dear (Name of Officer):

   Please be advised that I am resigning from my job as (title) effective (date).

   As of this date, I believe that (describe what salary, commissions, other benefits) are due and I look forward to discussing my termination benefits with you.

   I shall be returning all property belonging to the company (specify) by (date) and will be available to assist you in a smooth transition if requested.

   Thank you for your attention to these matters.

> Very truly yours,
> Your Name

Sent certified mail, return receipt requested

my clients be fired rather than resign, since potential damage claims and severance benefits may remain intact. If you are worried what others may think, you can always negotiate that the employer will tell outsiders that you "resigned for personal reasons" (even if you were fired).

7. *Keep quiet.* Tell friends and business associates of your decision to resign *after* telling your current employer, not before.

8. *Avoid bad-mouthing.* It is not a good idea to tell others about the circumstances surrounding a resignation, particularly if you are leaving on less-than-pleasant terms. Many employers have sued former

employees for defamation, product disparagement, and unfair competition on discovering that harmful oral or written comments were made. Additionally, when the statement disparages the quality of a company's product and at the same time implies that an officer or principal of the employer is dishonest, fraudulent, or incompetent (thus affecting the individual's personal reputation), a private lawsuit for personal defamation may be brought. Some companies withhold severance pay and other voluntary benefits as a way of getting even. Thus, avoid discussing your employer in a negative way with anyone.

9. *Return company property.* Disputes sometimes occur when property belonging to the employer is not returned. You probably must return such property (automobile keys, confidential customer lists, samples, etc.) immediately on resignation to avoid claims of conversion, fraud, and breach of contract.

Tip: If you return items by mail, get a receipt to prove delivery. A few states permit you to retain company property as a lien in the event you are owed money that the employer refuses to pay. However, since many states do not recognize this, speak to an employment lawyer before taking such action.

MAXIMIZING UNEMPLOYMENT BENEFITS

Each state imposes different eligibility requirements for collecting unemployment benefits (e.g., the maximum amount of money that may be collected weekly, the normal waiting period required before payments begin, the length of such benefits, and the maximum period you can wait before filing and collecting). States also differ on standards of proof required to receive such benefits. You must know such essential details before filing. Do this by contacting your nearest unemployment office for pertinent information.

The following are some of the questions to ask:

- How long did I have to work for my former employer in order to qualify?
- How quickly can I file?
- When will I begin receiving payments?
- How long will the payments last?

- What must I do (i.e., must I actively look for employment?) in order to continue receiving benefits?
- What must I prove in order to collect if my ex-employer contests my claim?
- When and where will the hearing be held?
- Will I have the opportunity to review the employer's charges and documentation opposing my claim (often contained in the official file) before the hearing?
- How can I learn whether witnesses will appear on the company's behalf to testify against me?
- How can I obtain competent legal counsel to represent me?
- How much will this cost?
- Will a record be made of the hearing? If so, in what form?
- Can the hearing examiner's decision be appealed?
- Can I recover benefits if I was forced to resign?
- Is the burden on the employer to demonstrate I was fired for a good reason (e.g., misconduct), or is the burden of proof on me to demonstrate I did not act improperly?
- Can I subpoena witnesses if they refuse to appear voluntarily on my behalf? Will the hearing examiner assist me in this regard?
- Are formal rules of evidence followed at the hearing?

Tip: Collecting unemployment benefits is not always a simple matter, especially if your claim is contested by an ex-employer. In most states, you can collect benefits if you were fired due to a business reorganization, massive layoff, job elimination, or other reasons that were not your fault. In many situations, you can even collect if you were fired for being unsuited, unskilled, or for overall poor work performance. However, you generally cannot collect if you voluntarily resigned from a job (unless you were forced to resign for a good reason—for example, you're required to work the midnight-to-eight shift when you have to care for your children) or were fired for misconduct.

The following are common examples of acts that justify the denial of unemployment based on misconduct:

- Insubordination or fighting on the job
- Habitual lateness or excessive absence
- Drug abuse on the job

- Disobedience of company work rules or policies
- Gross negligence or neglect of duty
- Dishonesty

Counsel Comments: Although these examples appear to be relatively straightforward, employers often have difficulty proving that such acts reached the level of misconduct. This is because hearing examiners typically seek to determine whether a legitimate company rule was violated and whether or not that rule was justified.

Each state treats terminations for cause differently with respect to unemployment compensation entitlement. Thus, always file a claim, even if you believe there is a good chance you may not qualify, because you may still be able to collect.

Generally, employees terminated for cause qualify for benefits if they were unable, rather than unwilling, to perform the job.

An article written for employers entitled "Unemployment Benefits: Contest Claims the Smart Way" (*You and the Law*, March 1996) states that employees terminated for misconduct may still qualify for benefits, but usually those benefits are limited. In such situations, some states postpone benefits for a number of weeks, while others reduce the amount of the payout. Some states impose steeper penalties for "gross misconduct" (defined as dishonest or criminal acts). In Maryland, for example, gross misconduct disqualifies applicants for the entire span of their unemployment. Workers are not eligible for unemployment again until they have gotten a new job and earned twenty times the weekly allowable benefit.

There are occasions when you may be entitled to receive unemployment compensation even when you voluntarily leave employment. This can occur if you had "good cause" for resigning. Determining good cause depends on the unique facts of a particular case, but it may be found by a department of labor or appeals board where there was a real, substantial, and compelling reason to leave your job.

For example, you may still be able to collect benefits if you leave a job because:

- You are the victim of a physical attack or provocation and reasonably fear for your safety

- You must do so pursuant to a doctor's orders (such as relocate to a warmer climate because of chronic bronchitis)
- The work is unreasonably dangerous
- The company changes your hours making it impossible for you to work (e.g., you are suddenly notified you must work the midnight to 8:00 A.M. shift, which you cannot do because you have young children and are a single custodial parent)

Tip: Recognize, however, that if you resign from a job to attend school full-time, start your own business, take an unauthorized vacation, or leave in anticipation of a firing, you will probably not be able to collect unemployment benefits.

Thus, check your state's law where applicable.

Preparing for a Hearing

Once you file for unemployment insurance benefits and learn that the employer is contesting your claim, it is your responsibility to follow the progress of the case carefully.

Tip: Consider whether you require representation by experienced counsel at the hearing (especially if you are considering suing the employer in court over other issues and do not want to lose the first battle). If you are anticipating receiving the maximum benefits allowed (which in some states can exceed $325 per week) and expect to be unable to find gainful employment for a long period of time (e.g., six months), it may be advantageous to hire a lawyer when the amount of money being contested is significant.

Many people do not know how to act at an unemployment hearing. Claimants are often told by unemployment personnel that a lawyer or other representative is not required and that prehearing preparation is unnecessary. They then attend the hearing and are surprised to learn that the employer is represented by counsel, who has brought witnesses to testify against their version of the facts. Some are unprepared for the grueling, possibly humiliating cross-examination lasting several hours that they are subjected to. Other claimants lose at the hearing because they don't understand the purpose of their testimony or what they must prove to receive benefits.

Plan on being able to attend the hearing on the date in question. If you cannot be present, speak to a representative responsible for scheduling, explain your reasons, and ask for another convenient date. This should preferably be done in person. Include future dates when you know you can appear. Call that individual the day before the old hearing date to confirm that your request has been granted.

An unemployment hearing is often no different from a trial. Witnesses must testify under oath. Documents, including personnel information, warnings, and performance appraisals, are submitted as exhibits. The atmosphere is rarely friendly. Thus, you must prepare in advance what you will say, how you will handle tough questions from the employer, and what you will try to prove to win the case.

Counsel Comments: I am sometimes amazed that employers fight unemployment claims so vehemently. The amount of insurance coverage they are required to pay does not increase dramatically when a claim is filed and/or granted. While it makes good sense to contest a claim where warranted, often it is done merely to get even. The following true case is a good example.

I once represented a taxi driver who was fired from his job. The employer claimed he walked off the job and was not entitled to unemployment compensation. However, my client proved that after he had a heated argument with the boss (which was justified) and was fired, he refused to turn in his car until he was able to use the car to retrieve his personal belongings.

The judge ruled that the client's actions were reasonable under the circumstances, and he was awarded unemployment compensation after a lengthy and contentious hearing. As I was leaving I asked the general manager why the company fought my client's claim in the manner it had. He responded that the company did this to everyone out of spite!

When preparing for the hearing, be certain that all your friendly witnesses (if any) will attend and testify on your behalf. If necessary, ask a representative from the unemployment office to issue a subpoena compelling the attendance of key disinterested witnesses (e.g., coworkers) who refuse to testify and voluntarily attend. If the unemployment representative has no power to do this, wait until the first day of the hearing. Explain to the judge or hearing examiner the necessity of compelling the appearance and testimony of key witnesses.

The judge may grant your request depending on its relevance and reasonableness.

Organize the case the day before the hearing to maximize your chances of success. If you have a lawyer, meet with him or her to learn the correct way to testify and what you must prove to win benefits. Collect all evidence so that it can be produced easily at the hearing. Practice what you will say. Prepare an outline of key points to be discussed and questions to ask each witness and employee of the ex-employer.

The Hearing

Arrive early on the hearing date and advise a scheduling clerk of your appearance. Bring your evidence and come properly attired (preferably in business clothes). In some states, you can review the entire contents of your file before the hearing; don't forget to ask for this. When your case is called, all witnesses will be sworn in. Show the judge your evidence and never argue with the hearing examiner. Listen to the judge's or your lawyer's questions before answering. Avoid being emotional and arguing with your opponent at the hearing.

After the employer finishes testifying, you will have the opportunity to cross-examine the witnesses and refute what was said. If the employer is represented by an attorney and you feel intimidated because you are not represented by counsel, tell the judge you are not familiar with unemployment hearing procedures. Ask the judge to intercede on your behalf if you feel your opponent's attorney is treating you unfairly.

Obtaining a Decision

Decisions are not usually obtained immediately after the hearing. You will probably be notified by mail (sometimes two to four weeks later). Be sure to continue filing for benefits while waiting for the decision. Many people forget to do this and lose valuable benefits.

Should You Appeal?

If you are notified that you have lost the decision, read the notice carefully. Most judges and hearing examiners give specific, lengthy reasons for their rulings. If you feel the ruling was incorrect or you disagree with the judge's opinion, you may want to file an appeal and have the case reconsidered. However, it is best to speak with an experienced employment lawyer to get an opinion before doing so. You may discover that your chances of success with an appeal are not as good as you think. Appeals are not granted automatically as a matter of right in many states. If the judges on the appeals board believe that the hearing judge's decision was correct factually or as a matter of law, the decision will go undisturbed.

Tip: The odds of winning an appeal are not in your favor if you lose at the initial hearing. The amount of time needed to review the transcript or tape of the proceedings, prepare an appeal brief, and reargue the case often makes it expensive and time-consuming. Depending on the particular facts of your case, appealing the hearing may not be worth it. However, if new material facts come to light, if relevant witnesses are willing to come forward and testify at an appeal hearing, or if the success of another case (such as a discrimination lawsuit that was previously filed) depends on a successful outcome of the unemployment matter, this could make a difference.

Typically, you have only a specified period of time (say thirty days) to file the appeal, so do this in a timely fashion to avoid having the appeal dismissed due to a technical error.

Tip: Speak to an employment lawyer if you have already received benefits and are now being asked to return the money because you lost the hearing. In some states, the failure to return benefits is a crime and you can be prosecuted. I have structured settlements for many clients in this situation that called for a small payout over time (with no interest charges imposed) to diminish the burden of having to pay all the money back immediately. People out of work with insufficient funds can do this with a lawyer's assistance, or even on their own, so inquire about this where appropriate.

Tom is terminated from a job for alleged misconduct. He files for unemployment compensation and expects the ex-employer will contest his claim. Surprisingly, no contest is filed and Tom begins receiving maximum benefits.

A year later, Tom is notified that the ex-employer demands a hearing to determine whether or not he was eligible for benefits. Tom cannot believe that the company has a right to do this many months later, but he learns this is legal. He appears at the hearing without a lawyer and loses.

Tom receives a letter from the state demanding the return of the $4,700 he received plus interest. The letter says that if he doesn't return the money, he may face criminal charges from the state's attorney general. Tom is scared and does not know what to do. He already spent the money, since he was out of work and needed to support his family.

He consults a skilled employment lawyer and hires him. The lawyer negotiates a settlement with a representative from the state unemployment insurance office. The settlement allows Tom to pay back the money at a rate of $50 per month with no interest. Tom is satisfied knowing he can afford such terms with no criminal penalties, especially since he has found a new job and is receiving a steady income.

CHAPTER 11

Job References and Defamation Lawsuits

John and three other employees were discharged from a major insurance company for failing to comply with their manager's request to falsify and alter certain expenditure reports and refund a portion of their expense money. This refusal caused them to be fired for "gross insubordination."

Following the termination, the employees sought other positions of employment. In response to inquiries about their previous jobs, the four ex-employees stated they had been fired for gross insubordination.

The Minnesota Supreme Court ruled that a defamation had occurred because the terminated employees, when asked, were required to repeat the reason they were given for their discharge. Any explanation they tried to give to prospective employers could not compensate for highly negative impressions caused by the words "gross insubordination." To make matters worse, the company policy of withholding information after a job referral request only added to the innuendos.

The former employees sued; each was awarded $350,000. The case is significant because it indicates that, in some states, em-

ployees fired on false charges of bad conduct can sue their former employers for defamation even if it is the workers themselves
who reveal the charges (since they may be compelled to disclose
the false allegations in interviews).

Employers across the country are facing a new kind of potential liability vis-à-vis employees: defamation actions, as fired employees are
increasingly suing former employers for libel and slander. It is estimated that up to five thousand claims are filed yearly, and lawsuits
commenced by discharged employees now account for approximately
one-third of all defamation actions, with the average winning verdict
exceeding $110,000. Furthermore, defending such actions can take
years and typically costs employers from $140,000 to $250,000 per
case.

In the employment context, defamation is defined as any false statement about an employee communicated by an employer to a third
party that harms that employee's reputation or deters others from
dealing with him or her in a business setting. A statement can be
defamatory if it holds an individual up to scorn or ridicule, accuses an
individual of committing a criminal offense or having a communica-
ble disease that is shunned by society (e.g., AIDS), or even questions
an individual's honesty or competence in certain cases.

Traditionally, defamation claims have arisen out of the termination
of employees. They are the result of the employer giving poor references, making false statements about fired employees, or giving false
information to employees about why an individual was terminated.

But the ability to sue an ex-employer for defamation doesn't arise
only for these reasons. It can also arise when false, damaging statements are revealed to nonessential third parties. For example, I once
represented a man who was fired after being falsely accused of drinking excessively at lunch. He obtained a copy of a memo confirming
this, which had been read by several coworkers. After the accusation
was shown to be untrue, my client recovered $25,000 in an out-of-
court settlement.

In another case, a stockbroker incurred the enmity of a company's
vice-president. A heated exchange between the two men culminated
in the employee's termination. Shortly afterward, two of the broker's
customers who had heard of his dismissal requested a meeting with

the vice-president to inquire about the status of their investments. The vice-president told them that the broker was about to lose his license, was in big trouble with the Securities and Exchange Commission, and would "never work again." Told of these remarks, the stockbroker sued his ex-employer for slander and stated that the company deliberately tried to destroy his career.

The employer argued that the vice-president's comments were a protected expression of opinion. However, the Texas Court of Appeals rejected this and the company's attempt to disclaim responsibility for the vice-president's utterances, since his status as a manager and an officer provided him with authority to speak for and bind the company. The court agreed with a jury's finding that awarded the stockbroker $212,875 for past and future damages to his reputation; $84,525 for lost damages; $19,791 for past mental anguish, humiliation, and embarrassment; and $1 million for other (punitive) damages.

Even more significant is that some courts have begun awarding damages to terminated individuals suffering from negative impressions that arise from an employer's silence or inaction. For example, one ex-employer successfully won a lawsuit against his former employer after claiming that his discharge, following the administration of a lie detector test, gave fellow employees the false impression that he had been discharged for participating in a wrongful activity. After it was demonstrated that the test results had been improperly evaluated by an unqualified and unlicensed polygraph examiner and that he was not guilty of any wrongdoing, the South Carolina Supreme Court agreed that this false impression amounted to defamation and awarded him $150,000.

Another court agreed that a defamation occurred by the method in which an employer packed and removed documents from a discharged employee's office after a termination. When asked by coworkers what was going on, the employer responded, "You don't want to know."

Courts are also recognizing valid causes of action by people who suffer damage to their reputations from statements in discharge letters, office petitions, warning letters, personnel files, and performance evaluations that contain false information or are used to deny a promotion. The same is true for false statements made at management or employee meetings or even when defamatory graffiti about an employee is written on company grounds and no attempt is made to remove it.

If a supervisor writes a memo stating that he lost confidence in an employee's work and charges the employee with incompetence, unreliability, untruthfulness, and poor attitude, the employee may have a valid defamation claim if the memo is circulated around the office and read by nonessential third parties, especially when damaging information is disseminated and the employer did not take adequate precautions to determine whether the derogatory information was accurate. For example, in one case a terminated employee sued his former boss for defamation when letters describing his poor performance were distributed and read by several executives. The employee was awarded $90,000 after proving that the information contained in the letters was false and deliberately disseminated to cause him harm.

Harshly criticizing an employee can make an employer vulnerable in a defamation lawsuit. Thus, if you are accused of stealing company property in front of others and slanderous remarks are made (e.g., "You are a crook"), your employer may be guilty of defamation if the remarks are proved false.

Protection can also extend to physical acts. One employee working for an automobile manufacturer was suspected of theft when leaving the premises. Hundreds of workers observed him being forcibly searched and interrogated. After proving the charges were unfounded, the man sued the company. He argued that the rough treatment observed by other workers held him up to ridicule and scorn, since the treatment implied he was guilty of theft; he was awarded $25,000 by a jury.

SLANDER AND LIBEL

The following legal causes of action fall under the larger heading of defamation.

Slander arises when an unfair and untrue *oral* statement is communicated to a third party that damages an individual's reputation. The spoken words must pertain to a person's poor moral character, unreliability, dishonesty, or financial instability (e.g., a statement that the person is filing for bankruptcy or is always being sued when this is false, or fails to live up to contractual obligations or business responsibilities).

Libel arises when an unfair and untrue statement is made about a person *in writing* (i.e., in a letter or memo). The statement becomes actionable when it is read by a third party and damages the person's business or personal reputation.

Counsel Comments: Mere statements that an employee was discharged from employment and truthful statements about that employee's work habits are not defamatory. Truth is a total defense against claims of libel or slander. Charging a worker with bad manners, being careless or being a troublemaker, not having sufficient skills, or not adequately performing a job will not typically qualify as defamation. However, statements that the individual was discharged for cause or unsatisfactory performance, incompetence, or insubordination, coupled with the employer's refusal to give a recommendation, may be potentially damaging and actionable as defamation.

Due to the potential exposure, most employers have become afraid of providing prospective employers with job references; the vast majority are instructed only to confirm an individual's name, job title, dates of employment, and positions held. This has caused problems to prospective employers who need to learn more about a candidate before offering a job so as to avoid liability in the emerging legal area of negligent hiring and retention.

For example, private day care and summer camp employers have an affirmative duty to conduct extensive background and character checks to ensure they do not hire convicted child molesters, and former employers have been sued for not disclosing a worker's propensity for prior violent acts. Companies may also be liable when they give a positive reference about employees in safety-sensitive positions or whose jobs involved the care or custody of others that later proves to be inaccurate.

In light of the conflict between the need of prospective employers to receive accurate job references and the rights of individuals to pursue defamation claims, a growing number of state governments have passed laws granting immunity to employers who disclose job reference information about an employee or former employee. Alaska, Arizona, California, Florida, Georgia, Kansas, Louisiana, Maine, Maryland, New Mexico, Oklahoma, and Tennessee are among the states that have immunity laws, and Rhode Island, Wisconsin, and Wyoming legislatures recently passed similar measures. Under most state laws, an employer who provides a reference on request is presumed to be acting in good faith and, unless lack of good faith is shown by clear and convincing evidence, is immune from all civil liability that may result.

Generally, however, these laws do not protect employers who provide information unrelated to job performance, knowingly provide false information, make a reference maliciously or one motivated by personal animosity, or violate state antidiscrimination laws (e.g., by giving a poor reference in retaliation against an employee who previously filed a discrimination charge against the company).

Counsel Comments: The problem with most of these new state laws is that employees have a difficult burden of proving that an employer gave a false reference maliciously or not in good faith. As a result, some commentators suggest that employers can talk poorly about someone with impunity, thereby creating a blacklisting and/or blackballing situation. Additionally, even in states without such laws, the law generally states that employers typically have a qualified privilege when discussing an ex-employee's job performance with a prospective employer. This means that the employer may be excused for disseminating information about an individual that later turns out to be false if the person responsible for disseminating the information did so in the course of his or her normal duties (e.g., a personnel supervisor who writes performance appraisals about individuals).

However, a qualified privilege can be lost or abused and an employer can be liable if an executive or personnel supervisor *knowingly* makes false defamatory comments about a former employee out of reckless disregard for the truth, ill will, or spite. This was illustrated in a recent case where a jury awarded an executive $6.3 million, which included $5 million in punitive damages.

In that case, the man's employer, an insurance company, was hit with a $21-million jury verdict in a separate lawsuit. An agent in the company's Texas office was accused of defrauding a Texas couple who bought an insurance policy. A week after the verdict came in, the company fired the executive (who ran the office) as a scapegoat. At the company's annual meeting, several executives stated that the verdict was a result of the failure of local management to follow rules and, without naming the executive, contended that "former management encouraged, condoned and participated in the fraud."

After this, the company told prospective employers that the executive was terminated for allegedly condoning forgeries. This made him unemployable. Even though the company argued that it had a qualified privilege to make statements it believed to be true, the jury agreed with the plaintiff and ruled that the privilege had been abused.

Tip: The first thing to remember in any defamation lawsuit is that you must prove that false statements were made to third parties. This is often difficult to do. For example, if you are told by an employment recruiter that he heard slanderous comments from your former employer, the recruiter would have to testify in court in order for you to prevail, and many people are reluctant to do this. Moreover, if your employer disseminates harmful information that is true, or you are fired for a legitimate reason that is properly documented and can be proved by the company, you may lose your case. (But if the company treats you harshly in front of others after the discharge, such as escorting you out of the building with a police officer, your case may be strengthened.)

Even if an employment lawyer determines that commencing a lawsuit in this area is not in your best interest, the lawyer may be able to compel an employer to stop talking negatively about you to others under the threat of litigation. Sometimes all it takes is for the lawyer to write a strong letter (called a cease-and-desist letter) to the employer demanding that all offensive conduct stop. That is why it is critical to consult an employment lawyer immediately to analyze your situation.

STRATEGIES TO PROTECT YOUR RIGHTS

The following suggestions can help you protect your rights in this area.

1. *Avoid signing a release.* When you sign a release form allowing an employer to investigate and/or discuss your background with others, the law generally allows the employer to be absolved from liability for providing negative information about you to a prospective employer even when the comments are made maliciously. The sample applicant consent form on page 220 illustrates this. Avoid signing any such waiver prior to or after taking a job or being fired if you can help it.

APPLICANT CONSENT FORM TO INVESTIGATE AND DISCLOSE DATA

I, (Name of Applicant), hereby allow ABC Company the right to contact and investigate my former and current employers, and all other pertinent parties, including, but not limited to, educational institutions where I enrolled, to fully investigate my background.

I understand that as part of the interview process, since I am applying for the position of (specify), ABC Company requires all applicants to disclose pertinent data concerning previous work history, police and military records, and educational activities.

The purpose and procedures used in this investigation have been fully described to me and I completely understand the reasons and potential uses of such investigations. I authorize ABC Company to use any and all information acquired to make decisions regarding my employment, which may be disclosed to third parties.

I understand and agree that if any material facts are discovered which differ from those facts stated by me on my employment application, at my interview, or at any time prior to my commencing employment at ABC Company (if I am offered a position with ABC Company), I will not be offered the job. Furthermore, I understand and agree that if material facts are later discovered which are inconsistent with or differ from facts I furnished before taking the job, I will be disciplined, including immediate discharge without warning.

The cost of this investigation will be paid by ABC Company. Nonetheless, I hereby indemnify, release and forever discharge and hold ABC Company and its subsidiaries and affiliated companies, agents and employees, as well as all third parties supplying such information, harmless from any and all claims, demands, judgments and legal fees arising out of or in connection with this investigation, the results, or any lawful use of the results or disclosure thereto.

_____

Signature of Applicant

_____

Printed Name of Applicant

Social Security Number: _____

Date: _____

Name of Witness: _____

2. *Review the company's reference policies.* These are sometimes contained in an employee handbook or a personnel policy statement or memo. If your employer has disseminated policies in writing, such as that no references of any kind will be given after a firing or that the company will favorably assist departing employees in pursuing and finding new employment, and the company failed to act in accordance with such policies, you may have the right to sue and allege breach of an implied or express contract.

3. *Negotiate to receive a favorable reference after a firing.* You can do this before accepting an important job, during negotiations about a contract extension, or as part of a severance package after termination. While not commonly addressed in an initial employment contract, future references practices can be discussed and agreed on. For example, the parties may agree that in the event of a resignation or termination not for cause, the employer will actively assist an employee in obtaining another job and/or provide a favorable reference. Such statements or promises made by an employee at the job interview can constitute an enforceable contract in certain situations.

You might also negotiate the right to receive a favorable reference as a condition of staying on a particular job after the expiration of an initial contract term or agreeing to do something extra, such as relocate to another division in a distant state. Your agreement to do something extra could be construed as sufficient consideration to make the employer's promise binding and enforceable.

Finally, as part of a severance negotiation, the parties could agree on a favorable reference and cover story in exchange for your promise not to sue. Once this has been agreed, employers typically require you to sign a release promising not to sue. Never sign such a document without first consulting an employment lawyer.

4. *Take action if you are given a negative reference in retaliation for making or filing a discrimination claim.* Many employers will provide negative references to prospective employers out of spite after an ex-employee files a charge of gender, age, or race discrimination. Employment attorneys increasingly confront the issue of retaliation, which stems from the way employers handle workers who have reported on-the-job discrimination or harassment under antibias laws. Some lawyers believe there is always retaliation after a person files a complaint or charge.

Although retaliation claims are sometimes difficult to prove, they can be identified by the negative consequences an employee suffers

when the timing of the firing is clear. The reason that asserting a retaliation claim can be helpful is that even if no defamation is proved
and the employee eventually loses his or her discrimination case, a retaliation claim is a separate legal cause of action and can proceed to a
trial. For example, one woman who lost a sexual harassment case was
nevertheless awarded $73,400 by a federal jury that believed she suf-
fered compensable retaliation after her charge was filed with the
EEOC.

The Supreme Court recently ruled that minority or female workers who claim they were fired because of bias can sue former employers for retaliating with poor job references. The decision was a
victory for a salesman who was fired from his job at Shell Oil. He
filed a claim with the EEOC alleging that he was fired because he
was black. While the claim was pending, he applied for another job,
and a Shell supervisor gave him a poor rating. He then filed another
claim with the EEOC alleging post-termination retaliation discrimination. When a lower court ruled that the law did not cover him
because he was no longer employed by Shell, he appealed. Eventually, the Supreme Court agreed that the supervisor had given him a
negative reference to punish him for filing the discrimination
charge.

Tip: Because the Supreme Court has now spoken on this issue, its
ruling strengthens the law against workplace bias and will make
bosses more reluctant to offer negative references about former employees who made formal allegations of discriminatory treatment
before being fired. If you are a minority worker who desires to file
a legitimate claim of work bias, you may now do so, since the
chances of "post-employment retaliation" should be dramatically reduced as a result of this case. Speak to an employment lawyer for
more details.

5. *Act promptly if you discover that an ex-employer is making defamatory remarks that inhibit your chances of obtaining new employment.* By sending a
letter by certified mail, return receipt requested, you are taking an important step to protect your rights. The letter should document what
you have learned and put your former employer on notice that you
will take prompt legal action if the problem persists. The sample letter on page 223 illustrates this.

LETTER TO PROTEST DAMAGING AND
INCORRECT REFERENCES

Date

Name of Employer
Address

Dear (Name of Officer or Supervisor):

On (date) I applied for a job with (Name of Potential Employer). The interview went very well. I was led to believe that after some final items were confirmed, including contacting you to confirm essential facts about my former position with your company, I would be offered a job as (state title).

Surprisingly, I was not offered the job. After many requests, I learned that, during an interview with my prospective employer, you had stated that I "had a poor attitude" and was not eligible for rehire.

These facts about me are untrue. In fact, I had the opportunity to review the contents of my personnel file before I was dismissed and not one reference was made anywhere in the file to my alleged "poor attitude."

Therefore, you are instructed to (specify what you want, such as issue you a formal written apology, contact the prospective employer in writing and admit to this mistake, or cease and desist from making any such unfavorable remarks about your job performance to anyone in the future, particularly to potential employers). In the event you disregard this request, be assured I shall have my attorney take immediate steps to protect my rights, including filing a defamation lawsuit on my behalf.

Hopefully, this can be avoided, and I thank you for your immediate attention to this matter.

Very truly yours,
Your Name

cc: (Name of Potential Employer)

Sent certified mail, return receipt requested

Author's Note: Although you may be unable to obtain employment with the new prospective employer, sending a copy of this letter to the company may invite another discussion or interview.

If you receive no response or an unfavorable response to your letter, you should consider speaking with an employment lawyer for advice.

6. *Take immediate action if you believe you are being blacklisted or willfully prevented from obtaining new employment.* The majority of states prohibit and punish employers for maliciously or willfully attempting to prevent former employees from finding work. Some states, including Arkansas, Maine, Nebraska, New Mexico, and Utah, treat untruthful job references as a crime. For example, the Utah statute says that any person convicted of blacklisting is guilty of a felony and shall be fined not less than $55 nor more than $1,000 and imprisoned in the state prison not less than sixty days nor more than one year. Missouri permits civil actions against employers for compensatory damages for untruthful statements. The following states provide criminal penalties and civil damage lawsuits against former employers: California, Florida, Iowa, Kansas, Montana, North Carolina, and Texas. In California and Texas, triple damages are awarded in certain situations; Montana and North Carolina statutes provide for additional punitive damages.

Counsel Comments: Because the law may have changed while this book was being published, and the trend in many states with blacklisting statutes is to exempt employers and not prohibit employment references, check the law in your state to be sure.

In some states, including Connecticut, *any* dissemination of employment data to prospective employers (other than the dates of employment, last position held, and latest salary figures) or confidential medical information is illegal without the ex-employee's consent.

7. *Utilize your state's "service letter" statutes if applicable.* At least twelve states have enacted some form of service-letter statute. These states, which include Indiana, Kansas, Maine, Minnesota, Missouri, Montana, Nebraska, Nevada, Ohio, Oklahoma, Texas, and Washington, give workers additional legal protection. In some of these states, employers are required to give a terminated worker a written statement regarding the true cause of his or her dismissal. Once such an explanation has been received by the worker, the employer cannot furnish

prospective employers with any reason that deviates from those given in the service letter. In a few states, an employer can be sued for damages for refusing to tell you why you were fired, for providing you with false reasons, or for changing its story and offering additional reasons to outsiders during legal proceedings (i.e., at a trial or an arbitration).

In one case, after a sales manager was terminated, he sent a letter to his ex-employer requesting the true reason for his termination pursuant to the Missouri service-letter statute. He received a letter back that merely confirmed the date when he was fired. The sales manager filed a lawsuit and was awarded $1.00 in actual damages and $47,500 in punitive damages after a lengthy jury trial. The Missouri Court of Appeals ruled that the failure to provide a reason for the discharge was tantamount to the nonissuance of a letter, for which the statute allows punitive damages. The sales manager contended that the employer wanted to avoid admitting its bad-faith reason for discharging him, ostensibly to avoid paying substantial commissions he expected to earn.

Tip: In order to receive the benefit of a service-letter statute that may be available in your state, it is necessary to send a *written* request. Oral requests are generally not sufficient. The sample letter on page 226 is a good illustration of the kind of letter to send.

If you do not receive an answer to the letter within a reasonable period of time (e.g., thirty days), or if the employer furnishes you with reasons that are untrue, your state's service-letter statute may have been violated. You should then send a second, final demand letter stating that you intend to file a lawsuit under your state's law if no response (or an inaccurate response) is forthcoming, or that you will consult an experienced employment lawyer immediately to explore your options.

8. *Research your state's law.* Despite the many states that have recently enacted laws favoring employers by allowing them to assert special defenses or offering them immunity when they provide false post-employment references in good faith, some states still treat untruthful job references as crimes and/or permit civil actions against employers. As previously mentioned, a few states allow people harmed by false references to recover compensatory damages, punitive damages, and other legal remedies.

LETTER DEMANDING TRUE REASON FOR DISCHARGE

Date

Name of Officer or Employee
Title
Name of Employer
Address

Re: My Termination

Dear (Name of Officer):

On (date) I was fired suddenly by your company without notice, warning, or cause. All that I was told by (Name of Person) was that my services were no longer required and that my termination was effective immediately.

To date, I have not received any written explanation documenting the reason(s) for my discharge. In accordance with the laws of this state, I hereby demand such information immediately.

Thank you for your prompt cooperation in this matter.

Very truly yours,
Your Name

In a few states, such as Connecticut, any dissemination of private employment data (e.g., confidential medical information or comments on your personal life or habits) to prospective employers is illegal. For example, it may be illegal for an ex-employer to disclose that you previously filed a discrimination lawsuit or a workers' compensation claim. Pursuant to the federal Americans with Disabilities Act (ADA), the results of any medical examination or information concerning your current medical condition or history must be kept confidential on separate forms and in a file apart from your personnel records. It may also be illegal to disclose to others information concerning your credit history that may have been acquired pursuant to the federal Fair Credit Reporting Act.

Since the laws in each state vary, it is best to do your research and take prompt legal action where appropriate.

9. *Contact an employment attorney if the ex-employer failed to keep its promises.* Some employers have stated policies concerning job references that are contained in company manuals, handbooks, and other written documents. When an employer fails to honor such promises, it may be liable for breach of contract or breach of an implied contract under the laws of your state. Explore this option with your lawyer where applicable.

10. *Recognize that you have rights while working.* It is not necessary to be fired to receive protection in this area. For example, you have a valid claim for defamation when harmful records such as memos in personnel files, poor performance evaluations, false offhand remarks, improper theft investigations, or false accusations in front of workers are made and/or distributed to third parties. Many states, including Connecticut, Illinois, and Michigan, have passed strict laws prohibiting employers from divulging disciplinary information unless the individual in question receives a copy of such a statement.

Counsel Comments: There has been a recent trend allowing current and terminated workers access to and inspection of their personnel files. In some states, including California, Connecticut, Delaware, Illinois, Maine, Michigan, Nevada, New Hampshire, Ohio, Oregon, Pennsylvania, Washington, and Wisconsin, people may have the right to inspect their files on demand. Some states even allow people to demand that false negative information be deleted or that written rebuttals be placed in their files. Such rebuttals can refute, explain, or clarify incorrect or misleading information, company action, or comments, and may be read by prospective employers. And in some states, people are allowed to bring private lawsuits to expunge false information contained in such files.

Tip: If you work in a state that permits you to review and/or copy the contents of your personnel file, it is a good idea to request this from time to time. Usually, the inspections have to be done on your own time (e.g., at lunchtime) and in the presence of a manager or company officer. (Some states permit companies to screen and remove certain information before you view it. This includes information being gathered as part of a criminal investigation and personal facts about other employees.)

If possible, make copies of all relevant documents because they can be of help later on. For example, if you have received numerous favorable performance reviews, but are fired for "unsatisfactory performance," your lawyer could find the documents you have copied useful in negotiating a better severance package or fighting the firing in court. This is because an employer who fires you for poor performance but has a history of giving you raises, merit awards, extra bonuses, and excellent reviews is susceptible to a wrongful-discharge and/or a discrimination lawsuit (unless it can be proved that your work substantially deteriorated or suddenly suffered markedly after receiving raves and good reviews). A competent employment lawyer will surely raise the issue that if you were such a good employee (as your file supports), what was the true reason behind your discharge? This position can be used effectively to get you a better severance package and other benefits in the negotiating process.

In conclusion, all the strategies discussed in this chapter should be carefully considered whenever you believe false information or poor references have been given to prospective employers after a discharge. Be aware that employers frequently face greater exposure and potential damages in lawsuits from leaking harmful or confidential information after a firing than from the firing itself. Thus, always know your rights and enforce them as quickly as possible.

CHAPTER 12

Dealing with Restrictive Covenants, Trade Secrets, Gag Orders, and Other Post-Termination Restrictions

Many former employees of a major company filed sexual harassment lawsuits against the employer and several senior officers with the Equal Employment Opportunity Commission. They alleged constant intimidation and a pattern of harassment throughout the company.

Other current employees who wanted to leave the company negotiated large severance packages in return for their agreement not to file charges with the EEOC. After accepting the money, however, they claimed they had been fraudulently induced and coerced into signing releases with gag orders that prohibited them from talking about the company to outsiders.

After *BusinessWeek* magazine began investigating the company, the EEOC attempted to talk to many current and former employees to gain facts. Many former employees refused to cooperate, stating they were prohibited from doing so by contract. Stymied by their refusal to cooperate, the EEOC requested a federal court judge to rule that the gag orders violated public policy and should be declared unenforceable.

The judge partially ruled in the EEOC's favor. He decided that the interests of the EEOC to protect the general population from

sexual harassment in the workplace overruled the company's attempts to resolve its disputes by private settlement. However, the
judge said that a portion of the gag clause prohibiting an employee from discussing the employment situation or the terms of
the settlement with persons other than the EEOC (such as the
press) was valid.

Ever since corporate downsizing became commonplace, businesses
have been pushing the envelope in drafting separation agreements that
protect them from a variety of legal claims, including discrimination
and other lawsuits, and prohibit terminated employees from competing against them or using trade secrets and other confidential information that they learned on the job.

This chapter discusses a variety of topics that relate to the ability of
employers to restrict your ability to work or discuss important information after being fired as well as the obligations imposed on workers who make preparations to leave (such as interviewing or taking
steps to establish a competing business) while on company time.

RESTRICTIVE COVENANTS

Restrictive covenants, also referred to as covenants not to compete, are
clauses in written employment contracts, confidentiality agreements,
or termination agreements that are used for many purposes. Depending on the facts, when properly drafted and when state law allows,
such clauses may:

- Restrict an employee from working for a competitor of the former employer
- Restrict an employee from starting a business or forming a ven-
ture with others that directly competes against the former employer
- Restrict an employee from contacting or soliciting former or current customers or employees of the employer
- Restrict an employee from using confidential knowledge, trade
secrets, customer lists, and other privileged information learned
while working for the former employer

- Restrict an employee from any of the above in geographic or time limitations

The above points are illustrated by the following actual clauses often used in agreements:

For a period of one (1) year following the termination of your employment for any reason, it is agreed that you will not contact, solicit, or be employed by any person, firm, association, or corporation to which you sold products of the Employer during the year preceding the termination of your employment.

During the period of this Agreement and for a period of one (1) year thereafter, the Employee agrees that he or any company he is affiliated with, either directly or indirectly, shall not induce, hire, solicit, or otherwise utilize the services of any employee or sales rep currently employed by the Company.

Without a written contract containing a restrictive covenant, employees generally *cannot* be stopped from working for a competitor or starting a competing business after they resign or are fired from a job. This is especially true if they resigned for a good reason (e.g., were not being paid in a timely fashion) and have not stolen trade secrets or confidential information.

In situations where employees signed an agreement with a covenant-not-to-compete clause either before or after commencing work, the general trend is that such covenants may not be enforceable because they unfairly inhibit a person's ability to earn a living at his or her chosen profession.

The enforcement of any written covenant varies on a state-by-state basis and usually depends on a number of factors unique to each particular case. Many states, such as New York, have left the issue to the courts to decide. Other states, including Oregon, Louisiana, and Texas, have responded legislatively by enacting statutes regulating the enforceability of such clauses. In those states where restrictive covenants are not automatically illegal (as they are generally when they restrict independent contractors, sales reps and agents, brokers, and professionals such as doctors), the primary focus of a judge is usually the reasonableness of the covenant in terms of geographic scope, time restraints, and purpose.

An employer may increase the chances of having such a clause enforced when the covenant is short in terms of geographic location (i.e., the ex-employee is prohibited from calling on only a few large customers located within the county where the employer's main office is located, instead of the entire United States); when such customers were procured by the employer's efforts and not the employee's; and when the prohibition does not exceed six months to a year.

Thus, a restrictive covenant prohibiting a lighting-services employee from competing in the lighting retrofitting business within a hundred-mile radius of his former employer for five years after termination was found to be unreasonable and unenforceable by the Nevada Supreme Court.

Tip: A nonsolicitation provision may bar you from calling on specific customers but does not generally prohibit you from taking orders if customers independently call you. Remember this and act accordingly.

Counsel Comments: Courts sometimes respond more favorably to situations where companies have paid the employee *extra* consideration, such as $2,500 or an extra week's vacation before signing a contract containing such a provision, or negotiating a greater severance package in consideration for signing a contract with such a clause. And in some states, if the agreement provides that the ex-employee will receive his or her regular salary while the covenant is being enforced so that no loss of salary takes place during the restricted period, some judges may enforce the clause depending on other factors.

These factors often include an examination into whether the ex-employee's services are special, unique, or extraordinary; whether the restriction is necessary for the company to protect its business; and whether the person is in possession of trade secrets and other confidential information that, if disclosed or used in competition, would severely damage the company. (When the employer prepares a restrictive covenant that is signed by the employee and is found to be enforceable, the restrictions may also apply to competing businesses conducted by the employee's family members with background help from the employee even though they did not sign any agreements.)

Counsel Comments: In order to establish that an employee is "unique," the employer must generally show more than that the employee excels at his work or that his performance is of great value. The employer generally has the difficult burden of proving that the employee's services are of such character as to make his replacement impossible or that the loss of such services would cause the employer irreparable injury. This is often very difficult to prove.

Thus, for example, in a New York case where an employee who was fired took many of her former customers with her to a rival insurance business, the court held that there was nothing unique or extraordinary about the function of an insurance agent, even one who was highly talented and successful.

In some states, if you are required to sign an agreement containing a restrictive covenant after you begin working, the court may find such an agreement to be unenforceable because no additional consideration was conveyed. In Oregon, for example, a judge will not enforce it unless the company gives a corresponding benefit (e.g., an increase in salary, a bona fide promotion, or a beneficial change in job status). Other states may rule in the company's favor on this point, however, finding that the additional consideration was the ability to keep the job (which would be lost if someone refused to sign the document). Since state laws vary substantially as to what constitutes sufficient consideration to enforce covenants in these cases, speak with a knowledgeable employment attorney to explore your options.

Be aware that some kinds of noncompete pacts stand a better chance of being upheld than others. These include a situation where a business is sold and the seller (who was also an employee) agrees not to compete with the buyer for a specified period of time after the sale.

The following strategies can help protect you in this area.

1. *Avoid signing any agreement containing a restrictive covenant.* Even if you work and/or live in a state that generally does not recognize such clauses, it is still not a good idea to sign any agreement containing such a clause. The reason is that a restrictive covenant provision may have a chilling effect and impair your ability to get or keep another job.

Restrictive covenants carry the implied threat that the company may institute legal action after your resignation or termination. This may effectively discourage you from contacting prospective employers or customers in your industry, establishing a competing business, or finding a job. On numerous occasions, clients of mine were asked by prospective employers if they were legally bound by any future working restrictions. Many times they were forced to provide copies of existing contracts and as a result were unable to secure employment.

If you are sued and the company seeks a temporary injunction to immediately stop you from working, your legal fees and costs to successfully defend yourself in court could be prohibitive. The problem is that many employers think they are protected when they have employees sign noncompetition clauses. Although such protection may be illusory, companies often take great pains to go to court to find out if these clauses are enforceable and to demonstrate to current employees their resolve in not allowing others to do the same thing. Thus, even if you win, you will probably get stuck with a hefty legal bill. (Losing parties in this country typically are *not* required to pay for the prevailing party's attorney fees.)

The point to remember is that even if you think a prospective employer will foot the bill for your court fight, don't expose yourself to the risk of finding out.

Avoid signing any covenant that contains a liquidated damages provision. Such a clause may say, for example, that if you violate the agreement, you must return that portion of your compensation (e.g., extra salary or other money) you have received in consideration for signing an agreement not to compete, or you must forfeit benefits (e.g., valuable stock options) due to vest in the future. While perhaps not affecting the enforceability of the covenant itself, a forfeiture provision may represent a threat of substantial economic harm.

2. *Consult an employment attorney immediately if an ex-employer threatens to sue to enforce a restrictive covenant.* You may be surprised to learn that the employer will be unsuccessful in the event of a lawsuit. Courts in many states are now ruling that noncompete agreements are not enforceable (a) when they restrict a person's right to work (particularly if your trade is your only means of support), (b) when they are being used merely to guard the employer's turf, (c) when trade secrets (defined in the next section) are not involved, or (d) when you must work to support a family member with special needs (e.g., a spouse who is ill).

Do not take any action detrimental to your interest, such as signing a document admitting wrongdoing, until you have spoken with counsel. Many people are pressured by ex-employers to do things they later regret. Avoid being intimidated whenever possible.

3. *Determine if the employer has breached any obligations or duties owed to you.* When companies are in breach of important contract terms, the law generally presumes they have "unclean hands." Sometimes in such situations restrictive covenants will not be applied against you. In one case, for example, I defended several sales employees who had gone into business in competition with their ex-employer. Earlier, these individuals had contacted me to review an employment agreement that they had signed with the ex-employer. The agreement did contain a restrictive covenant, but during the consultation I learned that the employer, to save the company money, had reduced their salaries despite their written protests. I advised my clients that since the employer was obligated to pay a predetermined salary specified by contract, the failure to do so might release them from the covenant in the agreement.

The employees were sued after commencing business operations. At the trial, the judge heard testimony regarding this unilateral unjustified cut of pay. The judge agreed that the employer had unfairly reduced their compensation without consent and ruled that the restrictive covenant could not be enforced against them.

Tips: An employment lawyer may try to get some leverage by asserting legitimate counterclaims, such as that you were victimized by sexual harassment or age or race discrimination while working. Your defense can become stronger when you present evidence demonstrating you were treated wrongfully.

You can also gain leverage by stating that your customers do not want to get involved in litigation and that you will drag them in if the case proceeds. The company may be reluctant to harm its customers in this manner and may decide that the ill will created by a lawsuit is not worth it.

Always avoid bad-mouthing the ex-employer during litigation proceedings. It is important for a judge to view your case in a sympathetic way; the more you are viewed as the innocent party just trying to earn a living, the more likely the judge may rule that enforcing the covenant isn't fair.

Finally, the odds of winning your case can get better the longer the company delays in commencing action. If the employer waits several months after learning of your alleged misconduct, a judge may feel that it wasn't so important to the employer after all and deny the employer's request for injunctive relief.

4. *Retrieve a copy of any pertinent agreement you may have signed.* When people resign or are discharged and receive a formal demand that they refrain from certain acts (usually in the form of a cease-and-desist letter), often they cannot locate the agreement containing the restrictive covenant. This places them at a disadvantage. For example, they may be unable to obtain an accurate opinion from a lawyer if he or she cannot review the contract and may be forced to spend unnecessary legal fees trying to obtain a copy from the ex-employer. Thus, request copies of all documents that you sign and store them in a safe place for later review by you and your lawyer. Plan ahead and try to obtain copies from the company before you depart because it is much easier to do this while you are still there than after you are out the door.

5. *Research the law in your state.* Restrictive covenants that are unreasonable (e.g., are in force for five years) will not be upheld. But in some states, if the court finds the covenant to be overbroad in terms of geographic scope or time limitation, it has the ability to enforce the clause by merely reducing the time frame or territory (e.g., reducing it from two years to three months), and unless the employer acted in bad faith, courts in these jurisdictions may modify covenants to the extent necessary to protect the employer's interest without imposing undue hardship on the employee.

In other, "all or nothing at all" states, the covenant will be stricken in its entirety without any modification.

Each state has its own procedure and unique requirements for accepting a company's application to grant injunctive relief rather than award damages. This means that the court may issue an order (i.e., an injunction) prohibiting the individual from working for the company's competitor. If the employee fails to comply with the court's order, he or she may be held in contempt. However, in some states, during the pendency of the action, if the employee believes he is right, his attorney may request court permission to post a bond for the damages the employer might be awarded so that the employee can continue to work for the competitor.

Thus, research the unique law in your state to understand your rights.

TRADE SECRETS AND CONFIDENTIAL INFORMATION

Recently, it was reported that Dow Chemical and General Electric reached an out-of-court settlement over employee poaching. Dow had accused GE of systematically recruiting an engineer with no supervisory responsibility who worked with automakers in projects involving high-tech plastics.

In another case, after General Motors accused Volkswagen of stealing secrets when it recruited Jose Ignacio Lopez and seven of his GM associates, it was reported that GM received $1.1 billion to settle the matter.

Experts suggest that more companies and employees are willing to steal trade secrets, especially in high-tech industries, because many workers do not feel much loyalty in this era of corporate downsizing. Unfortunately, most employees do not understand that such conduct can lead to criminal liability in light of the passage of the federal Economic Espionage Act signed into law in 1996. Pursuant to this statute (discussed in detail later in this section), the U.S. Attorney General can authorize the FBI to pursue indictments when corporations allege that trade secrets have been misappropriated.

Sometimes ex-employees take valuable customer lists, trade secrets, and confidential information (such as prices and requirements of key customers) with them. When the company discovers this, a lawsuit may be filed to stop the ex-employee from using the information. In other instances, a former employer may attempt to stop an individual from using information that he acquired while working. Can this be done? The following information will give you a better understanding of the legalities in this area.

A trade secret may consist of any formula, pattern, device, or compilation of information used in business that gives a company an opportunity to obtain an advantage over competitors that do not know or use it. Although an exact definition is impossible, trade secrets are usually involved when:

- An employer takes precautions to guard the secrecy of the information
- An employer has expended significant money and effort in developing the information

- It is difficult to acquire the information outside the company (i.e., it isn't generally known to outsiders)
- Employees are warned that trade secrets are involved and that they are obligated to act in a confidential manner
- Employees are tied to restrictive covenants in written agreements that bar or limit them from revealing to others such information, especially to new or potential employers competing with the company

Employees and company executives consult me to determine whether a particular procedure or operating process constitutes a trade secret. Unfortunately, the answer is not always clear-cut. Generally, all or most of the preceding elements have to be present to establish that a given process or procedure is a trade secret and to determine whether it has been illegally conveyed when an employee is discharged or departs.

Lawsuits and injunctions brought by companies in this area are often quite complicated and costly to defend, even for victorious ex-employees, because each case must be analyzed and decided on its own particular facts and circumstances. Additionally, courts generally do not like to punish smart workers who learn on the job and try to better themselves thereafter by using their acquired knowledge on a new job. Only when an employer will be clearly damaged and lose its competitive advantage is it likely to be victorious in a lawsuit. And this is only after it demonstrates that a trade secret or confidential information has been or will be conveyed.

In one case, an employer lost an injunction action brought in an attempt to stop a competitor from using its customer lists. The situation arose when a former employee who had worked as a truck driver and occasional mechanic began working for a major competitor to the company's detriment. However, the court noted that at least three copies of its customer list were on open display at different locations of the company's premises, and it was obvious that anyone could see the list.

The Illinois Appellate Court stated that "there was no evidence of any effort on the part of the company to insure that its customer lists should be considered secret or confidential. When one adds that a significant number of the names were publicly known the company forfeited any right to bar competitors from using the names . . . even though those lists were the product of years of hard work."

However, another injunction lawsuit brought by an Illinois company was granted in the company's favor. In this case, the company filed the lawsuit after one of its key employees formed a competing business. Here the Illinois Appellate Court conceded that the company's processes were available to the public but were acquired by the competing business when the ex-employee copied, rather than developed, valuable formulas. This amounted to a breach of trust and pilfering of trade secrets by a former employee under circumstances entitling the employer to protection.

Counsel Comments: Even though a trade secret can be learned by outsiders through legitimate channels such as trade publications and scientific reports, this does not mean it loses its character as a secret. If the idea is taken by an outsider or appropriated by an ex-employee, a company may be able to bar its use. The defense that the secret could have been obtained legitimately may not matter; if the employee got it improperly, he or she may not be able to use it. For example, an ex-employee's failure to show any independent research or experimentation may make it difficult to prove he or she did not resort to stealing the secrets learned on the job.

An employee who leaves one job for another generally has the right to take with him all the skill and knowledge he has acquired as long as nothing he takes is the property of the employer. Courts distinguish between the skills acquired by an employee in his or her work and the trade secrets, if any, of the employer. The former may be used by the employee in subsequent jobs, the latter may not.

An employee's experience in executing a number of steps to produce a desired end is often not a trade secret. When sales employees become friendly with customers in the course of their employment, they are allowed to call on these customers for new employers. But in some instances, they may be prohibited from using their knowledge of unique customer buying habits, requirements, or other special information when soliciting their former employer's accounts. For example, if a salesperson knows that a particular customer will be in short supply of a specific product at a certain time, he may not be able to use that confidential information acquired while working for the former employer.

Perhaps the most frequently disputed issue concerning trade secrets involves customer lists. A "secret" list is not a list of companies or individuals that can be compiled from a telephone directory or other readily available source. A list becomes confidential when the names of customers can be learned by someone only through his or her employment—for example, when the salesperson secretly copies a list of customers that the company spent considerable time, effort, and money compiling and kept under lock and key.

Counsel Comments: Employers typically must consider all the aspects of a potential case before bringing suit, and they have the burden of proving that trade secrets are involved. The next hurdle in any lawsuit often is proving that such trade secrets were stolen or misappropriated. When bringing a lawsuit based on misappropriation of trade secrets, typically an employee will argue that the information acquired was common public knowledge obtained by going through directories, trade journals, books, and catalogs. Many times, the question before a court is not how the ex-employees *could* have obtained the knowledge, but how they did.

Tip: When an employer has made a special effort to remind employees of their obligation to protect the company's trade secrets, they may be held to a higher standard. For example, if posters are displayed in prominent areas reminding workers of their obligation to protect company secrets and this is published on a continuing basis in company journals, work rules, policy manuals, and memos, and if you are requested to sign periodic or yearly trade secret and confidentiality agreements similar to the one beginning on page 241, this may reduce the argument that you didn't know it was wrong to convey confidential information to a competitor.

The following suggestions may be helpful in this area.

1. *Avoid signing contracts containing trade secret prohibitions.* Any contract you sign that contains a trade secret policy will be slanted against you and increase the company's rights in this area. Employers commonly require employees to sign confidentiality agreements. Although the permissible scope of these agreements varies from state to state, they may be valid and can be used to convince a court that certain information is confidential and should be protected.

If you are asked to sign such an agreement before being hired, you

TRADE SECRETS AND CONFIDENTIAL INFORMATION
POLICY STATEMENT

The business of our Company involves valuable, confidential, and proprietary data and information of various kinds. Such data and information, called "Trade Secrets," concern:

• The names of Company customers and the nature of the Company's relationships (e.g., types and amounts of products acquired from the Company) with such customers;

• The Company's various computer systems and programs;

• Techniques, developments, improvements, inventions, and processes that are, or may be, produced in the course of the Company's operations; and

• Any other information not generally known concerning the company or its operations, products, suppliers, markets, sales, costs, profits, customer needs and lists, or other information acquired, disclosed, or made known to Employees or agents while in the employ of the Company, which, if used or disclosed, could adversely affect the Company's business or give competitors an advantage.

Since it would harm our Company if any of our Trade Secrets were known to our competitors, it is the company's policy that:

1. No Employee should, during or after his/her employment with the Company, use any Trade Secrets for his/her benefit, or disclose to any person, business, or corporation any Trade Secrets without the prior written consent of the Company.

2. Every Employee shall render exclusive and full-time services and devote his/her best efforts toward the performance of assigned duties and responsibilities (which may be changed at any time).

3. Every Employee should refrain from engaging directly or indirectly in any activity that may compete with, or result in a conflict of interest with, the Company, or that is not likely to be in the Company's best interests.

4. Every Employee should fully and completely disclose to the Company any inventions, ideas, works of authorship, and other Trade Secrets made, developed, and/or conceived by him/her alone or jointly with others, arising out of, or relating to, employment at the Company. All such inventions, ideas, works of authorship, copyrights, and other Trade Secrets shall be the sole property of the Company. The Employee agrees to execute and deliver to the Company such assignments, documents,

agreements, or instruments which the Company may require from time to time to evidence its ownership of the results and proceeds of the Employee's services and creations.

5. The Employee understands that he/she owes the highest duty of loyalty with respect to his/her duties. This means that he/she will, among other things, maintain a constant vigil over Company property, never make secret profits at the Company's expense (e.g., service customers of the Company but bill them for personal benefit, or receive kickbacks or special favors from customers, etc.), dress in a proper fashion, not use drugs or alcohol while on the job, and maintain a personal or Company automobile in good condition, together with a valid driver's license.

6. Every Employee shall avoid discussing any matter of a confidential nature, or which constitutes a Trade Secret, with any competitor or its employees. This includes discussions regarding customers, pricing, and policies. The Employee is reminded that any such discussions may cause the Company and the Employee personally, to have violated antitrust laws, including the Sherman and Clayton Acts. Sanctions of up to three (3) years imprisonment and fines up to $100,000 have been imposed on those who violate such laws.

7. Upon termination of employment, or at any time the Company may request, every Employee shall promptly return to the Company all memoranda, notes, records, reports, technical manuals, and other documents (and all copies thereof) in his/her possession, custody, or control relating to Trade Secrets, all of which written materials and other things shall be and remain the sole property of the Company. The failure to comply with this request shall be grounds for immediate dismissal. In addition, the Company shall not be obligated in any way to pay any severance upon termination to any Employee who fails to comply with the provisions of this paragraph specifically, and this memo generally.

8. Every Employee agrees to comply with the rules, regulations, policies, and procedures of the Company faithfully and to the best of his/her abilities. The Employee understands that the breach of any covenant contained herein may constitute substantial and irreparable harm to the Company, and the Company may seek injunctive relief and other relief which it deems necessary and appropriate under the circumstances to protect its rights and the Employee shall pay all reasonable attorney fees, costs,

and expenses incurred by the Company in the enforcement of any such action.

I (name of Employee) have received and read a copy of this Trade Secrets and Confidential Information Policy statement, understand all of its terms and agree to be bound by the provisions contained therein.

Printed Name: _____
Signature: _____
Date: _____

---

may have no choice if you want the job. The problem becomes more difficult after you have begun working. Many cases have been decided in favor of the company in this area. For example, five employees in Vermont who refused to sign a confidentiality, disclosure, and non-competition agreement that a new personnel policy imposed as a condition of continued employment had no claim against their employer after they were fired. The Vermont Supreme Court ruled that a handbook statement that dismissal would be considered after two unsatisfactory reviews did not preclude the employer from firing the workers for other reasons, including their refusal to sign the new confidentiality agreement.

Counsel Comments: If you are asked to sign such a document while working and refuse, you can probably be fired legally for "insubordination." Always consult an experienced employment lawyer for advice or to review any proposed trade secret agreement before you sign it.

2. *Be aware that the transfer or receipt of confidential information may constitute a crime.* Some states have passed laws making theft of trade secrets a criminal offense. Legislation was enacted in New Jersey, for example, making it a high misdemeanor to steal company property, including written material. Other states, including Arkansas, California, Colorado, Maine, Michigan, Minnesota, Nebraska, New Hampshire, New Mexico, Ohio, Oklahoma, Pennsylvania, Tennessee, Texas, and Wisconsin, have similar laws. The state of New York has gone even further in addressing this problem by declaring it a felony for anyone to steal property consisting of scientific material.

In the federal system, crimes involving misappropriation of intellectual property have been prosecuted under the National Stolen Property Act and mail and wire fraud statutes. A criminal RICO action may also be asserted. Pursuant to the National Stolen Property Act, if valuable written material is stolen and transported to another state, the Federal Bureau of Investigation and the Justice Department can assist employers in apprehending workers because it is a federal crime to sell or receive stolen property worth more than $5,000 that has been transported across state lines.

The Economic Espionage Act, which makes trade secret theft a federal crime, specifically addresses theft perpetrated via the Internet. Under Section 1832 of the act, it is a federal criminal act for any person to convert a trade secret to his or her own benefit or the benefit of others intending or knowing that the offense will injure any owner of the trade secret. The conversion of a trade secret is defined broadly to cover every conceivable act of misappropriation, and you can also be prosecuted for receiving or possessing trade secret information when you know it was given to you without the owner's authorization.

Penalties for violating this statute are steep. A person who commits an offense can be imprisoned up to ten years and fined up to $500,000. A corporation can be fined up to $5 million. The significance of this law is that those engaged in trade secret misappropriation can no longer be assured that liability will be limited to civil remedies and damages.

Since computers, E-mail, and other new technologies make it easier for employees at all levels to misappropriate valuable information and transfer it to others without removing bulky boxes, avoid the temptation to do so in light of this new serious federal law.

3. *Take your files home before being fired if you can do so.* What files may employees take with them when leaving a company? Generally, nothing that was developed while working for the company, including Rolodexes and business-generated reports, letters, diagrams, photographs, and all copies of such valuable materials that are necessary for the company's continued operations. You may retrieve personal information, but it may be scrutinized by a company official before you depart from the premises. To minimize problems, it is better to anticipate a firing and take nonconfidential materials away from the office before your official departure. You may thus avoid the possibility of

being searched and of not being able to remove such items at the time of your discharge.

4. *Limit what you say at the exit interview.* Many companies attempt to elicit information about what knowledge you've gained while working and how you intend to use it, especially when you are resigning from a job. At many companies, especially technology-intensive ones, there is a formal termination interview at which the question of confidentiality is mentioned. Avoid providing the employer with specifics at an exit interview because the less the employer knows of your plans, the better off you'll be. Be especially careful not to confirm that you possess trade secrets or that you have a continuing obligation to protect the company's secrets and agree not to disclose them to others.

If the employer identifies exactly what information it considers to be confidential and tells you that you are required not to use such information to its detriment, you may diplomatically object to such comments or state that you do not agree with the company's position. This may increase your rights by proving that you never agreed by your own conduct to be bound by the company's position.

5. *Never sign a letter or agreement at the exit interview stating that you have not taken confidential information.* However, if the employer offers you a significant increase in severance or other financial benefits, it may be worth signing such a document after you speak to counsel.

6. *Act properly.* If you are escorted to your office after being fired and told you can remove only clearly personal items, comply with this request. Do not scream or push anyone around. If you do, you will probably be escorted out of the building immediately and could face criminal charges for assault and battery. Stay calm and follow a supervisor's instructions. If you are not allowed to remove items that you believe belong to you, describe and identify those items in writing and have someone from the company agree that they will be stored safely until the issue can be resolved.

7. *Contact a lawyer immediately.* A competent lawyer can help you retrieve items that the employer does not want to release and aid you in many other important ways. You should always seek counsel immediately when you are accused of stealing or misappropriating confidential information or a company's trade secrets. Never admit fault without speaking to a lawyer, and you must defend such charges

promptly and aggressively. For example, your lawyer can immediately contact the company and state that the failure to resolve the issue amicably will give rise to a claim of defamation against the company because it is unfairly ruining your business reputation.

Since it is often unclear whether trade secrets are involved, and since the employer has the burden of proving that misappropriation occurred, do not agree to settle any matter without an employment lawyer's assistance. You may find, for example, that you *can* solicit your former employer's customers and use information in the customer lists and shipping histories if such information was easily obtainable by the general public. Although each case is decided on its unique factors and circumstances, many employers lose claims that they have a protectable interest sufficient to support enforcement of a contract's nonsolicitation and noncompetition provisions. In certain cases, the employer is unable to prove it suffered financial damage. Just proclaiming that it has lost a trade secret might get the court's attention but may not help the company prevail without more specific evidence.

Thus, know your rights and act accordingly in this area.

GAG ORDERS AND CONFIDENTIALITY AGREEMENTS

Confidentiality and nondisparagement clauses, commonly referred to as gag orders, are provisions in agreements or stand-alone agreements that prohibit departing employees from revealing the terms of a settlement or saying anything negative about the company to others who may also have been injured or to the press. Additionally, companies sometimes insert clauses into such agreements prohibiting ex-employees from seeking reemployment with the company, participating as a party or witness in any legal action or proceeding, or soliciting others to file suits against it. To ensure compliance, it is not uncommon for employers to insert penalties with such clauses, which state that if any material statement about the settlement is revealed to others, all monies previously given to the ex-employee must be returned and additional damages paid.

The following clauses were taken from actual agreements and illustrate these points:

Employee acknowledges and agrees to keep the terms of this Agreement strictly confidential. Employee will not disclose any term of this Agreement, including but not limited to the salary and severance pay provided to Employee by Employer, to any person or entity whatsoever with the exception of Employee's spouse, accountant, and attorney, unless ordered by a court of competent jurisdiction. Employee understands that this provision is of material importance to the Employer, and that damages for the breach hereof will be actual, but difficult to calculate. Accordingly, if Employee violates this provision in any manner, Employee will pay to Employer, as agreed-upon liquidated damages, the amount Employee has received or would receive from Employer as severance pay, and an additional amount equal to three (3) times the amount of severance pay. Employee acknowledges and agrees that the extra severance pay to be given is made in consideration for this promise and that this amount of liquidated damages is a fair estimate of the damages that the parties presently anticipate Employer will suffer in the event of a breach of this provision by Employee.

You agree that you will not participate, directly or indirectly, as a party, witness, or otherwise against the company unless compelled by a judicial subpoena.

You will not issue any communication, written or otherwise, that disparages, criticizes, or otherwise reflects adversely or encourages any adverse action against the company except if testifying truthfully under oath pursuant to subpoena or otherwise.

You agree never to apply for or otherwise seek reemployment with Employer at any time in the future.

Most employers prepare such clauses with the expectation they are enforceable due to the extra payments given to the ex-employee for settlement purposes. They do so to keep other employees from learning about the terms of a lucrative severance package and acting on this information. Believing that the terms of a settlement will remain confidential often encourages employers to settle formal charges of discrimination or other litigation that could affect hundreds of other unsuspecting employees.

When judges are asked to determine whether such clauses are valid, they typically weigh general policy which favors the private voluntary settlement of employment disputes versus the public's need to obtain valid information. While such provisions have generally been enforced in the past, the answer is not always clear-cut, depending on the unique facts of each case.

For example, in areas where public safety is involved, employers' claims that such confidentiality clauses are legal may not be upheld. In one recent case, a foreman who worked at a nuclear power plant was fired and then contacted the Nuclear Regulatory Commission to complain about numerous safety violations at the plant. He also filed a lawsuit against the company claiming that he was illegally terminated for whistle-blowing. The company proposed a settlement that contained numerous gag orders. These clauses would have restricted his ability to provide regulatory agencies with specific information and would not have allowed him to appear voluntarily as a witness in any judicial or administrative proceeding in which the company was a party. The proposed settlement also stated that if he was compelled to testify at any proceeding, he would use all reasonable steps to fight such a subpoena.

After the man's attorney rejected this proposal, his case continued. He then filed a lawsuit with the U.S. Department of Labor alleging that the proposed gag order violated his rights under the Energy Reorganization Act (ERA) by restricting free speech and his ability to testify about safety violations. He also claimed he was retaliated against after bringing this action.

The U.S. Department of Labor ruled in his favor. It found that the gag order proposal was an adverse employment action under the ERA and represented a serious threat to ensuring clear lines of communication between employees and regulatory agencies on matters of public health and safety.

Other rulings have allowed individuals to reveal discriminatory acts they observed or suffered to the EEOC even after signing separation agreements with gag orders, as the case mentioned at the beginning of this chapter reports.

Counsel Comments: In that case, however, the court did rule that a portion of the gag order prohibiting an employee from discussing her employment situation or the monetary terms of the settlement with the press or others was valid. Also upheld was a provision in which the departing employee agreed not to participate with the EEOC in a new suit or receive any further monetary damages that the EEOC might award in its own action.

To protect yourself in this area, remember the following.

1. *Know your rights.* There is a general presumption that gag orders and similar provisions will be valid, especially when you receive extra consideration (e.g., three more months' severance pay) as inducement to sign an agreement and the clause is clearly drafted. Thus, avoid signing any agreement if you do not want to be restrained from discussing the terms of the settlement with others or from suing the company at a later date (unless you are satisfied with the financial terms of the settlement).

2. *Consult an employment lawyer for advice.* Always seek counsel when presented with a comprehensive settlement agreement that requires you to waive rights of free speech and other protections. You may learn, for example, that it is illegal for a company to force you to sign such a document. If you previously signed an agreement with similar restrictions, you may learn from the lawyer that it is not valid when fraud, duress, or mistake was involved. For example, before signing any such agreement, you must be given ample time (generally at least twenty-one days) to review the document and consult an attorney of your choosing. Not being given this opportunity might vitiate the entire agreement.

Recently, an African-American woman was terminated for no apparent reason after working seven years for a real estate company. The woman was required to sign a simple general release in order to receive seven weeks' severance pay. The release did not contain language indicating that she had a period of time to consider the offer or consult with a lawyer.

After reluctantly signing the document and receiving the money, the woman learned that other white males at the company who were fired received, on the average, three weeks of severance for every year worked. Angered by such alleged disparate treatment, she retained me to protect her rights. As her lawyer I negotiated for the company to pay her an additional ten weeks' severance pay, despite the fact she had signed a waiver of all claims.

This case is instructive because it demonstrates that, under certain conditions, settlement agreements, waivers, and releases can be invalidated. In the case, I argued that my client had signed the waiver under duress (just so that she could collect the initial seven weeks of severance pay). Apparently, the company did not want to face the expense and consequences of a potential lawsuit based on gender and race discrimination as well as fraud, and decided to negotiate an amicable settlement.

3. *Be aware that not all liquidated damages clauses are enforceable.* Liquidated damages are an amount of money agreed on in advance by an employer and an employee in a written contract to be paid in the event of a breach or a dispute. If it is not possible to compute the amount of the loss, a judge may uphold the amount specified. However, in many circumstances, when the amount specified has no actual basis in fact (e.g., a clause states that in the event the employee reveals the terms of the settlement, he or she is liable to pay back the amount of severance previously received plus an additional amount equal to three times the amount), a judge may disregard it, viewing the amount merely as a penalty.

Sometimes, if an employee cannot discuss the terms of the settlement with anyone (including a spouse, attorney, and accountant), judges in some states may rule that the clause is unconscionable and therefore unenforceable.

4. *Keep your lips sealed.* By signing an agreement with a gag order, you are promising not to reveal the terms of the settlement to others. Thus, avoid the temptation of speaking about the settlement with anyone. That way, if you are sued for allegedly breaking your promise, you may eventually prevail in court (based on the facts).

Tip: If you previously told someone about the terms of a potential settlement, tell your lawyer about this. The lawyer may be able to modify language in the final draft of the settlement agreement that prohibits you from talking to others only *after* the document is signed. This can protect you if it is discovered that you discussed the pending settlement before you were aware that the company would insist on your continued obligation to secrecy (which was confirmed in the written agreement).

PREPARATIONS BEFORE LEAVING

Courts generally impose a duty of loyalty and good faith on employees in all industries. This duty exists throughout the worker's employment and is also present when the employee changes jobs and joins a new company.

The crackdown on so-called white-collar crimes has produced many mail fraud and related indictments against executives and employees who use their positions for personal gain at the expense of coworkers. An executive owes a duty of undivided loyalty to the company. Any activity that creates a possible conflict of interest must be brought to the attention of the company's president or board of directors for approval before the individual proceeds with a possibly conflicting or harmful action. This even includes situations where an executive secretly promotes a product his company previously rejected.

In one case, an executive had an undisclosed interest in a competing business while employed by another company. The court noted that he contributed substantial financial support to this business and aided in the development of the competing product.

Time and time again, courts have ruled against the self-serving employee who acts for private gain. Even though his employer decides not to use a particular product, an employee does not have the right to lend assistance of any kind to a potentially competing business.

A salesperson or employee can inform her customers that she intends to leave her job and work for a competitor. However, an employee cannot work for a competitor while still employed at her present company (especially if she is supposed to work full-time and is not an independent contractor).

In one case, a salesperson told customers that he intended to leave his company to work for a competitor. Although this was perfectly legal, he overstepped his authority by distributing the competitor's catalogs to these customers while still employed with the old firm. This, the court ruled, was improper; when he was terminated by his former company and sued, the individual was required to pay a considerable amount of money in damages for his disloyal actions, in-

cluding repayment of wages and commissions received during the period in question.

Employees are under no obligation other than their duty to give
loyal and conscientious service to an employer while in its employ.
Salespersons have the right to advise customers or clients that they are
going to quit and work for a competitor even while still working for
their present employer. In preparation for quitting a job, employees
can look for another job without advising their employers; advise customers, clients, and friends of the intention to leave and compete
(hopefully in the absence of a written restrictive covenant); and even
take minor steps to organize a new company while still working, such
as print stationery, set up telephones and faxes, and begin the process
of forming a corporation. What they cannot do is solicit business
while on the employer's payroll, talk against their present employer
and hurt its reputation, or lie down on the job by not taking orders
or working as diligently as before.

Generally, one company has the right to persuade another company's employees to join its ranks when the employees are not bound
by a contract or restrictive covenant. A defecting employee or executive can, however, be successfully sued for luring away key employees.

In one Massachusetts case, a manager was offered a lucrative post
with equity in a competing business. Before resigning his job, the
manager secretly solicited four key employees to join him in defecting.
After the four left, the company sued for damages caused by the
manger's disloyalty.

At the trial, the company stated that the defendant had been one of
its major officers, bearing the title of vice-president and general manager. While still performing these important functions, he enticed four
key employees to leave with him. Their departure had a devastating
impact on the company's productivity and sales. The manager responded that since he had never signed a covenant not to compete, he
was free to leave the company and go to work for whomever he
wished. Furthermore, since none of the other employees had signed
covenants, he should not be held responsible for their acts, since what
he did was not illegal.

The court concluded that the defendant had violated his duty of
loyalty and *he and the new employer* were required to pay damages. The
Massachusetts Judicial Supreme Court reacted strongly, saying, "The
defendants are liable for the breach of the manager's duty of loyalty by

not protecting the plaintiff against the loss of key employees. As Vice President and General Manager, defendant was responsible for staffing and hiring necessary replacements and his duty to maintain adequate managerial personnel forbade him from seeking to draw key managers away to a competitor."

Counsel Comments: Be aware that in most states you may not, before termination or resignation of employment, solicit employees to work with a competitor. This general rule is most clearly applicable if the supervisor-manager, as a corporate Pied Piper, leads his company's employees away, thus destroying the employer's business. In addition to suing an individual on the basis of breach of the fiduciary duty of loyalty and good faith, some lawyers commence lawsuits against the new employer based on a legal theory called tortious interference with contractual relations, when they induce a valued employee to break a contract and go to work for them.

Generally, if the key employee is under contract with a definite term (e.g., one year) and the employee breaks the contract before the expiration of the contract period, a lawsuit may be successful. However, when no formal contract exists, and the employee is merely hired at will (i.e., capable of being terminated or leaving at any time), such suits have less chance of success.

Tip: To avoid problems, avoid signing employment contracts with clauses that prohibit you from soliciting or utilizing the services of any other employee of the company after you depart. You may not be so constrained in the absence of such a contractual provision.

Be discreet about your future plans; do not reveal that you plan to work for a new employer while you are still on the payroll. Serving two masters or making significant preparations for the new employer while being paid by the current company can get you in trouble. In most states, you can be ordered to return all salary and other compensation you received during the disloyal period.

It is a good idea to confer with counsel before making preparations to leave an important job, especially if you are an executive, manager, or officer of the company. Ask a lawyer to tell you what you can and cannot do while working for the present company. For example, while it is probably permissible to merely begin the process of forming a separate corporation on your own, you cannot spend time negotiating a lease, hiring employees, and ordering supplies while on company time. Certainly, you should not take valuable company information and confidential materials with you. Your lawyer will be able to give you preventive advice in this area. As always, it is better to be safe than sorry.

CHAPTER 13

Employment Litigation and Alternatives

Tens of thousands of employment-related lawsuits are filed in state and federal courts annually. Common lawsuits are for discrimination complaints and breach of contract actions to collect wages, commissions, and benefits. Lawsuits are brought in either a state or a federal court, depending on the facts.

This chapter will provide you with an explanation of the various legal forums you may be exposed to when asserting your rights. Strategies will be provided to help win a case in court, after an appeal, through arbitration, and through small claims court, and how to settle a matter out of court through mediation. You will also learn how to deal effectively with the U.S. Department of Labor for wage and hour complaints and the EEOC or a state agency for discrimination violations, and how to assert a workers' compensation claim.

LITIGATION

The party commencing a lawsuit (called the plaintiff) must have proper subject matter and personal jurisdiction to avoid having the case initially dismissed. Having subject matter jurisdiction means filing the action in an appropriate court. For example, an ERISA benefits claim must be filed in a federal district court; a case involving significant wages cannot be filed in small claims court.

Tip: Speak to an employment lawyer to be sure you are filing your case in the proper court before starting a lawsuit.

It is also necessary to demonstrate personal (*in personam*) jurisdiction. Typically, if the person or business being sued (called the defendant) lives or works in the state where the action is filed, or has close ties with that state (e.g., ships goods into or travels to that state to conduct business), then personal jurisdiction may be determined to exist by a judge. It will also be necessary to select the correct venue (the proper county) where the lawsuit should be filed. For example, in a wrongful-discharge lawsuit, the proper venue is the county where the plaintiff or defendant resides. Since venue laws vary from state to state, ask your lawyer where the suit should be brought to avoid having the case dismissed.

Counsel Comments: Where applicable, ask your lawyer about the advantages and disadvantages of commencing the lawsuit in either state or federal court. Some experts believe that federal court judges are generally more highly regarded for their legal skills than state judges and that litigants are often able to obtain a trial quicker in federal court. However, if a dispute is with an employer located in your state, you may not be able to file a lawsuit in federal court unless you are asserting a discrimination charge or other matter dealing with federal laws (e.g., a wage and hour or overtime violation). Conversely, if you are being sued, it may be advantageous to keep the case in a state court to "slow down" its progress.

Before starting any action, it is important to analyze thoroughly whether your case has merit. For example, does the defendant have a strong defense? Will you be able to prove your case? Will the employer be interested in settling the matter before protracted and expensive litigation occurs? Carefully examine the strengths and weaknesses of any case before starting. Analyze whether the company has sufficient assets, such as money in the bank and property. After going through lengthy litigation and expense (if the matter is not settled out of court), you don't want to win the case but be unable to collect the award.

Tip: There are investigative companies that, for a fee, can advise you about the defendant's asset picture. Your lawyer can tell you where such companies are located. You may also find them listed in the yellow pages. Always discuss these concerns with your lawyer before you decide to litigate.

Courts

Depending upon one's choice and other factors, a trial may be conducted and decided by a judge only, or by a judge and jury. In some appellate courts and the United States Supreme Court, only judges are present to hear arguments and make decisions.

A court can preside only over matters to which it has jurisdiction. Courts of original jurisdiction are the first courts to preside over a matter. A court of appellate jurisdiction is a higher court that reviews cases removed by appeal from a lower court.

Each state has its own court system, which operates separately from the federal court system. There are basically two levels of state courts: trial courts and appellate courts. General trial courts are typically divided into two separate, distinct courts, one to hear criminal matters and one to adjudicate civil matters. Civil trial courts may be further divided depending on the amount of money or the subject matter at issue. In New York, for example, original jurisdiction small claims courts adjudicate civil matters up to $3,000; the civil court adjudicates matters up to $25,000, and the supreme court presides over civil matters involving more than $25,000.

The federal court system is divided into twelve districts or circuits and has jurisdiction when:

- A federal law, such as bankruptcy, copyright and patents, maritime, and postal matters, is at issue
- One state is suing another state
- A person or entity (i.e., a corporation) is suing a person or entity residing in another state and the amount in controversy exceeds $75,000

Within the federal system are separate limited jurisdiction courts that hear matters exclusively pertaining to bankruptcy (U.S. Bankruptcy Court), tax issues (U.S. Tax Court), suits against the federal government (U.S. Court of Claims), and disputes concerning tariffs and customs (U.S. Court of International Trade).

The United States Supreme Court is the country's highest court. It considers cases from the highest courts of each state, decisions of the U.S. Court of Appeals (the highest federal appeals court), and cases where the constitutionality of federal laws comes into play.

The vast majority of lawsuits, including unemployment and workers' compensation hearings, originate in state courts. If you are thinking of filing a lawsuit, speak to an employment lawyer or visit the clerk of any local court to determine where the correct place is to start. Each state has its own unique filing, procedural, and jurisdictional requirements, which must be correctly followed so that the case will not be dismissed. It is essential to get proper advice from a lawyer before starting any legal process.

Starting an Action

A civil lawsuit must be commenced (i.e., filed) within a certain period of time after the dispute arose to avoid dismissal on the basis of being untimely (called the statute of limitations). Each state and federal court has its own rules concerning the maximum amount of time you can wait before a lawsuit must be filed; it is crucial to know how much time you have before contemplating litigation. If you want to join with others in a suit (called a class action), it is necessary to contact the law firm representing the class within the required period of time to be able to join and be included in the lawsuit.

An employment lawsuit is started by preparing and filing a summons and complaint with the court. A summons is a single piece of paper typically accompanied by the complaint that, when served on the employer (i.e., the defendant), notifies it of a lawsuit. A complaint is a legal document that starts the lawsuit. It alleges pertinent facts and legal causes of action that the plaintiff will rely on in attempting to collect damages.

For a lawsuit to proceed, the summons and complaint must be served on the employer either in person (typically with the help of a process server or sheriff) or by certified mail, return receipt requested, in states that permit mail service. If the defendant is not notified of the existence of the lawsuit or if the complaint is not drafted accurately and fails to state a legally recognized cause of action, a judge may dismiss the case. If a lawsuit is dismissed without prejudice, it may be started over; lawsuits dismissed with prejudice may never be brought again.

Once the summons and complaint are served on the employer, they must be filed with the proper court together with the payment of the initial filing fee (which can be as much as $250 in some states). Filing these documents is rather easy. At the courthouse, a clerk accepts the fee and documents, stamps the papers to indicate the date and time received, and issues a receipt. The documents then become part of a file, which is stored at the court. The file is given to the presiding judge of the case when appropriate (such as during oral arguments before trial and at the trial). A judge, who is randomly assigned to preside over every filed case, will rule on various pretrial motions, move the case along to the trial, conduct the trial, and render a judgment based on the evidence when a jury is not involved.

After the complaint is served, the defendant has a period of time (usually no more than thirty days) to submit an answer. An answer is the defendant's reply to the plaintiff's charges in a civil lawsuit. Properly drafted answers typically deny most of the plaintiff's charges, list a number of legal reasons (called affirmative defenses) why the case should not proceed, and may or may not contain counterclaims. A counterclaim is a claim asserted by the defendant in a lawsuit. Sometimes the plaintiff loses the case and the defendant wins the case through its counterclaim.

Each case is decided by its unique facts. The fact that you are the plaintiff means only that you filed the lawsuit first; it does not guarantee success of the matter in any way. However, if the defendant fails to respond to the lawsuit by filing an answer, it may lose the case by default.

Tip: If you are sued, *always* consult an attorney after receiving a complaint to ensure that a timely answer will be filed.

Sometimes an employer is interested not only in obtaining damages but in seeking to stop an ex-employee from establishing a competing business or working for a competitor. An action called a preliminary injunction can be commenced. The employer as the moving party will request a hearing immediately after the lawsuit is filed. Such a request is called an order to show cause. If a judge rules in favor of the motion, the injunction will be granted. If a judge decides in favor of you (the defendant), the injunction will be denied, but, depending on the circumstances, the case may be allowed to proceed like any other lawsuit to ascertain damages.

Damages

Damages are compensation or relief awarded to the prevailing party in a lawsuit. Damages can be in the form of money or a directive by the court for the losing party to perform or refrain from performing a certain action. The following briefly describes various forms of damages.

Compensatory damages. This is a sum of money awarded to a party that represents the actual harm suffered or loss incurred. To collect compensatory damages, one must prove what the actual out-of-pocket losses are, since damages cannot be presumed. For example, projections of future lost profits will not be awarded unless they are definite and certain.

Incidental damages. Incidental damages are traditionally direct out-of-pocket expenses for filing a lawsuit and related court costs (e.g., process server fees). These direct costs of litigation are sometimes awarded to the prevailing party in a litigation as part of the party's loss.

Liquidated damages. This is an amount of money agreed on in advance by parties to a written contract to be paid in the event of a breach or dispute. If it is not possible to compute the amount of the loss, a judge may uphold the amount specified. However, in many circumstances, when the amount specified has no actual basis in fact, a judge may disregard it, viewing the amount merely as a penalty.

Nominal damages. This is a small amount of money (e.g., $1.00) awarded by the court. Sometimes a party may win the lawsuit but not have proved suffering or any actual damages.

Punitive damages. Also called exemplary damages, punitive damages represent money awarded as punishment for a party's wrongful acts beyond any actual losses. When punitive damages are awarded, a judge is often sending a signal to the community that similar outrageous, malicious, or oppressive conduct will not be tolerated. Under the laws of many states, punitive damages can be awarded only in certain types of lawsuits, such as personal injury and product liability actions, and not lawsuits to enforce employment contracts or business agreements.

Specific performance. This is a directive by the court for the party being sued (i.e., the defendant) to perform a certain action, such as sell a business or not work for a competitor pursuant to a clause in an employment contract. Specific performance is typically not awarded if monetary damages can make the party seeking the relief whole.

Injunction. This is a court order restraining one party from performing or refusing to perform an action or contract.

Mitigation of damages. This is a legal principle that requires a party seeking damages to make reasonable efforts to reduce damages as much as possible; for example, to secure comparable employment or file for unemployment benefits if a job cannot be obtained in the short term.

Pretrial Discovery

After the plaintiff or the plaintiff's lawyer receives the answer from the defendant, the discovery phase of the case begins. Lawyers use several pretrial devices, including interrogatories, depositions, and motions, to elicit information from the opposing side, gather evidence, and prepare for the trial. The discovery phase can last several years in a complicated breach of contract, defamation, wrongful-discharge, or discrimination case, and can be very expensive in terms of attorney fees and the costs of taking depositions, procuring documents, and paying for postage and related expenses.

Interrogatories are written questions sent to an opponent to be answered under oath. One problem with interrogatories is that the opposing party's attorney may draft the responses to prevent, insofar as possible, damaging statements from being conveyed.

Depositions often lasting several days are taken by both sides in complicated employment cases. A deposition is a pretrial proceeding in which one party is questioned under oath by the opposing party's lawyer. A stenographer is present to record all statements and preserve the testimony. Depositions are used to collect information and facts about the case, narrow the issues to be proved at trial, and discredit (impeach) the testimony of the witness.

Counsel Comments: It is essential that your lawyer properly prepare and advise you before your deposition is taken. Many cases have been lost due to unprepared responses elicited from a witness at a deposition. If your testimony is materially different (inconsistent) at the trial from statements you gave at the deposition, your credibility may be seriously undermined; giving a totally different statement about something at the trial could dramatically reduce the chances of success.

Incorrect answers at the deposition might also give the opposing attorney grounds to file a motion to dismiss the case in its entirety or throw out various causes of action. A motion to dismiss requests that even if the plaintiff's allegations are true and there is no genuine issue as to important facts, no legal basis exists for finding the defendant liable.

Sometimes attorneys file motions to get a ruling on admissibility of evidence or ask the court to assist in obtaining documents and records that have not been turned over by the other side (although promised).

Once the discovery phase of the case is completed, a judge will order a pretrial conference. Both attorneys are asked to appear to discuss the case and the possibility of settlement. Some judges make active attempts to settle cases at these conferences. If the conference is successful and the case is settled, the parties will prepare a written stipulation that describes the terms of the settlement. Typically, the judge will review and approve all settlements before they are implemented.

Tip: Think carefully before accepting any settlement. Most lawsuits take from two to five years to be tried. By accepting a fair settlement early on, you have use of the money, which can be invested to earn more money. You may eliminate large legal fees, court costs, and the possibility of eventually losing the case after a trial. However, if you have a good case, it may pay to wait before discussing and accepting a settlement. Most trial attorneys believe that large settlements are obtained for their clients by waiting until the case reaches the courthouse steps.

The decision on whether to accept a settlement should always be made jointly with your attorney, who knows the merits, pitfalls, and true value of the case better than you. However, do not allow a lawyer to pressure you into accepting a smaller settlement than you deserve. Some attorneys seek smaller immediate settlements out of laziness because the settlement represents money in the bank to them.

Instruct your attorney to provide you with a detailed explanation of the pros and cons of settling your case. Tell him that you prefer to control your affairs, including the decision of settling a claim. Do not let your attorney push you around. Your attorney cannot settle the case without your approval. If he does, he can be sued for malpractice. If you are not satisfied with your lawyer's advice or conduct, consult another attorney for a second opinion before settling the matter. Do this before taking action, because once you sign the settlement papers, you probably cannot change your mind and continue with the case, since release language contained in such documents generally prohibits you from doing so.

The General Release found in Chapter 2 (on page 32) is an example of the kind of document you might be asked to sign to settle an employment discrimination case.

If a matter cannot be settled, the judge will discuss with both attorneys how the case will proceed. The identity and order of witnesses and exhibits to be submitted at the trial will be agreed to before the trial begins. In many types of employment cases, either party can request that a jury decide the case rather than a judge. A jury trial usually involves twelve people, although some states allow as few as six. Some states permit a civil jury's decision to be less than unanimous.

The Trial

The first step of the trial begins with jury selection if a jury has been requested by either side. Prospective jurors are questioned (referred to as the *voir dire*) to see if they are qualified to sit on the panel. Lawyers seek answers to certain questions in the attempt to learn if a person has an open mind and is not biased. After attorneys for both sides dismiss certain people and retain others, the jury is picked and the trial begins. The plaintiff's lawyer will begin the trial with an opening statement. This is a speech designed to tell the judge or jury about the nature of the case, what the plaintiff intends to prove from the facts, and what kind of damages are sought.

After the defendant's attorney gives his opening statement, which essentially disagrees with the plaintiff's case, the trial begins. Witnesses are called by the plaintiff, and witnesses give their direct testimony under oath. The opposing attorney has the right to requestion (cross-examine) each witness in turn. All other evidence, such as documents and exhibits, is submitted, and other witnesses are questioned.

After the plaintiff's case is completed, the defendant presents its side of the case. When both sides are finished, each attorney gives a summation. This is a review of the facts, testimony, and other evidence. The following section briefly summarizes what you should know about evidence.

Evidence

Evidence is information in the form of oral testimony, exhibits, physical items, or affidavits used to prove a party's claim. Evidence can be presented in many forms. For example, exhibits are tangible evidence presented in a court proceeding for the purpose of supporting factual allegations or arguments. Testimony from expert witnesses may be introduced as evidence. In certain kinds of criminal cases, physical evidence such as fingerprints or hair samples can be helpful in proving who harmed a victim if no witnesses were present.

In a civil employment case, the plaintiff generally has the burden of proving its case by a legal standard called preponderance of the evidence ("more likely than not") through witnesses, charts, documents, photographs, and other forms of physical evidence. In a criminal case, the prosecution must prove a defendant's guilt beyond a reasonable doubt. This is a more difficult standard to achieve.

During the trial, one side will try to get evidence admitted into the court record for consideration by a judge or jury when deciding the case. The other party, through its lawyer, will seek to exclude such evidence through objections—for example, by stating that the evidence is irrelevant or inadmissible. A judge will either deny the objection and allow the evidence to be admitted or sustain the objection and exclude the evidence. The introduction of evidence in any case depends on a lawyer's arguments and the judge's interpretation of that state or federal court's rules. Certain types of evidence, such as hearsay evidence (a witness's testimony about what someone else said outside the courtroom), must be excluded (and may be excluded in advance of a trial).

Each party has the opportunity to discover what evidence the other intends to introduce at the trial to prove its version of the facts. This is done through depositions, where witnesses' testimony is taken under oath, and during discovery procedures, whereby records and other physical information is turned over to the other side for evaluation. In virtually all states, it is against the law to destroy evidence.

Tip: Because the success or failure of a case often depends on the type of evidence introduced and admitted (or excluded) from the record at a trial, it is important to hire an employment attorney who is very knowledgeable about the rules of evidence. For maximum success, always hire an employment lawyer who possesses competent trial skills.

The Judgment

If no jury is involved, the judge will render a decision. Typically, both parties have to wait a period of time (up to thirty days) before receiving the judge's written decision.

If a jury is involved, a judge will instruct its members as to what law is applicable to the facts and statements they have heard. The jury will then leave the courtroom and return with its determination. In rare cases, a judge may disregard the jury's findings and grant a motion for judgment notwithstanding the verdict (called a JNOV) when he or she believes there was insufficient evidence to support a jury's conclusion.

After the judgment is made, either party can appeal the decision by filing a written document called a brief. Information about appeals is discussed in the next section. It is also important to take proper steps to collect the judgment if the losing party doesn't pay. This may involve placing a lien on real estate property owned by the losing party or attaching such property to prevent the transfer, assignment, or sale without your consent. Speak to your lawyer for more information about how this can be accomplished.

Tip: Litigation is complicated, time-consuming, and subject to many hazards. Unless it is absolutely necessary, or your claim involves a small amount of money and you can handle it yourself using the small claims court, do not attempt to file papers and represent yourself (*pro se*) in a lawsuit without a lawyer.

Summary of Key Strategies to Follow in Any Lawsuit

1. Hire a lawyer skilled in conducting trials. Many attorneys do not litigate cases, which is a specialty.
2. Play an active role in all phases of the case. Request that your lawyer routinely send you copies of all incoming and outgoing correspondence on a regular basis. This will help you monitor and question the progress of your case.
3. Never ignore a summons and complaint if you are served. Ignoring a summons and complaint can result in the imposition of a default judgment with huge damages, penalties, and interest assessed against you without your filing a defense. Speak to a lawyer immediately to protect your rights.
4. Never ignore a subpoena if you are summoned to court to appear as a witness. A subpoena is an order requiring your presence to testify. If for some reason you cannot be present on the date specified, speak to the clerk of the court for advice and guidance. Ignoring a subpoena can result in a fine, imprisonment, or both.
5. Be prepared at all times. Competent lawyers work with their clients in anticipation of the upcoming deposition and trial. There should be no surprises in what you will testify to and what the opposing lawyer will ask you. Your lawyer should advise you how to react if you do not understand a question or do not wish to answer.
6. Consider alternative methods to settle your dispute. This includes arbitration and mediation (which are discussed in other sections of this chapter). Ask your lawyer to actively seek and encourage a settlement where warranted.
7. Determine if the opposing party has sufficient assets to pay a successful verdict before starting any action.
8. Assess the chances of winning or losing and how much a lawsuit will cost to commence or defend before getting in too deep.

Appeals

The vast majority of employment-related lawsuits never go to trial; they are either discontinued or settled. However, every case that is tried has a loser, and the losing party must decide whether or not to appeal the unfavorable decision.

An appeal is a request that a higher court review the decision of a lower court. In those states that have an intermediate appellate court, the losing party challenging a trial court decision first brings the appeal to the intermediate court. In the federal court system, the losing party brings the appeal to the court of appeals in the appropriate circuit. For serious criminal cases (i.e., felonies), the right to an appeal is mandatory. In civil employment cases, an appeals court may have the discretion not to consider the appeal in certain circumstances. After the appeal is decided by an intermediate appellate court, the case can be further reviewed by the highest state appeals court. In the federal system, after the appeal is decided by the United States Court of Appeals, the Supreme Court of the United States has the power and discretion to review and rule on the history of the case and the most recent appeal.

Appeals judges read the transcript of the trial together with legal documents called briefs to determine if the trial judge or jury erred in their decision. Typically, the intermediate appellate court will concern itself with issues of law as opposed to facts. It is rare that the appellate court will overturn a jury's factual decision. Rather, a verdict can be reversed if the wrong law was applied, incorrect jury instructions were given by the judge, or significant legal mistakes occurred, such as important evidence being mistakenly excluded by a judge from the trial.

The vast majority of employment-related civil cases are not reversed on appeal. Most decisions do not get reversed, but if a person or business has spent several years and thousands of dollars pursuing or defending a valid claim, the additional money spent on an appeal can be worth it, particularly if the delay caused by the appeals process works to a person's advantage.

Speak to a lawyer immediately if you receive an unfavorable trial verdict. There is a limited period of time (often thirty days) to file a notice that you intend to appeal. This must be done without delay to preserve your rights. To evaluate the chances of a successful appeal, it is necessary to carefully reconstruct (in an objective fashion) the reason the case was lost. Consider whether to hire the present attorney or retain a specialist in appeals matters. Although the current lawyer is familiar with the case, there are distinct advantages to hiring an attorney who makes a living writing briefs and arguing oral appeals (it is an art). Be certain you know how much the appeal will cost. Always sign a retainer agreement that clearly spells out attorney fees, costs, and disbursements.

The sample retainer agreement on page 268 illustrates the type of arrangement you may want to confirm in writing with your lawyer.

RETAINER AGREEMENT WITH ATTORNEY FOR APPEAL

Date

Name of Client
Address

Dear (Name of Client):

This letter confirms that you have retained me as your attorney to represent you to contest an appeal of a judgment granted in your favor by Justice (specify name) on (specify date) in the (specify trial court) and entered on (specify date) in the office of the Clerk. The appeal will be defended in (specify court).

You have agreed to pay to me promptly a retainer of (specify $) as a down payment for legal services to be rendered in this matter. This fee shall be applied against my standard hourly rate of (specify amount). If additional retainers are required, you agree to promptly pay same after receiving and reviewing accurate time sheets sent to you on a monthly basis. However, we have agreed that your final legal bill for all of my services will not exceed (specify $).

In addition to my fee, you also agree to pay for all incidental costs and disbursements incurred in connection with your appeal. Disbursements include, but are not limited to (specify, such as the cost of the trial transcript and the printing of briefs). All of these costs and disbursements are estimated to be (specify $) but the actual disbursements may vary from this estimate.

I promise to keep you informed of all developments as they occur and to send you copies of all incoming and outgoing correspondence immediately after it is generated/received. Additionally, I will supply you with drafts of the brief for your comments and approval before it is submitted.

I will personally handle the drafting of your brief and the arguing of any motions or the appeal in court if necessary.

I look forward to working with you on this matter. Kindly indicate your understanding and acceptance of the above terms by signing this letter below where indicated.

Very truly yours,
Name of Attorney

I, (Name of Client), have read and understand the above letter, have received a copy, and accept all of its terms:

_____
Name of Client

Counsel Comments: Remember that no matter which lawyer handles the appeal, appeals are generally costly, time-consuming, and sometimes do not produce anticipated results. Thus, evaluate the chances of success in an unbiased fashion and proceed cautiously.

ARBITRATION

Arbitration is a formal mechanism of resolving disputes that differs from litigation. Hearings are conducted by arbitrators rather than by judges and are not limited by strict rules of evidence. They can hear all relevant testimony when making an award, including some forms of evidence (e.g., hearsay, questionable copies of documents, etc.) that would be excluded in a regular court. Arbitrators have the authority to hear witnesses out of order. Their decision is usually final and unappealable. (Limited circumstances for appeals are mentioned later in this section.)

To obtain an arbitration, the law requires the employee and the employer to agree to the arbitration process beforehand in writing to prevent claims of unfairness by the losing side. Typically, in an employment contract, settlement agreement, or other document, the relevant clause may state some version of the following:

> Any controversy or claim arising out of or relating to this agreement or the breach thereof shall be settled by arbitration in accordance with the rules of the American Arbitration Association, and judgment upon the award rendered by the arbitrator may be entered in any court having jurisdiction thereof.

Sexual harassment and sex discrimination issues are currently being resolved in arbitration as well as by litigation. Often an employee prefers that her matter not be resolved through arbitration because punitive and other special damages are not granted in an arbitrator's award in many states. However, if you signed an employment agreement containing an arbitration clause, you may be forced to arbitrate your case (including claims made by a fired employee for age discrimination under the Age Discrimination in Employment Act).

Tip: Courts favor resolving cases through arbitration when agreed to beforehand by the parties. Thus, it is essential to understand the ramifications of signing any employment agreement or contract containing an arbitration clause.

> Angela is a salesperson working for an investment banking firm. She complains that her superiors created a hostile atmosphere designed to discriminate against female employees at the firm. She hires a lawyer and files a sex discrimination lawsuit in federal court.
>
> The employer seeks to stay the litigation and compel binding arbitration. It argues that she signed a Form U-4, common to people working in the securities industry. The Form U-4 contains a mandatory arbitration clause which states that the parties agree to settle all disputes via arbitration.
>
> Angela's lawyer argues she was never told that the Form U-4 precluded her from commencing an action for sex discrimination. However, the court rules against Angela and states that her matter must be resolved through arbitration. Angela is very disappointed because she cannot obtain a jury trial, reimbursement for her lawyer and expert-witness fees, or punitive and large compensatory damage awards via arbitration.

Advantages of Arbitration

1. *Expenses.* Substantial savings can be achieved through arbitration. Lawyer fees are reduced because the average hearing is shorter than the average trial (typically a day versus several days). Time-consuming and expensive pretrial procedures, including depositions, interrogatories, and motions, are usually eliminated. Out-of-pocket expenses are reduced because stenographic fees, transcripts, and other items are not required.
2. *Time.* Arbitration hearings and final awards are obtained quickly; cases are usually decided in a matter of months, compared to several years in formal litigation.
3. *Privacy.* The arbitration hearing is held in a private conference room, rather than a courtroom. Unlike a trial, the hearing cannot be attended by the general public.

4. *Expertise of arbitrators.* Arbitrators usually have special training in the area of the case. In an employment dispute in the entertainment industry, for example, arbitrators serving on the panel are typically respected lawyers or other professionals with significant experience in the industry. Their knowledge of trade customs helps them identify and understand a problem more quickly than a judge or jury.

5. *Increased odds of obtaining an award.* Some lawyers believe that arbitrators are more likely than judges to split close cases down the middle. The theory is that arbitrators bend over backward to satisfy both parties to some degree, since their rulings are final and binding. This tendency to compromise, if true, benefits employees with weaker cases.

Disadvantages of Arbitration

1. *Finality.* Arbitrators, unlike judges, need not give formal reasons for their decisions. They are not required to maintain a formal record of the proceedings. The arbitrator's decision is binding. This means that an appeal cannot be taken if you lose the case or disagree with the size of the award except in a few extraordinary circumstances where arbitrator misconduct, dishonesty, or bias can be proved.

2. *Arbitrator selection.* The parties sometimes agree that each will select its own arbitrator. In such cases, it may be assumed that the selected arbitrators are more sympathetic to one side than the other. However, arbitrators are usually selected from a list of neutral names supplied by the American Arbitration Association. This method all but eliminates bias.

3. *Loss of sympathetic juries.* Some knowledgeable lawyers believe that juries tend to empathize more with certain kinds of people, such as fired employees, minorities, and older individuals. Arbitrators are usually successful lawyers and businesspeople whose philosophical orientation may lean more toward companies than individuals.

4. *Loss of discovery devices.* Some claimants must rely on an adversary's documents and records to prove their case. For example, sales agents, authors, patent holders, and others often depend on

their company's (or licensee's) sales figures and accurate record
keeping to determine how much commission and royalties they
are owed. The same is true for minority shareholders who seek
a proper assessment of a company's profit picture. These people
may find a disadvantage in the arbitration process.

Trial lawyers have ample opportunity to view the private books and
records of an adversary long before the day of the trial. This is accomplished by pretrial discovery devices, which include interrogatories, depositions, and notices to produce documents for inspection and
copying. However, these devices are not readily available to litigants in
arbitration. In many instances, records are not available for inspection
until the day of the arbitration hearing. This makes it difficult to detect whether they are accurate and complete. And it is often up to the
arbitrator's discretion whether to grant an adjournment for the purposes of reviewing such records. Such requests may be refused.

Steps Leading to the Hearing

Commencing the hearing is a relatively simple matter once arbitration
has been selected as the method of resolving a dispute. You or your
lawyer sends a notice called a Demand for Arbitration to the employer.
See page 273 for an example of this notice.

Copies of the demand are sent to the American Arbitration Association (AAA), along with the appropriate administrative fee. The AAA
is most often selected to arbitrate disputes. It is a public-service nonprofit organization that offers dispute settlement services through the
national office in New York City and through dozens of regional offices in major cities throughout the United States.

The notice briefly describes the controversy. It specifies the kind of
relief sought, including the amount of monetary damages requested.
A response to the charges is then sent by the opposing party, usually
within seven days. This may also assert a counterclaim for damages.
Either party can add or change claims in writing until the arbitrator
is appointed. Once this occurs, changes and additional claims can be
made only with the arbitrator's consent.

After the AAA receives the Demand for Arbitration and reply, an
AAA administrator usually supplies the parties with a list of potential

DEMAND FOR ARBITRATION

American Arbitration Association
Commercial Arbitration Rules
Demand for Arbitration

Date:_____

TO: (Name) Name of Employer_____
     (of party upon whom the Demand is made)

     (Address) _____

     (City and State) _____ (Zip Code) _____

     (Telephone) _____

Named claimant, a party to an arbitration agreement contained in a written contract, dated _____, providing for arbitration, hereby demands arbitration thereunder. (Attach arbitration clauses or quote hereunder, such as)

"Any controversy or claim arising out of or relating to this contract, or any breach thereof, shall be settled in accordance with the Rules of the American Arbitration Association, and judgment upon the award may be entered in any court having jurisdiction thereof."

NATURE OF DISPUTE: Breach of contract action

CLAIM OR RELIEF SOUGHT: (amount, if any) $50,000 plus attorney fees as payment of salary through the termination date of employment agreement

TYPE OF BUSINESS: _____

Claimant __ Executive _____ Respondent Financial _____

HEARING LOCALE REQUESTED: _____
                              (City and State)

> You are hereby notified that copies of our arbitration agreement and of this demand are being filed with the American Arbitration Association at its New York City Regional Office, with the request that it commence the administration of the arbitration. Under Section 7 of the Commercial Arbitration Rules, you may file an answering statement within seven days after notice from the Administrator.
>
> Signed _____ Title _____
>   (May Be Signed by Attorney)
>
> Name of Claimant _____
> Home or Business Address of Claimant _____
> City and State _____ Zip Code _____
> Telephone _____
> Name of Attorney   Steven Mitchell Sack, Esq.
> Attorney's Address   135 East 57th Street, 12th Floor
> City and State   New York, NY 10022
> Telephone   212-702-9000 (ext. 34)
>
> To institute proceedings, please send three copies of this Demand with the administrative fee, as provided in Section 48 of the Rules, to the AAA. Send original Demand to Respondent.

arbitrators. The list contains the arbitrator's name, current occupation, place of employment, and appropriate background information. The parties mutually agree to nominees from this list. Potential arbitrators are obligated to notify the AAA immediately of any facts likely to affect their impartiality (e.g., prior dealings with one of the litigants) and disqualify themselves where appropriate. (If the parties do not agree beforehand to the number of arbitrators, the dispute is decided by one arbitrator unless the AAA determines that three arbitrators are appropriate.)

Once the arbitrator is selected, the AAA administrator schedules a convenient hearing date and location. There is no direct communication between the parties and the arbitrator until the hearing date; all requests, inquiries, etc., are received by the administrator and relayed to the arbitrator. This avoids the appearance of impropriety. The parties are free to request a prehearing conference to exchange documents and resolve certain issues. Typically, however, the parties, administrators, lawyers, and arbitrator meet face-to-face for the first time at the actual hearing.

The Arbitration Hearing

Most hearings are conducted in a conference room at an AAA regional office. A stenographer is present, if requested (the requesting party generally bears the cost). The arbitrator introduces the parties and typically asks each side to briefly summarize its version of the dispute and what each intends to prove at the hearing.

The complainant's case is presented first. Witnesses are called to give testimony (usually under oath). After witnesses finish speaking, they are usually cross-examined by the opposing party's lawyer. They may also be questioned by the arbitrator. The complainant introduces all its witnesses, documents, and affidavits until it has finished presenting its side of the case.

The opposing party then introduces its witnesses and documents to defend its case and/or prove damages. After the opposition has concluded its case, both sides are usually requested to make a brief summary of the facts (i.e., what they felt was proved at the hearing). Sometimes the arbitrator may request that legal briefs be submitted that summarize the respective position of the parties before rendering a final decision.

Arbitrators are generally required to render written decisions within thirty days unless the parties agree to some other time period. The arbitrator can make any award that is equitable. He or she can order the losing party to pay additional costs, including AAA filing fees and arbitrator fees. Legal fees may be awarded if the arbitration clause so provides. See page 276 for an example of an Award of Arbitrator.

Arbitrators volunteer their time for hearings lasting under two full days; they are paid a reasonable per diem rate (up to $1000) for additional hearings. If the parties settle their dispute prior to a decision, the parties may request that the terms of the settlement be embodied in the consent award.

AWARD OF ARBITRATOR

In the Matter of Arbitration between

_____

Sally Smith
And
Doe Corporation Inc.   Case No.

_____

I, the undersigned Arbitrator, having been designated in accordance with the Arbitration Agreement entered into by the above named Parties, and dated (specify), and having been duly sworn and having heard the proofs and allegations of the Parties, AWARD as follows:

1. Within ten (10) days from the date of this AWARD, Doe Corporation Inc. ("Doe") shall pay to Sally Smith ("Smith"), the sum of Twenty Five Thousand Eighteen Dollars ($25,018.00), plus interest in the amount of Two Thousand Two Hundred Dollars ($2,200.00), for breach of contract.

2. The counterclaim of Doe against Smith is hereby denied in its entirety.

3. The administrative fees of the American Arbitration Association totaling Eleven Hundred Dollars ($1,100.00) shall be borne equally by the Parties. Therefore, Doe shall pay Smith the sum of Five Hundred Fifty Dollars ($550.00) representing one half (50%) of the filing fees previously advanced by Smith to the AAA.

4. Each Party shall pay one half (50%) of the Arbitrator's fee in this arbitration.

5. This AWARD is in full settlement of all claims and counterclaims submitted in this arbitration.

_____
Signature of Arbitrator

Dated: _____

Arbitrators have no contact with the parties after the hearing is concluded. The parties are notified in writing by the AAA administrator and are sent a copy of the award. The decision in a typical employment case is brief—usually no formal reasons are given to explain why a particular award was rendered or the basis on which damages were calculated.

It is practically impossible to appeal a losing case. The arbitrator has no power once the case is decided. The matter can be reviewed only by a judge, and judges cannot overturn the award on the grounds of insufficient evidence. The only ways a case can be overturned on review are:

- For arbitrator dishonesty, partiality, or bias
- When no valid agreement was signed by both parties that authorized the arbitration process
- When an issue was ruled on which the arbitrator was not authorized to decide

Awards are modifiable only if there was a miscalculation of figures or a mistake was made in the description of the person, property, or thing referred to in the award.

How to Increase the Chances of Success in Arbitration

Since the arbitrator's award is final and binding, it is essential to prepare and present a case properly the first time around, because you won't get a second chance. The following strategies may help increase the chances of success.

1. *Hire a lawyer.* People have the right to appear themselves (*pro se*), but it's best to have a lawyer represent you at the hearing, particularly if the dispute involves a large amount of money or complicated legal questions. The familiar expression "He who represents himself has a fool for a client" is certainly applicable in arbitration. Seek the services of an experienced lawyer who is familiar with the intricacies of the arbitration process. This can be discovered by asking the lawyer how many times he or she has represented clients in arbitration within the past several years. If the answer is "never" or "only a few times," look elsewhere for representation.

2. *Prepare for the hearing.* It is important that both you and the lawyer submit evidence to prove the case, so:

- Organize the facts. Gather and label all documents needed at the hearing so they can be produced in an orderly fashion.
- Prepare a checklist of documents and exhibits so that nothing will be forgotten during the presentation.
- Make copies of all documents for the arbitrator and adversary.
- If some of the documents needed are in the possession of the other party, ask that they be brought to the hearing or subpoenaed.
- Interview witnesses.
- Be sure that friendly witnesses will attend and testify; if there is a possibility that additional witnesses may have to appear, alert them to be available on call without delay.
- Select witnesses who are believable, who understand the case and the importance of their testimony, and who will not say things at the hearing to surprise you.
- Coordinate the witnesses' testimony so your case will seem consistent and credible.
- Prepare witnesses for the rigors of cross-examination.
- If a translator is required, make arrangements in advance.
- Prepare a written summary of what each witness will hopefully prove and refer to it at the hearing.
- Anticipate what the opponent will say to defeat your claim and be prepared to refute such evidence.
- Practice your story to put yourself at ease and help organize the facts.
- Prepare a list of questions your lawyer should ask the opponent at the hearing.
- Dress appropriately by wearing conservative business clothes.
- Act professionally and show respect for the arbitrator.
- Listen to the arbitrator's questions and instructions; never argue with the arbitrator.
- If a question is posed while you are speaking, stop talking immediately.
- Answer all questions honestly and directly.
- Avoid arguing with your opponent at the hearing; interrupt his or her presentation only when absolutely necessary.

Finally, if you are fortunate and obtain a judgment, most losing parties voluntarily comply with the terms of an unfavorable award. However, if your opponent decides not to pay, you can enforce the judgment in a regular court. Speak to a lawyer for more details.

MEDIATION

Mediation is an alternative to resolving employment disputes via formal litigation or arbitration. A neutral intermediary (the mediator) defines the conflicting interests of the parties, explains the legal implications, and attempts to help the parties reach and prepare a fair settlement. When settlements are achieved, they are typically reached more quickly and cheaply because opposing parties have not hired opposing counsel to fight it out in court.

Traditionally, mediation was commonly used in union collective bargaining contract proceedings. Now more private nonunion employment-related cases are being resolved this way. For example:

- When an employer alleges it was justified in firing an executive for cause prior to the expiration of the stated term in an employment agreement
- When a worker threatens to file a lawsuit alleging sex harassment
- When there is a significant dispute over the terms of an important clause in an employment contract
- When a worker is issued a final warning because of alleged deteriorating performance prior to a discharge
- When the EEOC is involved in various stages of investigating a discrimination charge, the parties may prefer to work out their problems in the privacy of a business suite instead of a crowded public courtroom and negotiate the terms of a settlement based on their best mutual interests. If a mediator (usually a trained lawyer, businessperson, or retired judge) is hired to assist in the process, he or she will not make decisions for the parties but will help them reach an agreement within the realistic limits of their budget.

Resolving a dispute by mediation requires that both parties agree to mediate the dispute. It also requires a good-faith effort by the parties to resolve the dispute, not to determine who is right and who is wrong. Nonbinding mediation may not work when one party strongly believes it is entitled to punitive or extra damages that can be awarded only by a judge via litigation.

How Mediation Works

Various community associations, private enterprises, and the American Arbitration Association offer mediation services. The AAA is most often selected to assist parties in the mediation process. It is a public-service, nonprofit organization that offers dispute-settlement services to business executives, employers, trade associations, unions, and all levels of government. Services are available through AAA's national office in New York City and through twenty-five regional offices in major cities throughout the United States. A list of various mediation and dispute-resolution organizations is included at the end of this chapter.

Once both parties agree to try to solve their differences through mediation, a joint request for mediation is usually made through an AAA regional office. The request identifies the parties involved in the dispute, gives their current addresses and phone numbers, and briefly describes the controversy and the issues involved. The employee and the company should include whatever information is helpful to appoint a mediator.

The AAA assigns a mediator from its master list. The parties are then given information about the mediator. Typically, the mediator has no past or present relationship with the parties. A mediator is free to refuse the appointment or resign at any time. Likewise, the parties are free to stop the mediation or ask for the services of a different mediator. If a mediator is unwilling or unable to serve, or if one of the parties requests that the mediator resign from the case, the parties may ask the AAA to recommend another mediator. The mediator is compensated on an hourly or a daily basis. Both parties are informed of potential mediator fees and are sometimes requested to sign a document evidencing approval of the compensation arrangement and an agreement to share fees.

Before choosing a mediator, inquire if the mediator's approach is suited to your needs. Ask the following questions at the initial interview:

- How does the mediator operate?
- How much experience and training does the mediator have?
- What is the mediator's background?
- How many sessions are required?
- How much will mediation cost?

After the initial interview takes place and the mediator is found to be acceptable, he or she will arrange the time and place for each conference with the parties. At the first conference, the parties will be asked to produce information required for the mediator to understand the issues, and either party may be asked to supplement this information. The mediator will explain what the parties should expect. Good mediators explain that the process is entirely voluntary, that they are not judges and have no power to dictate solutions, and that the parties are free to terminate the mediation process at any time.

A mediator does not have authority to impose a settlement but will attempt to help the parties reach a satisfactory resolution of their dispute. Although usually trained in law, the mediator is not supposed to give legal advice. While parties do not have to be represented by counsel at the mediation sessions, most claimants and employers retain lawyers in employment and business disputes.

The mediation conferences are private. The mediator will meet with both parties and then sometimes with each privately. Other persons, including witnesses, may attend only with the permission of the parties and at the invitation of the mediator.

Counsel Comments: The mediator is hired as a consultant, jointly retained, to help the parties work their way through their problems to resolution. At some point, the mediator may make a recommendation or proposal. The parties can agree or disagree or come to a compromise of their own. The mediator will draft a report confirming the agreement. The report is then given to the parties for submission to their attorneys for incorporation into a formal document, such as a settlement agreement.

If the parties fail to agree, or do not agree with the mediator's recommendation, they can break off the mediation, consult another mediator, give up, settle their dispute without a mediator, or go to court. The following is a typical mediation scenario from start to finish:

1. The mediator and the parties meet at an initial conference. The mediator's role is explained, and the responsibilities and rights of the parties are set forth.
2. The mediator designs a schedule for the sessions.
3. The parties sign a formal retainer agreement with the mediator.
4. A method is adopted for obtaining whatever information is required for the mediator to understand the parties' problems.
5. The mediator identifies the various areas of agreement, defines the issues to be resolved, and assists the parties in their negotiations.
6. A final settlement may be proposed.
7. The mediator arranges for the terms of the settlement to be transmitted to the attorneys of the parties for filing in court, if necessary.

Counsel Comments: Some mediators do not possess sufficient skills or training to be effective. Others have been criticized for not ending the process when the interests of each party are not receiving balanced treatment. If the mediator is a lawyer, he or she often has to make an adjustment in attitude. Unlike the lawyer, who tells the client what to do, a mediator must allow the parties enough freedom to structure their own unique solutions to problems. Mediation by attorneys has raised the concern of whether one lawyer can adequately advise two parties with opposing interests and whether a mediator can invoke the attorney–client privilege in any future litigation.

For example, if lawyers are present with the parties at mediation sessions and incriminating or damaging statements are made by a client, a lawyer may seek to prevent a judge or jury from ever hearing such statements in court if the mediation fails. Whether a judge will allow such oral testimony to be admitted in court depends on various factors, including whether the parties formally agreed beforehand that such statements were confidential and could not be introduced in subsequent court hearings.

Tip: To avoid problems, interview the mediator carefully; be sure to hire the mediator only on the basis of a written retainer agreement.

If you believe the process is not working or do not feel comfortable with the person hired, terminate the relationship immediately and discuss further options with your lawyer or other professional adviser. Understand that mediation will not work unless both parties are willing to cooperate and recognize the savings and other benefits to be achieved versus litigation, such as:

- Eliminating the anxiety of preparing a case before going to court
- Avoiding potential poor publicity
- Maintaining privacy
- Obtaining a quicker result
- Eliminating uncertainty as to outcome when the case is tried in court
- Demonstrating the desire to maintain a good business relationship

If either party has a great need to even the score, mediation will probably fail. Speak to your professional adviser to determine if mediation is a proper means of resolving any employment dispute before resorting to litigation or arbitration. Once you are involved in mediation with a company representative, inquire if that person has sufficient authority to resolve and settle the matter on the company's behalf when a resolution is imminent. Finally, since your lawyer may be able to meet and question important witnesses, the benefits of learning more about your adversary's case may make the exercise worthwhile even if a settlement is not forthcoming. (In some employment lawsuits, nonbinding court-ordered mediation is required before a trial begins. Speak to your lawyer for more details.)

In conclusion, it is often beneficial to submit to nonbinding mediation when you believe you will be treated fairly: for example, if you will have a say in choosing the mediator, be given access to relevant documents, have the right to be represented by a lawyer at all stages of the proceeding, and have the right to receive the same kind of damages you are entitled to get in court (reinstatement, back pay, front pay, and possibly punitive damages).

Before accepting mediation, do some final research. Was it fair for other employees of the company? Has it worked in the past?

Recently, I represented a terminated executive with a five-year employment contract. Prior to proceeding with binding arbitration (called for in the parties' employment contract), the parties attempted to settle the dispute through nonbinding mediation. I thought that the exercise was quite beneficial because I was able to discuss the facts of the case with opposing counsel and hear what the other side's key witnesses, including the company president, were prepared to testify to at the hearing.

The mediator recommended that the parties settle the matter and assisted in structuring an informal offer worth more than $1.5 million. The client decided not to accept the offer. A disagreement arose between me and my client, resulting in my discharge. After more than twenty-five days of hearings in subsequent arbitration, I learned my ex-client was awarded a judgment of only $46,000!

Tip: Even if you do not believe you will be treated fairly in mediation, you may be required to submit to nonbinding mediation before filing a lawsuit. Be aware of this and act accordingly.

SMALL CLAIMS COURT

Before considering filing a lawsuit in small claims court for a small amount of wages or money that is owed you, attempt to resolve your dispute in a reasonable fashion. It is often best to write a demand letter to your employer or ex-employer and send it certified mail, return receipt requested. In addition to documenting your claim, the letter will advise the company that if the matter is not corrected to your immediate satisfaction, you will take further action. If there is no response to your letter, send a follow-up letter reporting that your initial letter has not been answered. The letter should also state what your next step will be if this letter is ignored.

If you cannot get satisfaction in such a matter through personal negotiations, you might consider suing in small claims court. Small claims courts, which help you collect wages, commissions, and money in an inexpensive manner without your having to hire a lawyer, hear over 1 million cases a year in the United States. They can be used in many situations. For example, you may want to sue for money damages when your ex-employer has failed to pay you salary you are owed or reimburse you for expenses incurred on the company's behalf. Many small claims courts have night sessions, and matters are resolved quickly, sometimes within a month from the time an action is filed. The maximum amount of money you can recover varies from state to state and generally ranges between $2,000 and $5,000.

The following guidelines describe the procedures of a typical small claims court. However, the rules vary in each city and state. Before you contemplate starting a lawsuit, call the clerk of the local court and ask for a written explanation of the specific procedural rules to be followed.

Who Can Be Sued?

Small claims court can be used to sue any person, business, partnership, corporation, or government body owing you money. If you sue in small claims court and recover a judgment, you are precluded from suing again to recover any additional money owed to you. Thus, if your claim greatly exceeds the maximum amount of money that might be awarded in small claims court, consider hiring a lawyer and instituting suit in a higher court.

Do You Have a Valid Claim?

In order to be successful, you must have a valid claim. This means that you must:

- Identify the person or business that damaged or caused you harm;
- Calculate the amount of damages you suffered;
- Show that there is some basis in law to have a court award you damages; and
- Be sure that you were not the main cause of your own harm, that you haven't waited too long to start the action (statute of limitations), and that you did not sign a written release.

Where to Sue

Call your local bar association, city hall, or the county courthouse to discover where the nearest small claims court is located. In some states, small claims court is called justice court, district court, municipal court, or justice of the peace court. In most states, suit must be brought in the county in which the person or business you are suing lives or does business. Confirm this with the small claims court clerk and ask what days and hours the court is in session. Also find out the maximum amount of money you can sue for, what documents are needed to file a complaint, the filing fee, and whether this can be paid by cash, check, or money order.

What Can You Sue For?

You can sue only to collect money. Thus, before you begin to sue in small claims court, estimate the amount of money you want to collect. When calculating the amount of your claim, include all incurred expenses, including gasoline bills, tolls, telephone costs, losses due to time missed from work, sales tax, and interest, if applicable. Save all your receipts for this purpose.

Starting the Lawsuit

You begin the lawsuit by paying a small fee (about $5) and either going to the court in person or mailing in a complaint that states the following information:

- Your name and address
- The complete name and address of the person, business, or company you are suing (the defendant)
- The amount of money you believe you are owed
- The facts of your case
- The reasons you (the plaintiff) are seeking redress

If you are filing a claim on behalf of an individually owned business, you must list the name of the owner in addition to the name of the business. If you are filing a claim on behalf of a partnership, you must list the name of the partnership as the plaintiff. (Some states do not allow a corporation to sue someone in small claims court.)

Be sure to write the accurate and complete name and address of the defendant on the complaint. Write the corporation's formal name rather than its "doing business as" (d/b/a) name. Thus, if you are suing a corporation, contact the country clerk's office in the county where the corporation does business to obtain its proper name and address. Better still, call the department of corporations or the secretary of state in your state to obtain such information.

At this time, you may also be required to prepare another form called a summons, which notifies your ex-employer of the lawsuit. Sometimes the clerk will do this. Ask the clerk whether the court will mail the summons by registered or first-class mail, personally serve the defendant on your behalf, or whether you must hire a professional process server. If a professional process server is required, ask what is necessary to prove that service was accomplished. You may have to pay the process server an additional fee (between $20 and $50). However, if you win your case, you can ask the judge to include the process server's fee in the award. When the clerk gives you a hearing date, be sure that it is convenient and you have no other commitments.

The Defendant's Response

When the person or company you are suing receives the summons, the defendant or his or her attorney can:

- Deny your claim by mailing a written denial to the court
- Deny your claim by personally appearing in court on the day of the hearing
- Sue you for money you supposedly owe (this is called a counterclaim)
- Contact you to settle the matter out of court

If an offer of payment is made, ask to be reimbursed for all filing and service costs. Notify the court that you are dismissing the action only after you receive payment. (If you are paid by check, wait until the check clears.) Do not postpone the case. Tell the employer that unless you are paid before the day of the trial, you are prepared to go to court and either commence with the trial or stipulate the offer of settlement to the judge.

If a written denial is mailed to the court, ask the clerk to read it to you over the phone or go to the court and read it yourself. This is your right and may help you prepare for your opponent's defense. The following is an example of a simple denial in an answer: "I deny each and every allegation in the face of the complaint." Now you must prove your allegations in court to recover your claim.

Your Duties as the Moving Party

It is up to you to follow the progress of your case. Call the clerk and refer to the docket number to discover whether the defendant received the complaint and whether it was answered. If you discover that the defendant did not receive the complaint by the day of the trial, request that the clerk issue a new complaint to be served by a sheriff or process server. Go to court that day anyway, to be sure that the case is not dismissed because of your failure to appear.

If the complaint is personally served and your employer does not appear at the trial, he or she will be in default and you may be awarded a judgment automatically. In some states, you still have to prove your case in order to be successful. Moreover, defendants sometimes file motions (legal affidavits) requesting the court to remove the default judgment on the grounds that there was a valid reason for not attending the hearing. If this motion is granted, your trial will be rescheduled.

If you are unable to come to court on the day of the trial, send a certified letter, return receipt requested, to the clerk, asking for a continuance. The letter should specify the reasons you will be unable to appear and include future dates when you will be able to come to court. Send a copy of this letter to your opponent. When you receive a new date, send your opponent a certified letter, return receipt requested, informing the employer of the revised date. Requests for continuances are sometimes not honored. Call the clerk on the day of the original trial date to be sure that your request has been granted. Be prepared to send a friend or relative to court to ask for a continuance on your behalf if a continuance has not been obtained by the day of the trial.

Preparing for Trial

You have several weeks to prepare for trial. Use the time wisely. First, be sure that your friendly witnesses, if any, will attend the trial and testify on your behalf. Select witnesses who are believable and who will not say things that will surprise you. In some states, you can present the judge with signed affidavits or statements of witnesses who are unable to appear at the trial. Some states also permit judges to hear testimony via conference telephone.

If necessary, the clerk can issue a subpoena to ensure the attendance of important witnesses who you believe may refuse to attend and testify. A subpoena is a document that orders a person to testify or produce books, papers, and other physical objects on a specified date. If the subpoena is issued and the person refuses to appear, a judge can direct a sheriff to bring the witness into court or even impose a jail sentence for a willful violation of the order.

When you come to court for the trial, check to see if the clerk has received any subpoenaed documents. If such records are crucial to your case and have not been received, you can ask for a continuance. If you have subpoenaed an individual and do not know what he or she looks like, ask the clerk to call out the name to determine if he or she is present so you can proceed with the trial.

To maximize your chances of success, organize your case before the trial. Gather and label all your evidence so that you can produce the documents easily. You may also wish to speak with a lawyer or call a lawyer's referral service for legal advice. Many communities have such advisory organizations, and they are willing to inform you, without charge, about relevant cases and statutes. This may help you know to what damages you are legally entitled. You may cite these laws, if applicable, at the hearing.

The Trial

Arrive early, locate the correct courtroom, find the name of your case on the court calendar, and check in with the clerk. You should be properly attired, preferably in business clothes. Come prepared with all relevant documents. Examples are:

Receipts and canceled checks
Correspondence
Contracts
Letters of protest demanding unpaid wages
Unpaid invoices
Contemporaneous memos of promises or statements made to you
Signed affidavits or statements from friends and witnesses unable
to appear at the hearing
An accountant's statement of lost wages
Prior years' tax returns
Diagrams or charts
Copies of applicable statutes, cases, and regulations

When your case is called, you and the employer will be sworn. The
judge or court-appointed arbitrator, magistrate, commissioner, or volunteer attorney will conduct the hearing and ask you questions. Be
relaxed. Keep your presentation brief and to the point. Tell why you
are suing the employer and what monetary damages you are seeking.
Show your evidence. Bring along a short written summary of the case.
You can refer to it during the trial, and if the judge does not come to
an immediate decision, he or she can use your outline for reference.
Talk directly to the judge and respond to his or her questions. Show
respect. Always refer to him or her as "Your Honor" or "Judge." Listen to the judge's instructions and never argue. If the judge asks you a
question while you are speaking, stop immediately. Then answer the
question honestly and to the point. Be diplomatic rather than emotional. Also avoid arguing with your opponent in court and never interrupt his or her presentation.

After both sides finish speaking, you will have the opportunity to
refute what the employer has told the judge. Do not be intimidated if
the employer is accompanied by a lawyer. Simply inform the judge
that you are not represented by counsel and are not familiar with small
claims court procedures. Ask the judge to intercede on your behalf if
you feel that the employer's attorney is treating you unfairly. Most
judges will be sympathetic, since small claims courts are specially designed for you to present your case without a lawyer.

If you are a defendant, follow the same procedures as the plaintiff:
prepare your testimony, contact your witnesses to be sure that they
will appear at the trial and testify on your behalf; collect your exhibits

and documents; arrive early on the day of the trial and check in with the clerk. If you have any doubts about your case, try to settle with the plaintiff before the judge hears the case. Request that the case be dismissed if your opponent fails to appear. Your opponent will speak first if he or she appears. Wait until he or she is finished speaking before telling your side of the story. Point out any inconsistencies or flaws in your opponent's story. Conclude your remarks by highlighting the important aspects of the case.

Tip: Some states require that you send a "thirty-day demand letter" before filing an action. The letter should briefly describe your money loss and what you want the employer to do to remedy the situation. Add that you are giving the employer thirty days to make a good-faith response. Otherwise, you will begin legal action. Send the letter certified mail, return receipt requested, and consider sending copies to your state attorney general's office and your attorney. If the letter is answered and the ex-employer refuses to pay, you may learn what position it intends to take at the trial. If your letter is ignored, that is evidence in court.

Counsel Comments: In certain states, an employer's willful failure to pay earned vacation money, wages, or other accrued compensation or promised benefits may cause it to be liable for extra statutory damages (such as an additional 25 percent) plus legal costs and expenses. Check your state's law to ascertain whether this applies to your case. If it does, tell the judge about the existence of your state's law and request these additional penalties. (If you are successful but the additional penalties put you over the small claims court limit, you may be awarded only the maximum amount of money permitted and may have to forfeit the balance exceeding this cap. Be aware of this.)

Obtaining Judgment

Some small claims court judges render oral decisions on the spot. Others issue a decision in writing several days after the hearing. This gives them time to weigh the testimony and exhibits. If your opponent fails to attend the hearing, judges usually render a judgment of default immediately after your presentation.

If you win the case, make sure you know how and when payment will be made. Check to see that all your disbursements, including court costs, filing fees, service of process, and applicable witness fees, are added to the amount of your judgment. Send a copy of the decision by certified mail, return receipt requested, to your opponent, together with a letter requesting payment. Some states require that payment be made to the court; others allow payment to be made directly to you.

Do not hesitate to act if you do not receive the money. First, contact the clerk and file a Petition for Notice to Show Cause. This will be sent to the defendant, ordering the employer to come into court and explain why it has not paid. You should also file an Order of Execution with the sheriff's, constable's, or clerk's office in the county where the defendant is located or owns a business. This will enable you to discover where the employer has assets. The sheriff or other enforcement agent has the power to go out and collect the judgment by seizing personal property, freezing the defendant's bank accounts, placing a lien on any real estate, or even garnisheeing an individual's salary where appropriate. The clerk of your small claims court should tell you exactly what to do to collect your judgment.

By bringing suit in small claims court, you usually waive your right to a trial by jury. However, the defendant can surprise you. Some states allow defendants to move a small claims court case to a higher court and/or obtain a trial by jury. If this occurs, you will need a lawyer to represent you, and his or her services could cost as much as your claim in the dispute.

Some states do not allow losing plaintiffs to appeal. If you can appeal, however, an appeals court will overturn the decision of a small claims court judge only if there is strong proof that the judge was biased or dishonest. This may be difficult to prove.

FILING A DISCRIMINATION CLAIM

If you believe you have been victimized by employment discrimination, consider filing a discrimination charge with the EEOC and/or your state agency. In some states, filing a charge with either the EEOC or a state agency will be treated as filing with both. Speak to a labor lawyer for advice because some state statutes provide greater protection and some state agencies have more powers than the EEOC.

EEOC offices are listed in the telephone directory under United States Government, or you can call 800-669-4000. State agencies can be located by calling your state's department of labor or an EEOC office in your area. Listings of EEOC field offices and state human rights commissions are found at the end of this chapter.

Typically, you must give your name if you want an investigation to proceed, but you cannot be retaliated against for filing a charge.

Although some state agencies permit a longer period (e.g., up to 300 days depending on state law), to be timely you must file a charge with the EEOC within 180 days of the date the last incident occurred.

Although you may file a private lawsuit in federal court, once you file a charge with the EEOC you cannot litigate the matter privately until the EEOC dismisses your case (finds "no probable cause") or rules in your favor. In either situation, you then have ninety days to file a private lawsuit after receiving a final disposition notice (called a right-to-sue letter) from the EEOC.

The law entitles victims of discrimination to recover a variety of damages. This may include reinstatement or job hiring; receiving wage adjustments, back pay, and double back pay; receiving promotions and future pay; recovering legal fees, filing costs, and fees paid for expert witnesses; receiving punitive damages and compensatory damages up to $300,000 depending on the size of the employer; and other damages depending on the facts of your case. Remember, it is illegal to be fired because you belong to a protected class, such as being a woman, over forty, a minority, handicapped, or a religious observer.

Tip: Obtaining a favorable decision does not automatically mean that you will receive big bucks. The employer may appeal a state agency or EEOC decision and force you to sue it in federal court. This could effectively stall any financial recovery for many years.

Once you decide to file a charge, you must call the nearest local office of the EEOC or state human rights agency where you live or work for an appointment. Unless the matter is urgent (i.e., you must file the claim within three days or have it be thrown out as being untimely and you will be barred from suing in court or obtaining any kind of relief from your employer's unlawful conduct in the future), you may have to wait for an appointment. This can take several weeks or even months.

Be prepared for the appointment. Recall the names and addresses of all witnesses, other employee–victims, and key company workers who treated you unfairly (e.g., the name of your supervisor). It is a good idea to keep a diary that documents the date, time, and place of any discriminatory acts and illegal statements made and who overheard these remarks. Collect and save copies of all relevant documents and materials before the appointment. This may include letters of reference, performance reviews, and other favorable documents. Bring this information with you when you meet the investigator. Present your evidence objectively to increase the odds your complaint will be accepted and acted on by the EEOC investigator.

To start the ball rolling, it is necessary to file a formal charge. No one can stop you from filing a complaint; the law forbids employers from threatening reprisals or retaliation (such as loss of a promotion) when action is taken. The following facts must be included in the complaint:

1. Your name
2. The names, business addresses, and business telephone numbers of all persons who committed and/or participated in the discriminatory acts(s)
3. Specific events, dates, and facts to support why the act(s) was discriminatory (e.g., statistics, whether other employees or individuals were discriminated against, and if so, the persons victimized and by whom)

The complaint must be signed and sworn to by the complainant. However, it is not necessary for the complaint to be lengthy or elaborate. The main purpose is to allege sufficient facts to trigger an investigation. That is the advantage of filing charges with an appropriate agency; charges of discrimination are initiated and investigated at no cost to you. An investigator from the EEOC or state agency prepares and types the complaint. The example of an EEOC charge of discrimination below illustrates the brevity of a valid complaint:

I am a female. On (date) I was notified by my supervisor (name) at (name of employer) that I was fired. I asked (name) to tell me why I was fired; he said it was because I called in sick six times in the past year. I know of several male employees who called in sick more than six times and who were not fired.

Based on these facts I believe I have been discriminated against on the basis of my gender.

Tip: Be sure the form is filled out completely, signed, and notarized. Don't worry if you did not include all pertinent information, since you are allowed to amend the charge at a later date. I am often consulted by terminated workers who are concerned that the initial charge does not adequately discuss all the pertinent facts and causes of action. Sometimes I recommend additional language to be inserted in an amended charge, which is done by an EEOC investigator at a later date. Always get a copy of the charge before leaving the appointment so that you can refer to it later.

Do not be dissuaded from filing a charge. Tell the investigator you insist that the claim be accepted even if you are told the case is poor or is not timely.

If your claim seems plausible, the EEOC or state agency develops the claim on your behalf. A copy of the complaint, together with a request for a written response, is then sent to the employer. The employer must respond to the charges within several weeks. This is done either by a general denial of the claim or by the filing of specific facts and reasons to support the employer's position.

After charges and countercharges have been examined by an investigator, the employer and the complainant may eventually be invited to attend a no-fault conference if the investigator believes the complainant's charges possibly have merit. Cases that are deemed to be too far-fetched or insufficient on their face are dismissed before the no-fault conference. If you receive a notice from the EEOC that your case has been dismissed (sometimes referred to as lacking probable cause), it must advise you of your rights. The right-to-sue letter will state that if you want to proceed with your case, you must file a formal lawsuit in federal court within ninety days or forfeit your claim.

The purpose of a no-fault conference is to discuss your case. At that time, the investigator may make arrangements to visit the employer's premises, examine documents and other pertinent records, and interview key employees and witnesses. Because an employer may have an incentive to dispose of the matter early on to save excessive legal fees, lost manpower time, and potential damages, approximately 40 percent of all complaints are disposed at the settlement conference.

Tip: Although it is not necessary to retain a lawyer to represent you at or before the no-fault conference, the chances of settling your case are much higher with a lawyer present. An employer will bring its counsel, and you may be intimidated. Additionally, an experienced lawyer can evaluate your claim and advise how much it is realistically worth. Since many EEOC claims take years to be heard, a lawyer will advise you whether a settlement offer is valid and should be accepted, particularly after considering the lengthy delays that are frequently involved.

The conference is conducted by an investigator. Pressure may be placed on the employer to offer a monetary settlement or some other form of restitution (such as a promotion) to avoid the large legal expenses that would be incurred in the course of an ongoing investigation and eventual hearing. Then, too, some employers may be fearful that the investigator will examine their business records, including employment applications, interoffice memos, and pay records if a settlement is not reached.

If your case cannot be settled at the conference, many options are available, including:

- Hiring a lawyer privately and suing the employer in a civil lawsuit, typically in federal court
- Representing yourself *pro se* (without a lawyer) and suing the employer in federal or state court
- Having the agency act on your behalf to protect your rights and proceeding to a fact-finding hearing and determination
- Having the EEOC or Department of Justice commence a lawsuit for you and/or others similarly situated in a class-action lawsuit
- Hiring a lawyer and commencing a private lawsuit in state court and, if applicable, alleging other causes of action as well as violations of discrimination laws

The advantage of suing an employer privately is that you may receive a quicker settlement. The EEOC and other agencies have many thousands of claims to process and follow; your case could take years before it is acted on. Even if you receive a favorable decision (referred to as a finding of probable cause), the employer can appeal the agency's decision, adding years to the delay before an administrative trial is commenced. A lawyer working for you may be able to move the matter along more quickly. However, private lawsuits can be very expensive. That is why it is best initially to contact the nearest district office of the EEOC or state agency and speak with an intake person or investigator, or contact a lawyer and discuss your options before taking action.

Tip: State and local laws are often more favorable than federal law in terms of the standards of proof required, the amount of damages awarded, and other factors. It may be advantageous to file charges with these agencies instead, so do not automatically assume your case must be filed with the EEOC. Talk to an employment lawyer to discuss your options and maximize a claim.

When you retain a lawyer, he or she may first contact the employer by letter. The letter may specify the potential charges and invite the employer to discuss settlement before the matter proceeds to the next step. Cases are often settled this way before a formal discrimination charge is filed. The letter on page 28 of Chapter 2 illustrates the kind of letter that a lawyer may send on your behalf.

Additional information and strategies on how to properly hire and work effectively with a lawyer are discussed in the next chapter.

Final Tips: No matter what course of action you consider, do not delay unnecessarily. In many situations, you must file a formal complaint within 180 days of the time the alleged act(s) occurred to avoid the expiration of the statute of limitations. Some complainants take their time and unfortunately discover their cases are dismissed because they waited too long to file.

To determine the status of the investigation and action taken in your case, regularly call the EEOC officer assigned to it. Be assertive and follow the progress of your case. Whenever you receive a request for information, provide this immediately to the investigator.

If you are unhappy with the progress of the investigation or how the case is being handled, consult a lawyer for guidance and advice. Consider joining a class-action lawsuit if one already exists against your employer or ex-employer. By doing so, however, you may have to withdraw from your private action.

Finally, be patient. The EEOC and state agencies often take years to render a decision, and the employer may delay the final outcome years more by refusing to settle and appealing the case further. Some investigators leave the agency while working on your case, and a new investigator has to be assigned, causing further delay. Thus, recognize that in most situations, even with a good case, you may not receive justice for many years.

Summary of Steps to Maximize a Discrimination Claim

1. If you believe that you have been victimized by employment discrimination, consider filing a discrimination charge with the EEOC and/or your state agency. In some states, filing a charge with either the EEOC or a state agency will be treated as filing with both. Speak to an employment lawyer for advice, because some state statutes provide greater protection and some state agencies have more powers than the EEOC.

2. Locate the nearest EEOC field office and your state's human rights commission. (See the lists at the end of this chapter.) EEOC offices are also listed in the telephone directory under United States Government, or you can call 800-669-4000. State agencies can be located by calling your state's department of labor or an EEOC office in your area.

3. Typically, you must give your name if you want an investigation to proceed, but you cannot be retaliated against for filing a charge.

4. Although some state agencies permit a longer period (e.g., up to 300 days depending on state law), to be timely you must file a charge with the EEOC within 180 days of the date the last incident occurred.

5. Although you may file a private lawsuit in federal court, once you file a charge with the EEOC you cannot litigate the matter privately until the EEOC dismisses your case (finds no probable cause) or rules in your favor. In either situation, you then have ninety days to file a private lawsuit to be timely after receiving a

final disposition notice (called a right-to-sue letter) from the EEOC.

6. Obtaining a favorable decision does not automatically mean that you will receive big bucks. The employer may appeal a state agency or EEOC decision and force you to sue it in federal court.

7. Regularly call the EEOC officer to determine the status of the investigation and action taken in your case. Be assertive and follow the progress of your case. Whenever you receive a request for information, provide this immediately to the investigator.

8. If you are unhappy with the progress of the investigation or how the case is being handled, consult an attorney for guidance and advice. Consider joining a class-action lawsuit if one already exists against your employer or ex-employer. By doing so, however, you may have to withdraw from the action.

9. Be patient. The EEOC often takes years to render its decision, and the employer may delay the final outcome years more by refusing to settle and appealing the case further.

Final Tips About Winning a Discrimination Case

Filing a discrimination charge is only the first step; proving your case is an entirely different matter. While the advice and guidance of a skilled employment lawyer is always necessary, acting on the following tips can improve your chances of success.

1. *Develop the facts beforehand.* Collect and save all pertinent documentation before filing a formal charge or being fired. Copies of favorable letters of reference and performance reviews in your possession, for example, may make it more difficult for the employer to argue that you were fired for poor work performance.

2. *Try to prove your case through direct evidence.* Statements made by supervisors or managers about your age, gender, or color that are overheard by others can be more effective in proving your case than relying on circumstantial evidence (such as statistics that tend to demonstrate a pattern of discrimination). Maintain a diary listing damaging statements made to you or about you, especially discriminatory comments others tell you they heard.

3. *Be able to refute the employer's defenses with logic.* In court, the em-

ployer will typically respond to your charges by attempting to prove that its actions were the result of legitimate, nondiscriminatory factors. This may include firing you for financial reasons, not because you were pregnant, over forty, or black. You will then have the challenge of offering evidence to show that the excuse is merely a pretext (or a cover-up) for discrimination. Although this is often difficult to do, you can prevail by proving the employer's reason is factually untrue, insufficient to have actually motivated your discharge, done in retaliation for your complaining about or filing a formal charge of discrimination, or implausible.

CLASS-ACTION LAWSUITS

In a situation where a number of people in a protected group, including minorities, older workers, handicapped workers or women, were similarly discriminated against or were injured by the same or similar conduct of an employer, those people may join in bringing a "class action" against the employer. Typically, in a class-action lawsuit, several members of the protected group bring the action on behalf of the entire affected class of employees or job applicants. This is usually done through one law firm experienced in conducting litigation on behalf of many plaintiffs in one case. (Sometimes the EEOC may sue for the group.)

The advantage of bringing a class-action lawsuit is that legal costs are spread among many hundreds or thousands of claimants. This allows large or complex cases to proceed against major companies when it would not be economically feasible or practicable for one or several individuals to do so on their own.

As an example, it was reported that the large supermarket chain Publix recently agreed to pay $81.5 million to settle a class-action lawsuit by 150,000 women who accused the big grocery chain of relegating them to dead-end, low-paying jobs. The settlement applies to all women who worked at any of the 535 Publix stores in Florida, Georgia, South Carolina, and Alabama since 1991.

The suit was brought in 1995 by eight women who accused Publix of passing them over for raises and repeatedly denying them management jobs. They and four others who quickly joined the case said they watched as men with less experience and less seniority got promotions. Some said their requests were met with unwanted sexual advances from managers. The EEOC later joined the suit, and it was expanded to a class action covering past and current employees.

In order to qualify and proceed as a class-action lawsuit, numerous stringent rules must be satisfied. For example, if you and several other workers have suffered similar wrongs or injuries by an employer, that may not be enough to certify a class-action lawsuit. In that event, each individual would have to file a separate lawsuit, and their cases could either be processed separately or consolidated into one action by a judge at the trial stage. The difference with a class-action lawsuit is that it typically involves hundreds of workers alleging similar injuries.

Speak to a law firm that specializes in handling class-action lawsuits for more details. It may also be a good idea to contact the American Bar Association in Chicago or the American Civil Liberties Union in New York for information on law firms in your area specializing in organizing and handling class-action lawsuits.

FILING A CHARGE WITH THE DEPARTMENT OF LABOR

A local or regional office of your state's labor department or federal Department of Labor is the agency to contact when you have not received your wages or vacation pay or if you have overtime complaints. These agencies are in the government listings of your telephone directory under Department of Labor.

Like discrimination complaints, you must act quickly in many instances to avoid the tolling of your charge due to a failure to timely file pursuant to the applicable statute of limitations. For example, in overtime cases brought pursuant to the federal Fair Labor Standards Act, you can collect only the unpaid overtime that has accrued for two years prior to filing a charge (commencing from either the last time your employer failed to give you a paycheck or underpaid you, or you discovered this was the case). This may be extended to three years in certain situations where you can prove that the employer willfully refused to pay overtime. Thus, it is important to act quickly.

In some states, the labor department will not assist you in collecting unpaid wages if you earn more than a certain amount per week (e.g., $400). In such a case, you might then be forced to sue the employer privately and/or hire a lawyer to assist you in collecting unpaid wages.

The best way to determine if the labor department will actively assist you in prosecuting your claim is to call a local office and schedule an appointment with a representative or investigator. Bring all your correspondence, documentation, and proof with you at the initial appointment. This will make it easier for an investigator to evaluate your claim. If your case has merit and the agency will assist you, find out what steps it will take on your behalf. Inquire how long it will take before you collect.

Tip: It is important to call the investigator handling your matter on a regular basis (e.g., once every two months) to oversee the progress of the case. As with complaints filed with the EEOC or state discrimination agencies, do not expect to resolve the matter quickly, since there may be a backlog of thousands of cases similar to yours.

If you need further assistance, if the agency is not handling your matter properly, or if you feel the labor department is not responsive to your needs, it may be necessary to hire a lawyer to commence a private lawsuit for unpaid wages or overtime on your behalf. Information and strategies on how to work effectively with an employment lawyer are contained in the next chapter.

WORKERS' COMPENSATION CLAIMS

Each state has enacted its own particular laws with respect to workers' compensation benefits, which provide aid for employees who suffer job-related injuries. Your state's workers' compensation commission (also sometimes called the industrial relations commission) administers and enforces workers' compensation laws.

Always alert your employer immediately in writing sent certified mail, return receipt requested, if you are injured on the job. Under compensation laws in most states, each employer must promptly provide medical, surgical, optometric, or other treatment for injured employees as well as provide hospital care, crutches, eyeglasses, and other appliances necessary to repair, relieve, or support a part of the body. Your company's medical team may eliminate unnecessary treatment, but injured employees may select their own physician for authorized treatment, provided that physician is authorized by the state's workers' compensation board.

Tip: Do not be afraid to report an accident or file a claim in writing. Most states prohibit companies from firing, demoting, or otherwise punishing an employee for filing or pursuing a valid workers' compensation claim. Do this as quickly as possible so your case is not dismissed as being untimely. While you are receiving medical treatment, save all receipts of drug purchases, trips to the doctor (including tolls and cab fares), and all related purchases. You are generally entitled to full reimbursement for all direct out-of-pocket expenses, including payment for doctors, hospitals, rehabilitation, and related therapy costs. Dependents are entitled to receive death benefits in case of death, and you will be compensated for the loss of a limb or body part (such as an eye) based on a predetermined schedule. You are also entitled to compensation for loss of wages and income. The type of disability you suffered (e.g., temporary, permanent, partial, and/or total disability) will determine the amount of money you receive each week and how long you will receive such benefits. Each state has maximum limits for weekly benefits that typically do not exceed 75 percent of a worker's regular weekly salary.

Do not hesitate to consult a lawyer specializing in workers' compensation injuries or a personal-injury lawyer, particularly if your employer refuses to provide benefits and pay your medical bills. A lawyer can protect your rights in many ways. For example, if anyone other than your employer or coworker was even partly responsible for the accident, you may be free to file your own liability insurance claim against that person or business. If for any reason your accident is not covered by workers' compensation because you are an independent contractor or because the company has no coverage, you may be able to file a lawsuit against your employer in the same fashion that you could sue anyone who causes you personal injury. In such a case, additional damages such as attorney fees, money for mental pain and suffering, loss of companionship to a spouse, and even punitive damages may be awarded.

Under certain circumstances, you may also be able to collect Social Security benefits, retirement benefits or unemployment compensation, and health insurance payments while you are collecting disability benefits. A labor lawyer or one who specializes in workers' compensation law can advise you. A knowledgeable lawyer may be required to argue your case at the hearing stage before an administrative law judge, especially when the issues are not clear-cut (such as when and where the accident occurred), to determine initially if workers' compensation is applicable. Lawyers handling workers' compensation matters are generally quite knowledgeable about medical conditions and dealing with doctors. Resolving an issue of whether an accident caused a partial or permanent disability can involve tens of thousands of dollars in future wages. (Typically, workers' compensation lawyers work on a contingency-fee basis.) It may also be necessary to retain the services of a lawyer if you want to pursue an unsuccessful verdict at the appeals stage. Thus, consult a specialist for advice and guidance.

Hiring a lawyer is very important in situations where your employer opposes a claim and it is necessary for you to present your case before the workers' compensation commission at informal and/or formal hearings and appeals. The lawyer will assist you in preparing for the hearing and presenting witnesses, medical documentation, and other evidence at the hearing. This can be done at the initial informal hearing and then at subsequent formal hearings if the matter is not settled. You may also need a lawyer to guide you through the appeals process if your employer contests a favorable decision on your behalf or if you lose the case or are awarded far less in benefits than you deserve.

Once you begin receiving benefits, many states require you to update your condition periodically to ascertain your continued eligibility for benefits. Subsequent hearings may be required to determine whether your benefits should stop or be reduced, especially if the employer believes you are capable of returning to work.

Thus, always seek the advice of a competent lawyer to assist you through the process of filing and hopefully winning a workers' compensation case. Information and strategies on how to hire and work effectively with a lawyer is contained in the next chapter.

AGENCIES AND ORGANIZATIONS
TO CONTACT

Federal Agencies and
Private Organizations

For Civil Rights Violations

American Civil Liberties Union
132 West 43rd Street
New York, NY 10036
(212) 944-9800

Commission on Civil Rights, Washington, DC
National Association for the Advancement of Colored People,
Washington, DC
National Organization for Women, New York, NY

For Discrimination Complaints

American Civil Liberties Union
132 West 43rd Street
New York, NY 10036
(212) 944-9800

Equal Employment Opportunity Commission
1801 L Street NW
Washington, DC 20506
(800) 669-EEOC
(800) 669-4000 (for a list of regional offices)
(202) 663-4264

U.S. Department of Labor
200 Constitution Avenue NW
Washington, DC 20210
(202) 219-6666

Concerning the Elderly

American Association of Retired Persons
601 E Street NW
Washington, DC 20049
(800) 424-3410

National Council on the Aging, Washington, DC
Social Security Administration, Washington, DC
Equal Employment Opportunity Commission
1801 L Street NW
Washington, DC 20506
(800) 669-EEOC
(202) 663-4264

For Discrimination Concerning the Handicapped

Equal Employment Opportunity Commission
1801 L Street NW
Washington, DC 20506
(800) 669-EEOC
(202) 663-4264

U.S. Department of Transportation, Washington, DC

Pension and Welfare Benefits Administration
1730 K Street NW, Suite 556
Washington, DC 20006
(202) 254-7013

Social Security Administration, Washington, DC

State Attorney General's Office

President's Committee on Employment of People with Disabilities
1331 F Street NW
Washington, DC 20004-1107
(202) 376-6200

For Safety and Health Complaints

Occupational Safety and Health Administration
Frances Perkins Building
200 Constitution Avenue NW
Washington, DC 20210
(202) 219-6091

U.S. Department of Labor
200 Constitution Avenue NW
Washington, DC 20210
(202) 219-6666

For Information on Labor Unions

AFL-CIO, Washington, DC
(202) 637-5000

National Labor Relations Board
1099 14th Street NW
Washington, DC 20210
(202) 273-1991

Pension Information

Division of Public Disclosure
U.S. Department of Labor
Room N5507
Washington, DC 20210
(202) 219-8771

Pension Rights Center
918 16th Street NW, Suite 704
Washington, DC 20006
(202) 296-3778

Pension Benefit Guaranty Corporation
Case Operations and Compliance
1200 K Street NW
Washington, DC 20005
(202) 326-4000

Pension and Welfare Benefits Administration
1730 K Street NW, Suite 556
Washington, DC 20006
(202) 254-7013

Mediation and Dispute
Resolution Organizations

The following organizations may be able to provide you with additional information about specific areas of dispute resolution. Many offer catalogs of publications, as well as brochures containing general information.

American Arbitration Association
140 West 51st Street
New York, NY 10020
(212) 484-4000

American Bar Association
Section on Dispute Resolution
740 15th Street NW
Washington, DC 20009
(202) 662-1680

National Institute for Dispute Resolution
1901 L Street NW, Suite 600
Washington, DC 20036
(202) 862-7200

Council of Better Business Bureaus
4200 Wilson Boulevard, Suite 800
Arlington, VA 22203
(703) 276-0100

EEOC Field Offices

Albuquerque EEOC
505 Marquette NW, Suite 900
Albuquerque, NM 87102-2189
(505) 766-2061

Atlanta EEOC
75 Piedmont Avenue NE, Suite 1100
Atlanta, GA 30335
(404) 331-0604

Baltimore EEOC
City Crescent Building
10 South Howard Street, 3rd Floor
Baltimore, MD 21201
(410) 962-3932

Birmingham EEOC
1900 3rd Avenue North, Suite 101
Birmingham, AL 35203-2397
(205) 731-0082

Boston EEOC
1 Congress Street, 10th Floor
Boston, MA 02114
(617) 565-3200

Buffalo EEOC
6 Fountain Plaza, Suite 350
Buffalo, NY 14203
(716) 846-4441

Charlotte EEOC
5500 Central Avenue
Charlotte, NC 28212-2708
(704) 567-7100

Chicago EEOC
500 West Madison Street, Room 2800
Chicago, IL 60661
(312) 353-2713

Cincinnati EEOC
Ameritrust Building
525 Vine Street, Suite 810
Cincinnati, OH 45202-3122
(513) 684-2851

Cleveland EEOC
Tower City, Skylight Office Tower
1660 West 2nd Street, Suite 850
Cleveland, OH 44113-1454
(216) 522-2001

Dallas EEOC
207 South Houston Street, 3rd Floor
Dallas, TX 75202-4726
(214) 655-3355

Denver EEOC
303 East 17th Avenue, Suite 510
Denver, CO 80203-9634
(303) 866-1300

Detroit EEOC
477 Michigan Avenue, Room 1540
Detroit, MI 48226-9704
(313) 226-7636

El Paso EEOC
The Commons, Building C, Suite 100
4171 North Mesa Street
El Paso, TX 79902
(915) 534-6550

Fresno EEOC
1265 West Shaw Avenue, Suite 103
Fresno, CA 93711
(209) 487-5793

Greensboro EEOC
801 Summit Avenue
Greensboro, NC 27405-7813
(919) 333-5174

Greenville EEOC
SCN Building
15 South Main Street, Suite 530
Greenville, SC 29601
(803) 241-4400

Honolulu EEOC
677 Ala Moana Boulevard, Suite 404
PO Box 50082
Honolulu, HI 96813
(808) 541-3120

Houston EEOC
1919 Smith Street, 7th Floor
Houston, TX 77002
(713) 653-3377

Indianapolis EEOC
101 West Ohio Street, Suite 1900
Indianapolis, IN 46204-4203
(317) 226-7212

Jackson EEOC
Cross Roads Building Complex
207 West Amite Street
Jackson, MS 39201
(601) 965-4537

Kansas City EEOC
911 Walnut, 10th Floor
Kansas City, MO 64106
(816) 426-5773

Little Rock EEOC
425 West Capitol Avenue, 6th Floor
Little Rock, AR 72201
(501) 324-5060

Los Angeles EEOC
255 East Temple Street, 4th Floor
Los Angeles, CA 90012
(213) 251-7278

Louisville EEOC
600 M. L. King Jr. Place, Room 268
Louisville, KY 40202
(502) 582-6082

Memphis EEOC
1407 Union Avenue, Suite 621
Memphis, TN 38104
(901) 722-2617

Miami EEOC
1 Northeast 1st Street, 6th Floor
Miami, FL 33132-2491
(305) 536-4491

Milwaukee EEOC
310 West Wisconsin Avenue, Suite 800
Milwaukee, WI 53203-2292
(414) 297-1111

Minneapolis EEOC
330 South 2nd Avenue, Room 430
Minneapolis, MN 55401-2224
(612) 335-4040

Nashville EEOC
50 Vintage Way, Suite 202
Nashville, TN 37228
(615) 736-5820

Newark EEOC
1 Newark Center, 21st Floor
Newark, NJ 07102-5233
(201) 645-6383

New Orleans EEOC
701 Loyola, Suite 600
New Orleans, LA 70113-9936
(504) 589-2329

New York EEOC
7 World Trade Center, 18th Floor
New York, NY 10048
(212) 748-8500

Norfolk EEOC
252 Monticello Avenue, 1st Floor
Norfolk, VA 23510
(804) 441-3470

Oakland EEOC
Oakland Federal Building, North Tower
1301 Clay Street
Oakland, CA 94612-5217
(510) 637-3230

Oklahoma City EEOC
531 Couch Drive
Oklahoma City, OK 73102
(405) 231-4911

Philadelphia EEOC
1421 Cherry Street, 10th Floor
Philadelphia, PA 19102
(215) 656-7000

Phoenix EEOC
4520 North Central Avenue, Suite 300
Phoenix, AZ 85012-1848
(602) 640-5000

Pittsburgh EEOC
1000 Liberty Avenue, Room 2038A
Pittsburgh, PA 15222
(412) 644-3444

Raleigh EEOC
1309 Annapolis Drive
Raleigh, NC 27608-2129
(919) 856-4064

Richmond EEOC
3600 West Broad Street, Room 229
Richmond, VA 23230
(804) 771-2692

St. Louis EEOC
625 North Euclid Street, 5th Floor
St. Louis, MO 63108
(314) 425-6585

San Antonio EEOC
5410 Fredericksburg Road, Suite 200
San Antonio, TX 78229-9934
(210) 229-4810

San Diego EEOC
401 B Street, Suite 1550
San Diego, CA 92101
(619) 557-7235

San Francisco EEOC
901 Market Street, Suite 500
San Francisco, CA 94103
(415) 744-6500

San Jose EEOC
96 North 3rd Street, Suite 200
San Jose, CA 95112
(408) 291-7352

Savannah EEOC
410 Mall Boulevard, Suite G
Savannah, GA 31406
(912) 652-4234

Seattle EEOC
909 1st Avenue, Suite 400
Seattle, WA 98104-1061
(206) 220-6883

Tampa EEOC
Timberlake Federal Building Annex
501 East Polk Street, 10th Floor
Tampa, FL 33602
(813) 228-2310

Washington, DC EEOC
1400 L Street NW, Suite 200
Washington, DC 20507
(202) 275-7377

State Human Rights Commissions

Alabama
Civil Rights & EEO Office
649 Monroe Street
Montgomery, AL 36131
(334) 242-8496

Alaska
Human Rights Commission
800 A Street, Suite 202
Anchorage, AK 99501-3628
(907) 276-7474

Arizona
Civil Rights Division
1275 West Washington
Phoenix, AZ 85007
(602) 542-5263

California
Fair Employment & Housing Commission
1390 Market Street, Room 410
San Francisco, CA 94102-5377
(415) 557-2325

Colorado
Civil Rights Division
1560 Broadway, Suite 1050
Denver, CO 80202
(303) 894-2997

Connecticut
Human Rights & Opportunities Commission
90 Washington Street
Hartford, CT 06106
(203) 566-3350

Delaware
Human Relations Division
820 North French Street
Wilmington, DE 19801
(302) 577-3485

District of Columbia
Human Rights Commission
51 N Street NE, 6th Floor
Washington, DC 20002
(202) 724-0656

Florida
Civil Rights Division
303 Hartman Building
2021 Capitol Circle SE
Tallahassee, FL 32399-2152
(904) 488-5905

Georgia
Fair Employment Practices Office
156 Trinity Avenue SW, Room 208
Atlanta, GA 30303
(404) 656-1736

Hawaii
Labor & Industrial Relations Department
EEO Officer
830 Punchbowl Street
Honolulu, HI 96813
(808) 548-4533

Idaho
Human Rights Commission
PO Box 83720
Boise, ID 83720-0040
(208) 334-2873

Illinois
Human Rights Department
100 West Randolph Street, Suite 10-100
Chicago, IL 60601
(312) 814-6245

Indiana
Civil Rights Commission
100 North Senate Avenue, Room N-103
Indianapolis, IN 46204
(317) 232-2600

Iowa
Human Rights Department
Lucas State Office Building
(515) 281-7300

Kansas
Civil Rights Commission
900 SW Jackson Street, Suite 851-S
Topeka, KS 66612-1252
(913) 296-3206

Kentucky
Human Rights Commission
Heyburn Building, 7th Floor
332 West Broadway
Louisville, KY 40202
(502) 595-4024

Louisiana
Civil Rights
PO Box 3776
Baton Rouge, LA 70821
(504) 342-2700

Maine
Human Rights Commission
State House, Station 51
Augusta, ME 04333
(207) 624-6050

Maryland
Human Relations Commission
6 St. Paul Street, 9th Floor
Baltimore, MD 21202
(410) 767-8600

Massachusetts
Commission Against Discrimination
John W. McCormack State Office Building, Room 601
1 Ashburton Place
Boston, MA 02108
(617) 727-3990

Michigan
Civil Rights Department
Victor Office Building
201 North Washington Square
Lansing, MI 48913
(517) 335-3165

Minnesota
Human Rights Department
500 Bremer Tower
7th Place & Minnesota Street
St. Paul, MN 55101
(612) 296-5665

Mississippi
Appeals Board
301 North Lamar Street, Room 100
Jackson, MS 39201
(601) 359-1406

Missouri
Human Rights Commission
3315 West Truman Boulevard
Jefferson City, MO 65102-1129
(573) 751-3325

Montana
Human Rights Division
PO Box 1728
Helena, MT 59624
(406) 444-3870

Nebraska
Equal Opportunity Commission
PO Box 94934
Lincoln, NE 68509
(402) 471-2024

Nevada
Equal Rights Commission
151 East Tropicana Avenue, Suite 590
Las Vegas, NV 89158
(702) 486-7161

New Hampshire
Human Rights Commission
163 Louden Road
Concord, NH 03301
(603) 271-2767

New Jersey
Civil Rights Division
383 West State Street, CN089
Trenton, NJ 08625
(609) 984-3100

New Mexico
Human Rights Division
1596 Pacheco Street
Santa Fe, NM 87502
(505) 827-6823

New York
Human Rights Division
55 West 125th Street
New York, NY 10027
(212) 870-8790

North Carolina
Human Relations Commission
217 West Jones Street
Raleigh, NC 27603
(919) 733-7996

North Dakota
Equal Employment Opportunity
600 East Boulevard Avenue
Bismarck, ND 58505
(701) 328-2660

Ohio
Civil Rights Commission
220 Parsons Avenue
Columbus, OH 43215
(614) 466-2785

Oklahoma
Human Rights Commission
2101 North Lincoln Boulevard, Room 480
Oklahoma City, OK 73105
(405) 521-3441

Oregon
Civil Rights Division
State Office Building, Suite 1045
800 NE Oregon Street, #32
Portland, OR 97232
(503) 731-4873

Pennsylvania
Human Relations Commission
PO Box 3145
Harrisburg, PA 17105
(717) 787-4410

Rhode Island
Human Rights Commission
10 Abbott Park Place
Providence, RI 02903
(401) 277-2661

South Carolina
Human Affairs Commission
PO Box 4490
Columbia, SC 29240
(803) 253-6336

South Dakota
Human Rights Division
State Capitol
910 East Sioux
Pierre, SD 57501
(605) 773-4493

Tennessee
Human Rights Commission
400 Cornerstone Square Building
Nashville, TN 37243
(615) 741-4940

Texas
Human Rights Commission
8100 Cameron Road, Building B, Suite 525
Austin, TX 78754
(512) 837-8534

Utah
Labor Division & Anti-Discrimination Division
160 East 300 South, 3rd Floor
Salt Lake City, UT 84114
(801) 530-6921

Vermont
Public Protection Division
109 State Street
Montpelier, VT 05602
(802) 828-3171

Virginia
Human Rights Council
PO Box 717
Richmond, VA 23206
(804) 225-2292

Washington
Human Rights Commission
711 South Capitol Way, Suite 402
Olympia, WA 98504
(360) 753-6770

West Virginia
Human Rights Commission
1321 Plaza East, Room 104-106
Charleston, WV 25301-1400
(304) 558-2616

Wisconsin
Equal Rights Division
PO Box 8928
Madison, WI 53708
(608) 266-0946

Wyoming
Labor Standards & Fair Employment Division
Herschler Building, 2nd Floor East
Cheyenne, WY 82002
(307) 777-6381

CHAPTER 14

How to Hire and Work Effectively with Your Employment Lawyer

The time to determine whether you need an employment lawyer is before you consider any action. Common situations that might call for help include:

- Before deciding to resign from a lucrative job
- Before considering filing a discrimination case with the EEOC or a state agency or filing a private action in federal or state court
- Before seeking damages due to an employer's alleged breach of contract
- Before considering going into a competing business against your ex-employer when you previously signed an agreement containing a restrictive covenant
- Before considering filing a lawsuit to recover earned commissions, overtime, wages, bonus, severance, vacation pay, or medical, pension, or profit-sharing benefits
- Before negotiating severance and other benefits resulting from a firing
- Before signing a release or any settlement agreement presented to you by an ex-employer
- After being warned of a pending termination but before the actual firing, to consider your options and strategies

- After being denied unemployment benefits
- After learning that prospective employers are receiving negative references about you

Employment laws are unduly complicated, and people often need lawyers to guide them properly. Thus, the best time to evaluate whether you need an employment lawyer is *before* legal action is contemplated or necessary. The best way to decide if a lawyer is necessary is to speak to one. Hopefully, you won't be charged for brief information given over the telephone.

FINDING THE RIGHT LAWYER

You should select your employment lawyer with care. The right choice can mean the recovery of thousands of dollars and/or the satisfactory resolution of a conflict or other problem and peace of mind. The wrong choice can cost you money and aggravation.

One way to find a lawyer is to ask around for recommendations. If you don't know of an employment lawyer, ask friends, associates, and relatives if they can recommend someone, or call a local or state bar association. These associations are listed in the phone book, and some maintain lists of attorneys who agree not to charge more than $25 for the first half hour of consultation. If experience is important, tell the person handling your call that you want to contact an experienced practitioner.

Be wary of lawyer advertising. Some lawyers mislead the public with their ads. One common method is to run an ad that states that a particular matter costs only $xx. When a potential client meets the lawyer, he or she learns that court costs and filing fees are $xx, but attorney's fees are extra. Also beware of advertisements that say the attorney is a "specialist." Most state bar associations have not adopted specialist certification programs.

Once you have obtained the name of a potential lawyer, call him or her, describe your problem, and ask whether an interview should be scheduled. Recognize that many lawyers who competently represent clients in one area (e.g., real estate) are not qualified to represent them in an employment matter, because most attorneys become familiar with certain types of cases that they handle promptly, efficiently, and profitably. When lawyers accept matters outside the realm of their daily practice, the chance of their making mistakes or not handling matters promptly increases. Ask the lawyer what proportion of his time is spent working in the field of law related to your problem. If the lawyer says he does not commonly handle such matters, ask for the names of other lawyers he is willing to recommend. Clients often receive excellent assistance through lawyer referrals.

THE INITIAL INTERVIEW

After you find a lawyer who will discuss your case with you, set up an initial interview. This interview will help you obtain a sound evaluation of your legal problem and help you decide if you should hire this lawyer. This is also the time to discuss important working details, such as the fee arrangement. Bring all pertinent written information to the initial interview (e.g., copies of contracts, checks, rebuttals to performance reviews, and letters of protest). Tell the lawyer everything related to the matter. Communicate all relevant information without inhibition, because the discussion is privileged and confidential.

Once the lawyer receives all the pertinent facts, he or she should be in a position of advising if the matter has any legal validity or consequences depending on state and/or federal law. You should also be advised whether the matter can be resolved through legal assistance. If so, inquire how quickly the lawyer believes the matter can be resolved, what must be done, and how much the lawyer intends to charge for the contemplated services.

Counsel Comments: For example, after recently terminated employees meet with me for an initial comprehensive consultation, I can accurately advise them whether their employer has violated the law and the chances of obtaining more money in a negotiated out-of-court settlement. I tell my potential clients the steps I intend to take after being retained, such as what the initial demand letter will say, when it will be delivered to the employer, and why this and other steps are to be taken. Based on my experience in handling similar matters in the past, I try to give all my clients realistic odds of their success. For example, I may tell a potential client that there is a 75 percent chance of receiving an extra $5,000 in a settlement but only a 25 percent chance of receiving an extra $50,000.

If you are considering a lawsuit, or if you are being sued and need the lawyer to assist in defense of your case, the lawyer will then:

- Decide whether the case has a fair probability of success after considering the law in the state where the suit will be brought
- Give an estimate as to how long the lawsuit will last
- Make a determination of the approximate legal fees and disbursements
- Explain what legal papers will be filed, when, and what their purposes are
- Discuss the defenses an opponent will probably raise and how to deal with them

If the lawyer sees weaknesses in your case and believes that litigation will be unduly expensive, he or she may advise you to compromise and settle the claim without resorting to litigation. In any event, the chosen course of action should be instituted without delay in order to receive remuneration as quickly as possible and to ensure that the requisite time period to start the action (i.e., the statute of limitations) will not have expired.

For all matters, the lawyer should advise what legal work needs to be done, how long it will take, and how much it will cost. Some lawyers neglect to give honest appraisals. Clients are then misled and spend large sums of money on losing causes. Be wary if the lawyer states, "You have nothing to worry about." Prudent attorneys tell clients that airtight cases do not exist and that the possibility of unforeseen circumstances and developments is always present.

Tip: Request an opinion letter that spells out the pros and cons of a matter and how much money you may have to spend to accomplish your objectives. Even if you are charged for the time it takes to draft the letter, an opinion letter can minimize future misunderstandings between you and your employment lawyer and help you decide whether or not to proceed with a lawsuit or legal intervention.

It is important to leave the interview feeling that the lawyer is open and responsive to your needs, is genuinely interested in helping you, will return your telephone calls promptly, and will prepare and handle your case properly. Although it is difficult to predict how well an attorney will perform, there are certain clues to look for during the interview:

- Does the lawyer present an outward appearance of neatness and good grooming?
- Are you received at the appointed interview hour or kept waiting? Some lawyers believe that if clients are kept waiting, they will think the lawyer is busy and, therefore, good. Keeping you waiting is merely a sign that the lawyer is not organized or is inconsiderate.
- Does the lawyer leave the room frequently during the interview or permit telephones calls to intrude? You deserve his or her complete attention.
- Does the lawyer demonstrate boredom or lack of interest by yawning or finger tapping?
- Is he or she a clock watcher?
- Does the lawyer try to impress you by narrating other cases he handled? Lawyers do not have to boast to obtain clients.

Tip: Most important, does the lawyer fail to discuss the fee arrangement up front? Some lawyers have a tendency to wait until all work is done before submitting large bills. The failure to discuss fee arrangements at the initial interview may be a sign the lawyer operates this way.

Successful lawyers win cases and make money for their clients. Don't be fooled by appearances. Plush offices, fancy cars, and expensive clothes may be a reason you will pay exorbitant fees for routine legal services. Don't be overly impressed by the school from which the lawyer graduated. Most law schools do not give their graduates practical training, and many less prestigious "local" law schools provide superior concrete skills, which is what you are paying for.

Be sure the lawyer of your choice will be working on the matter. People often go to prestigious firms expecting their matter to be handled by a partner. They pay large fees and sometimes wind up being represented primarily by a junior associate. Be sure the retainer agreement states that the matter will be handled by attorney X (the employment lawyer of your choice).

The major factor in determining whether you should hire a particular lawyer is his or her experience and expertise in handling legal problems like yours. Use a lawyer who devotes at least 50 percent of his or her practice to problems like yours. Avoid inexperienced lawyers if possible. Novices charge less, but often require more time to handle a problem. If you are being charged on an hourly basis, you may pay the same amount of money and not obtain the expertise of a pro.

Hire a lawyer to whom you can relate. Ask the lawyer about his or her outside activities and professional associations. Inquire if you can speak to any of his or her previous clients; references may help you learn more about the lawyer. If you do not feel comfortable with the first lawyer you meet, shop around and schedule appointments with others.

Confirming the Arrangement

After you decide to retain a particular lawyer, you should discuss a variety of points concerning fees to eliminate potential misunderstandings.

Clarify the Fee

Most lawyers generally charge a modest fee for the first visit to the office. Fees should be charged only when time is spent working on a matter. Charges are based on the amount of time and work involved, the difficulty of the problem, the dollar amount of the case, the result, the urgency of the problem (for example, an arbitration hearing the lawyer must handle several days after being retained will command a higher fee than the same hearing that takes place in a month), and the lawyer's expertise and reputation in handling your type of problem. Operating expenses and office overhead are elements that may also affect the fee arrangement.

As an example, I typically agree to handle a severance negotiation matter on a modified contingency basis. The client typically pays a sum of money (no more than $1,000) up front as a retainer. This retainer is applied against a contingency fee (no more than one-third) of all money, collected as a result of my efforts, exceeding what may initially have been offered to the terminated worker directly. The sample retainer letter on pages 331–332 illustrates this arrangement.

MODIFIED CONTINGENCY-FEE RETAINER AGREEMENT

Law Offices of Sack & Sack
135 East 57th Street 12th Floor
New York, NY 10022
Telephone (212) 702-9000
Telecopier (212) 702-9702

Steven M. Sack
Jonathan S. Sack★
★Also admitted in N.J. & D.C.

Date

Name of Client
Address

Re: Name of Employer

Dear (Name of Client):

This letter will confirm the terms of my engagement as your attorney regarding the above. I have met with you several times and thoroughly reviewed your file to learn the pertinent facts with respect to your current problems. For those and additional services to be rendered, you paid a consultation fee of One Hundred Fifty Dollars ($150.00) and a retainer of One Thousand Dollars ($1,000.00).

I will now contact the above *in negotiations* in the attempt to collect additional severance and other post-termination benefits on your behalf beyond those monies directly offered to you in the proposed (date) settlement agreement. For my efforts and in the event negotiations are successful, this office shall be paid a contingency fee of ONE THIRD (33.33%) of the gross amount of any money offered to me in settlement exceeding said benefits and less the $1,000.00 previously paid to me. Specifically included in the computation of my fee shall be a discounted value of any nontaxable monies, benefits, and outplacement assistance paid for by the employer that I obtain on your behalf.

All settlements will require your approval before I conclude same. Additionally, you understand that despite my efforts on your behalf there is no assurance or guarantee of the success of the outcome of my negotiations since the company may refuse to pay any additional compensation. Nevertheless, you have requested my law firm's intervention in this matter and I will promptly keep you posted with all developments as they occur.

The aforementioned contingency arrangement is not for any legal work rendered in formal litigation. In the event that negotiations are unsuccessful, we will discuss the possibility of my representing you in a formal litigation under mutually acceptable terms after our discussion and separate written agreement regarding fees.

I will personally handle all negotiations on your behalf.

If the above terms of this letter are acceptable and confirm our understanding and discussions, please sign below in the space where indicated and immediately return the original letter back to my office, keeping the copy for your records.

Thank you for your interest and attention, and if you have any questions or comments, feel free to call.

Very truly yours,
Steven Mitchell Sack

I, (Name of client), have read the contents of the above retainer letter, discussed the terms with Mr. Sack, understand the contents and all of the terms thereof, and have received a copy of this retainer letter for my files:

_____ Date: _____
Name of Client

Frequently, lawyers cannot state exactly how much they will charge because they are unable to determine the amount of work that will be involved. In that case, ask for an estimate of the minimum and maximum fee you can expect to pay. If it seems high, do not hesitate to question it. If necessary, state that you intend to speak to other lawyers about fees.

The fee arrangement is composed of several elements, which you must clearly understand. Costs are expenses that the lawyer incurs while preparing a case or working on a matter (e.g., photocopying, telephone, and mailing expenses and fees paid to the court for filing documents). Be certain the fee arrangement specifically mentions in writing which of these costs you pay.

Employment lawyers use different forms of fee arrangements. In a flat-fee arrangement, the lawyer is paid a specified sum to get the job done. Most employment lawyers offer a number of services that are performed on a flat-fee basis (e.g., review or preparation of an employment contract and other standard services). In a flat-fee plus time arrangement, a sum for a specified number of hours is charged. Once the lawyer works more hours than are specified, the client is charged on an hourly basis.

Most lawyers use an hourly rate, which can range from $150 to $300 or more. Under this arrangement, you will be charged at a fixed hourly rate for all work done. If you are billed by the hour, ask if phone calls between you and the attorney are included. If so, ask that you be charged only for calls exceeding a certain number per month. This can be justified by arguing you should not be charged when the lawyer fails to clarify a point, obtain additional information, or discuss news regarding the progress of the case. (See pages 334–335 for a sample hourly retainer agreement.)

In a contingency-fee arrangement, the lawyer receives a specified percentage of any money recovered via a lawsuit or settlement. Many employees favor contingency-fee arrangements because they are not required to pay legal fees if their case is unsuccessful. However, some types of contingency fees are not permitted—for example, when the fee paid to the lawyer exceeds the maximum allowable percentage (generally 40 to 45 percent). If the lawyer proposes a high contingency fee, never accept such an arrangement and hire him.

Spell out contingency arrangements in writing to prevent problems. The agreement should state who is responsible for costs in the event you are unsuccessful. All provisions should be explained so that they are clearly understood; be sure to save a copy for your records.

There are distinct advantages and disadvantages to using different fee arrangements. For example, in a flat-fee arrangement, you know how much you will be charged but not how much care and attention will be spent on the matter. The hourly rate might be cheaper than a flat fee for routine work, but some dishonest lawyers "pad" time sheets to increase fees. In addition, although contingency-fee arrangements

HOURLY RETAINER AGREEMENT

Date

Name of Client
Address

Re: Retainer Agreement Regarding Doe v. Doe

Dear (Name of Client):

This letter confirms that you have retained me as your attorney to (state precise nature of engagement, such as to negotiate a settlement agreement with your ex-employer if that is reasonably possible; or, if not, to represent you in a breach of contract lawsuit). You agree to pay to me promptly an initial retainer of (specify $, such as $1,500). If I devote more than 10 hours to this case based upon accurate time records commencing from the initial conference, which I will prepare and send to you on a monthly basis, you shall pay additional fees counted at the rate of (specify $, such as $150/hour).

If you should decide to discontinue my services in this matter at any time, you shall be liable for my time computed at the rate of $150/hour.

These fees do not include any work in appellate courts, any other actions or proceedings, or out-of-pocket disbursements. Out-of-pocket disbursements include, but are not limited to, costs of filing papers, court fees, process servers, witness fees, court reporters, long-distance telephone calls, travel, parking, and photocopies (billed at 10 cents per copy) normally made by me or requested by you, which disbursements shall be paid for or reimbursed to me upon my request after I furnish you with evidence of same.

I promise to keep you informed of all developments as they occur and to send you copies of all incoming and outgoing correspondence immediately after it is generated/received. I will personally handle all negotiations of your matter, preparing all necessary papers and documents and arguing your case in court if necessary.

I look forward to working with you on this matter. Kindly indicate your understanding and acceptance of the above terms by signing this letter below where indicated.

Very truly yours,
Name of Attorney

I, (Name of Client), have read and understand the above letter, have received a copy, and accept all of its terms:

_____ Date: _____
Name of Client

are beneficial to clients with weak cases, they sometimes encourage attorneys to settle "winner" cases for less money than could be obtained by going to court. This is why, no matter what type of fee is agreed on, it is essential to hire a lawyer who is honest and has your best interests in mind at all times.

Ask for a receipt if you pay for the initial visit or a retainer in cash. If a retainer is required, inquire whether the retainer is to become part of the entire fee and whether it is refundable. The retainer guarantees the availability of the lawyer to represent you and is an advance paid to demonstrate your desire to resolve a problem via legal recourse.

Ask if the retainer and other fees can be paid by credit card. Be sure interest will not be added if you are late in paying fees. Request that all fees be billed periodically. Insist that billing statements be supported by detailed and complete time records that include the number of hours (or partial hours) worked, a report of the people contacted, and the services rendered.

Tip: Some lawyers may be reluctant to do this, but by receiving these documents and statements on a regular basis, you can question inconsistencies and errors before they get out of hand, be aware of the amount of the bill as it accrues, and pay for it over time. The sample monthly billing statement on page 336 is the kind of bill that my office prepares for all my clients who are charged on an hourly basis. Insist on nothing less.

MONTHLY BILLING STATEMENT

Date

Name of Client
Address

Final statement for all services rendered in the matter of the contract negotiation between (Name of Client) and (Name of Employer) at the rate of $200 per hour per agreement:

1.	1/05/2000	Initial Meeting with Client	
		10:30–11:15	NO CHARGE
2.	1/06/2000	Review of initial proposed Agreement	
		7:30–7:55 a.m.	25 min.
		Tel. conv. with Client	
		9:05–9:15	10 min.
3.	1/07/2000	Tel. conv. with Employer's Attorney	
		9:40–9:45	5 min.
		Tel. conv. with Client	
		8:45–8:50; 9:50–9:55	10 min.
4.	1/08/2000	Draft of Revised Agreement including	
		tel. conv. with client	
		6:50–8:05 a.m.	75 min.
		Fax Agreement to Employer's Attorney	
		Final Discussion with Employer's Attorney	
		2:05–2:25	20 min.

Total time spent on Matter from January 5, 2000, through January 8, 2000:   165 min. or
                                                          2.75 hours

Amount earned: $550.00

Additional Tip: Insist that the lawyer send you copies of all incoming and outgoing correspondence so that you will be able to follow the progress of the case. Add this provision to your retainer agreement to ensure that you will receive copies on a regular and continuous basis.

Understand what legal fees are tax-deductible. Legal fees are deductible provided they are ordinary and necessary business expenses. This means that the cost of legal fees paid or incurred for the collection, maintenance, or conservation of income (which includes hiring a lawyer to collect wages or more severance pay) can be deducted. Deductions are also allowed for legal fees paid to collect, determine, or refund any tax that is owed. Ask the lawyer whether the fees you will pay are deductible. Structure the fee arrangement to maximize tax deductions and ask for a written statement that justifies the bill on the basis of time spent or some other allocation to support the claim. Keep the statement in a safe place until tax time and show it to your tax preparer. Accountants and other professionals often clip copies of the statements directly to the return so that the IRS won't question the deduction.

The following is a summary of deductible legal fees:

- Attorney fees paid to negotiate severance pay and other post-termination benefits
- Attorney fees paid to obtain a tax ruling
- Attorney fees paid to negotiate an employment agreement
- Attorney fees paid to fight the enforcement of a restrictive covenant precluding you from earning a living
- Attorney fees and costs paid to file a lawsuit to collect wages, commissions, bonus, or other compensation
- Attorney fees paid to oppose a suspension or disbarment of a professional license
- Attorney fees for services tending to increase or protect taxable business income (e.g., defending inherited stock)

Other Items to Clarify in the Initial Interview

Will the lawyer be available? Complaints often arise because of poor communication. At the initial interview, ask the lawyer what his normal office hours are. Advise him that availability is very important to you. Request that he return phone calls within twenty-four hours. Insist that his secretary or associate return phone calls if he will be unavailable for extended periods of time, but make it clear that you will not call him unnecessarily.

Will the lawyer work on the matter immediately? The legal system is often a slow process. Don't stall it further by hiring a procrastinating lawyer. Insist that the lawyer begin working on the matter as quickly as possible. Ask for an estimate of when the matter will be resolved. Include this in the retainer agreement for protection.

Are there hidden conflicts of interest? Lawyers must avoid even the appearance of impropriety. For example, when a lawyer represents you but previously represented your former employer in another case, there is an inherent conflict that limits his ability to zealously promote your best interests. Ask the lawyer up front if he perceives any potential conflict of interest (e.g., is he related to or was he ever employed by the company you are suing?). A lawyer must decline representing a client when his professional judgment is likely to be affected by other business, financial, or personal interests. If a lawyer is disqualified, his associates and partners are also forbidden to serve you.

How will funds be handled? Lawyers are obligated to keep client funds in separate accounts. This includes unearned retainer fees. The rules of professional conduct state that an attorney cannot commingle client funds with his own and that bank accounts for client funds must be clearly marked as "Client Trust Accounts" or "Escrow Accounts."

A lawyer must notify clients immediately when funds are received, and clients must also receive an accurate accounting of these funds. This consists of a complete explanation of the amount of money held by the lawyer, its origin, and the reason for any deductions. Insist on nothing less.

Tip: Ask for a copy of all checks received before the lawyer deposits the funds into his trust account. Tell the attorney to place your funds in an interest-bearing escrow account. Later on, when the funds are remitted, be sure the interest is included in the amount returned to you.

PROBLEMS ENCOUNTERED AFTER A LAWYER IS HIRED

You have the right to change lawyers at any time if there is a valid reason. Valid reasons include improper or unethical conduct, conflicts of interest, or malpractice by the lawyer. If you are dissatisfied with the lawyer's conduct or the way the matter is progressing, consult another lawyer for an opinion. Do this before taking action, because you need a professional opinion to tell whether the current lawyer has acted correctly or incorrectly.

Never fire your lawyer until you hire a replacement, because you may then be unrepresented and the case could be prejudiced or dismissed. If you fire the lawyer, you may be required to pay for the value of work rendered. You may also have to go to court to settle the issue of legal fees and the return of your papers, since some lawyers assert a lien on a litigation file. However, these potential problems should never impede you from taking action if warranted.

If you have evidence that the lawyer misused funds for personal gain or committed fraud, you may file a complaint with the state grievance committee or local bar association. Don't be afraid to do this. All complaints are confidential. You probably cannot be sued for filing a complaint if it is later determined that the lawyer did nothing wrong.

Another alternative is to commence a malpractice lawsuit against the lawyer. Legal malpractice arises when an attorney fails to use "such skill or prudence as attorneys of ordinary skill commonly possess and experience in the performance of the tasks they undertake." This doesn't mean you can sue if your lawyer gets beaten by a better lawyer. You can sue only if he renders work or assistance of minimal competence and you are damaged as a result. You can also sue for malpractice when there is a breach of ethics (e.g., the failure to remit funds belonging to a client) in addition to suing for breach of contract and/or civil fraud.

The following are examples of lawyer malpractice:

- Settling a case without your consent
- Procrastinating work on a matter (e.g., neglecting for a lengthy period to prepare a stipulation of settlement and the client dies)
- Charging improper fees
- Failing to file a claim within the requisite time period (the statute of limitations)
- Failure to keep you advised of major developments in a matter to your material detriment
- Failing to disclose that a conflict of interest exists

Consult another lawyer before embarking on any course of action to learn if you have a valid claim. An honest and unbiased attorney will also tell you what steps should be taken to protect your rights.

Counsel Comments: More lawyers are now willing to testify against each other. If your complaint to a state's disciplinary board is viable, it will be investigated (the process may take months). An investigative committee will decide whether the case should be given a hearing. After an investigation, the board may make recommendations for disciplinary action against the professional, including a formal reprimand, suspension from practice, or revocation of the attorney's license (which is rare).

You can also file a private lawsuit against the professional requesting that such an investigation ensue. In such a lawsuit, the lawyer, who will generally carry malpractice insurance, will be defended by lawyers from his insurance carrier. Whether or not malpractice has actually occurred is a question of fact to be decided by a judge or jury. Due to the complexity of most malpractice cases, and the fact that the lawsuit will typically be vigorously defended, it is critical to seek advice from a skilled lawyer.

SUMMARY OF STEPS TO TAKE TO USE A LAWYER EFFECTIVELY

1. Speak to a lawyer before action is contemplated to determine if one is needed.
2. Schedule an interview if necessary; inquire if you will be charged for it.
3. Bring relevant documents to the interview.
4. Do not be overly impressed by plush surroundings.
5. Be sure the lawyer of your choice will be handling the matter.
6. Hire an experienced practitioner who devotes at least 50 percent of his or her working time to employment matters.
7. Look for honesty and integrity in a lawyer.
8. Insist on signing a retainer agreement to reduce misunderstandings.
9. Have the agreement read and explained to you before signing and save a copy for your files.
10. If the lawyer cannot state exactly how much you will be charged, get minimum and maximum estimates. Include this in the agreement.

11. Be certain you understand how additional costs are calculated and who will pay for them.
12. If an hourly rate is agreed on, negotiate that you will not be charged for a few telephone calls to your lawyer.
13. Inquire if you can pay the bill by credit card.
14. Structure the fee arrangement to maximize tax deductions and savings.
15. Insist on receiving copies of incoming and outgoing correspondence and monthly, detailed time records.
16. Be sure the lawyer will be available, that he or she will immediately commence work on your matter, and that there are no potential conflicts of interest.
17. Insist that all funds received by the lawyer on your behalf be deposited into an interest-bearing escrow account. Don't forget to ask for the interest later on. Better still, insist that all settlement checks from employers be made payable only to you (or jointly if the lawyer insists) and never solely to the lawyer.
18. Do not allow the lawyer to pressure you into settling a case or making a rushed, uninformed decision.
19. Consult another lawyer before deciding to fire your present one, file a complaint with a grievance committee, or commence a malpractice lawsuit.
20. Do not expect miracles.

LEGAL RESEARCH

At different points in this book, I have advised you to "research or know your state's law." This does not mean that you must actually go to a law library and do your own research. Although knowledge is power, a little knowledge is often dangerous. It is always preferable that you speak to a competent lawyer, a legal referral service or group (e.g., the American Civil Liberties Union), an appropriate federal or state agency, or a court clerk for more details whenever possible.

However, understanding and specifically knowing the law can only help when you are negotiating with your employer, presenting your workplace problem to a state or federal investigator, preparing a court case, arbitration, or mediation, or working with your lawyer. Thus, it may be a good idea to do your own research as an extra measure of security if you have free time and are so inclined.

Although most public libraries and colleges have general legal reference books, the best place to go is probably a local bar association office library or a law school near you. To learn when (and if) the law library is open to the public, phone the library, explain your problem, and ask what reference sources you should consult.

Tip: When you go to a law library, it's a good idea to speak to any students who may be there studying or researching a matter. Law students are generally helpful in providing answers to your questions and may even retrieve source books for you. If you find their assistance helpful, offer to buy them lunch or dinner for their trouble. You will be amazed by the amount of free assistance you may receive from such a gesture!

The way to start your research should be to read the actual federal or state statute (law) that deals with your problem. For example, if you believe you were fired because of your age, you might want to read the actual Older Workers Benefit Protection Act, Title VII, the Civil Rights Act of 1991, and corresponding state antidiscrimination laws. Sometimes the statutes come with useful commentary, such as a legislative history of the bill and/or purpose of the law.

You may also want to review cases with similarities to yours that have been tried in your state and hopefully in the same court system. Most judges and state and federal agencies desire to follow the decision of cases with similar fact patterns.

For example, suppose you are being sued by an ex-employer that claims you are legally obligated to return an overdraw (i.e., money that you received that exceeds your commission earnings). If you or your lawyer are able to find a similar case in point where a judge in your state ruled that a draw paid before a commission is earned is deemed to be nonforfeitable salary and should not be returned unless the employee signed a promissory note or other agreement providing that the draw was to be considered a loan, you would stand a better chance of prevailing.

Tip: Be thorough and current in your research. For example, be sure that there are no new cases that have reversed or negated your case's significance.

Ask the librarian to help you find any major treatises (i.e., law review articles) about the particular labor or employment problem you face. These articles are written by honor law students, law professors, or practicing attorneys, and are instructive because they explain the significance of legal developments and often cite various leading cases you can read. Consult the *Current Law Index* and the *Index to Legal Periodicals* to help you find articles on topics that pertain to your matter. Hopefully, you will find pertinent articles written by people in your state that discuss your state's laws and court decisions. This can help your research immeasurably.

CHAPTER 15

Conclusion

Congratulations. Now that you have read this book, you have a better understanding of knowing what to do and how to react when you get fired. Being terminated from a job is devastating emotionally and financially, especially when it is unexpected. But following the numerous strategies I've mentioned will make you better prepared for this event if it unfortunately happens.

It is best to prepare now for the eventuality of a firing, however remote the possibility. This can be done by updating your résumé regularly and talking to friends in the industry about a possible job change. Know the marketplace for your talents and target companies who are profitable, growing, and in a hiring mode. Always be discreet with your inquiries.

When you are told of the horrible news, ask for more time before the effective termination date. Each additional day you receive pay and benefits is critical. Extra pay gives you more time to consider your options, helps your personal cash flow situation, and, although remote, may give you an opportunity to persuade management to change its decision. Don't be afraid to plead, beg, or be emotional where warranted. It's hard to be the bearer of bad news, so play on that difficulty for your benefit. While it may be hard to continue to work under these conditions, being there is probably better than not working at all or being home feeling sorry for yourself. Maintaining a work routine is important for your morale and may help you find alternate suitable employment quicker.

Ask for a face-to-face meeting with the key decision maker. Where possible, request to speak with the most sympathetic ally at the company. When you get a meeting, you may be able to pry open the door for reconsideration. If unsuccessful, it will be a good opportunity for you to negotiate more post-termination benefits and learn the reason for the firing.

As I have discussed, try to appeal to the company's sense of decency and fair play during the negotiations. If the decision can't be changed, accept it gracefully and comply with all requests for an exit interview, such as returning company property or assisting with the training of a replacement. Keep your cool. Since your last impression may be your most important one, thank superiors for the experience and opportunity of working and learning from them. Do not be sarcastic. Try to be warm to all of your coworkers because you never know when the tables will be turned or when you may need to call upon people for a multitude of favors. Treat this difficult experience as an opportunity to mend the fence. Try to leave on a positive note, because no one likes a sore loser.

Seek competent legal advice if you do not agree with the company's decision. Do not tell the company you will be speaking to a lawyer, because it's nobody's business.

Inquire if you can arrange to continue to work as a consultant. If your job performance was not the reason for the termination, you and the company may be able to mutually benefit from your familiarity with its operations during a transition phase. This way you may be able to net more after-tax dollars and enjoy the opportunity to work out of your house and be your own boss. The experience can also make you more productive at your next job and serve as a great cover story—you wanted a change of pace. Today it is common to be entrepreneurial.

Don't forget to speak to management about your cover story. Know what your employer will say about you to future prospective employers. Where beneficial, try to get your immediate supervisor (if you left on good terms) to field calls on your behalf. Hopefully, this person or the company generally will stress your accomplishments and positive work ethic. But don't be disappointed if you are told that no reference, either positive or negative, will be given, because this is common in today's workplace.

Where applicable, prepare a letter of reference on company letter-head and have it signed before you leave for the last time. A sample letter of reference is on page 166 of this book.

To avoid misunderstandings, confirm the offer of severance and post-termination benefits in writing. If the company won't commit the offer to writing, send a confirming memo outlining what was of-fered and/or agreed to. Refer to the sample memos in this book as a guide.

If you are presented with a severance agreement to sign, tell the employer you will need time to review it and consider your options. Avoid saying anything more and do not show your displeasure with the offer. Take the agreement home and study it. Consult with your accountant or professional adviser and speak to a knowledgeable em-ployment lawyer where applicable. By signing a release in exchange for the offered post-termination entitlements, you may be giving up claims that are far more valuable than what is offered. Remember that most severance offers are typically negotiable and you can often get more by having a lawyer negotiate a better package on your behalf. Often there are many aspects of your compensation not included in the initial severance offer, such as continued medical and outplace-ment benefits. Think about what you are giving up by leaving peace-fully, and think about what you will need in the coming months.

Never sign the agreement if you suspect you have been treated il-legally. Get sound legal advice when you believe you were fired to be deprived of large commissions, vested pension rights, a year-end bonus, vacation pay, medical coverage, or other expected financial benefits.

You generally cannot be fired after returning from an illness, preg-nancy, or jury duty, or after complaining about a safety violation or other wrongdoing. You may also have rights when you are fired in a manner inconsistent with company handbooks, manuals, written con-tracts, and disciplinary rules. It is also illegal to be fired if you are over forty, belong to a protected minority, are a female, have strong reli-gious beliefs, or are handicapped primarily because of such personal characteristics.

If you are fired as part of a massive layoff with other large numbers of workers or your plant is closed without getting at least sixty days' notice or sixty days' severance pay, speak to a lawyer immediately. This is also true if you received a verbal promise of job security or other rights that the company failed to fulfill, if you are a long-term worker and the punishment "does not fit the crime" (especially when younger workers were not similarly treated), or when you are fired in a manner inconsistent with provisions in a written employment contract (assuming you received one).

If possible, try to make copies of all pertinent documents in your personnel file while working. For example, if you have received excellent performance reviews and appraisals and the file indicates you received merit salary increases, your lawyer may be able to use this material to fight the firing or negotiate more severance and other benefits than the company first offers.

The lawyer may also advise you to think twice before accepting the company's offer of allowing you to resign. This is because when you resign, you may be waiving your claim to unemployment and other post-termination benefits.

If you have been with a company for a long time, your lawyer or yourself should attempt to receive severance based on the number of years worked multiplied by, say, four weeks for every year worked. If you have only been employed for a short time, suggest that the company pay you severance equal to the length of time you already worked or based upon a percentage of your total compensation. If you did not see it coming, argue that because the company failed to give you notice, you were denied a benefit given to other fired workers. Pay in lieu of notice is another way of getting what you want, which is more money.

Hopefully, you or your lawyer will remain persistent yet professional at all times. Whatever is finally offered, you must consider receiving it now in a lump sum or as a payout over time. Payouts are good for tax purposes, continuation of benefits, and for vesting and crediting purposes. You may or may not be able to simultaneously collect unemployment insurance benefits during a payout, depending on state law. A lump sum payment is better if you have a new job lined up already or if you do not need the medical coverage. Having the money in hand at your disposal is often better than remaining on the leash, depending on your personal circumstances. The strings attached may require you to cooperate with your old company or not compete, when all you may want now is to get away as far and as fast as possible. And, where appropriate, ask for a "bridge" to retirement so that you may avail yourself of lifetime retiree benefits.

Other final issues to discuss include ongoing medical benefits paid by the employer, outplacement assistance or payment in kind in cash, and continued use of an office, secretary, and telephone. All of these topics are covered in greater detail in the book.

Hopefully, you tried to protect your rights where applicable by reviewing, preparing, and sending the numerous sample letters in the book to preserve and enforce your rights. These letters can be used whenever you think your rights have been violated.

Before sending such a letter, always obtain the proper name and address of the employer. This can be done by copying the full corporate name that appears on your paycheck. If you receive checks from two different companies or business entities, determine which is the appropriate company to send the letter to. When in doubt, send the letter to each company to increase the chances of a timely response.

To whom should the letter be sent? Preferably, the president of the company or a senior executive who will pass the letter on to the appropriate individual in human resources, benefits, or payroll. When in doubt, send the original to the president and copies to a few key people (no more than three) within the organization. By the way, if you were on good terms with a key person, it might be best to send the letter to him or her first to increase the chances of a favorable response. If you receive a negative response, you can always send a second letter to the president.

Be precise when drafting the letter because any ambiguity will be construed against the letter-maker, and avoid spelling or grammar mistakes. An unprofessional-looking letter will not have the impact of a clearly drafted document. Thus, review the letter before sending it out; have the letter proofread by someone else to minimize mistakes. Make and save a copy of the letter before it is sent. Store the copy in a safe place. Always send the letter by certified mail, return receipt requested, to prove delivery. You may also fax the letter or hand-deliver it using a messenger service. If so, save the receipt to prove that the letter was received.

If no response or an unacceptable response is received, this book contains names and locations of many federal and state agencies to contact to get help. For example, the Equal Employment Opportunity Commission (EEOC) and the Department of Labor (DOL) employ investigators and intake personnel who will meet with you for free to discuss your case. The telephone numbers and locations of pertinent agencies are listed at the end of Chapter 13. Often, these agencies will contact your ex-employer and try to reach a quick settlement of your matter.

If you do not receive prompt assistance from these agencies, think the process will work too slowly, or wish to discuss the matter with an attorney, reread Chapter 14 on how to consult, hire, and work effectively with an employment lawyer.

Hundreds of thousands of workers are fired unfairly or illegally each year. Millions of dollars are forfeited by people who fail to assert themselves or recognize what they are legally entitled to. Fortunately, the law has changed to safeguard the rights of workers. Although the law varies from state to state and each case warrants individual attention based on its particular facts, the information contained in this book will give you a better idea if your rights have been violated after receiving a pink slip.

As you now have learned, many of the strategies in this book will help you maximize the chances of asserting yourself properly and/or winning a lawsuit when you have to fight back. I wrote *Getting Fired* for workers throughout the United States in all industries, and have tried to reduce complicated case decisions, administrative agency rulings, and legislation into simple action strategies to follow. These guidelines are usable no matter what state your employer is located in.

Remember, the body of employment law has been created to further fairness and justice. It is there to protect you provided the right steps are taken and the right moves are made. Always reread appropriate portions of this book where applicable. Know the law and discuss your situation with a competent employment lawyer or professional adviser.

Thanks for reading this book and, above all, good luck!

Glossary

Abuse of process: A cause of action that arises when one party misuses the legal process to injure another.

Accord and satisfaction: An agreement between two parties, such as the employee and his or her company, to compromise disputes concerning outstanding debts, compensation, or terms of employment. Satisfaction occurs when the terms of the compromise are fully performed.

Action in accounting: A cause of action in which one party seeks a determination of the amount of money owed by another.

Admissible: Capable of being introduced in court as evidence.

Advance: Sometimes referred to as "draw," it is a sum of money that is applied against money to be earned.

Affidavit: A written statement signed under oath.

Allegations: Written statements of a party to a lawsuit that charge the other party with wrongdoing. In order to be successful, allegations must be proved.

Answer: The defendant's reply to the plaintiff's allegations in a complaint.

Anticipatory breach: A breach of contract that occurs when one party—i.e., the employee—states in advance of performance that he or she will definitely not perform under the terms of his or her contract.

Appeal: A proceeding whereby the losing party to a lawsuit requests that a higher court determine the correctness of the decision.

Arbitration: A proceeding whereby both sides to a lawsuit agree to submit their dispute to arbitrators rather than judges. The arbitration proceeding is expeditious and is legally binding on all parties.

Assignment: The transfer of a right or interest by one party to another.

Attorney in fact: A person appointed by another to transact business on his or her behalf; the person does not have to be a lawyer.

At-will employment: *See* Employment at will.

Award: A decision made by a judicial body to compensate the winning party in a lawsuit.

Bill of particulars: A document used in a lawsuit that specifically details the loss alleged by the plaintiff.

Breach of contract: A legal cause of action for the unjustified failure to perform a duty or obligation specified in an agreement.

Brief: A concise statement of the main contents of a lawsuit.

Burden of proof: The responsibility of a party to a lawsuit to provide sufficient evidence to prove or disprove a claim.

Business deduction: A legitimate expense that can be used to decrease the amount of income subject to tax.

Business slander: A legal wrong committed when a party orally makes false statements that impugn the business reputation of another (e.g., imply that the person is dishonest, incompetent, or financially unreliable).

Calendar: A list of cases to be heard each day in court.

Cause of action: The legal theory on which a plaintiff seeks to recover damages.

Caveat emptor: A Latin expression frequently applied to consumer transactions; translated as "Let the buyer beware."

Cease-and-desist letter: A letter, usually sent by a lawyer, that notifies an individual to stop engaging in a particular type of activity, behavior, or conduct that infringes on the rights of another.

Certificate of incorporation: A document that creates a corporation.

Civil court: Generally, any court that presides over noncriminal matters.

Claims court: A particular court that hears tax disputes.

Clerk of the court: A person who determines whether court papers are properly filed and court procedures followed.

Closely held business: A business typically owned by a small number of owners.

Collateral estoppel: *See* Estoppel. Collateral estoppel happens when a prior but different legal action is conclusive in a way to bring about estoppel in a current legal action.

Common law: Law that evolves from reported case decisions that are relied on for their precedential value.

Compensatory damages: A sum of money, awarded to a party, that represents the actual harm suffered or loss incurred.

Complaint: A legal document that commences a lawsuit; it alleges facts and causes of action that a plaintiff relies on to collect damages.

Conflict of interest: The ethical inability of a lawyer to represent a client because of competing loyalties, e.g., representing both employer and employee in a labor dispute.

Consideration: An essential element of an enforceable contract; something of value given or promised by one party in exchange for an act or promise of another.

Contempt: A legal sanction imposed when a rule or order of a judicial body is disobeyed.

Contingency fee: A type of fee arrangement whereby a lawyer is paid a percentage of the money recovered. If unsuccessful, the client is responsible only for costs already paid by the lawyer.

Continuance: The postponement of a legal proceeding to another date.

Contract: An enforceable agreement, either written, oral, or implied by the actions or intentions of the parties.

Contract modification: The alteration of contract terms.

Conversion: Unlawfully keeping or retaining property belonging to another.

Counterclaim: A claim asserted by a defendant in a lawsuit.

Covenant: A promise.

Creditor: The party to whom money is owed.

Cross-examination: The questioning of a witness by the opposing lawyer.

Damage: An award, usually money, given to the winning party in a lawsuit as compensation for the wrongful acts of another.

Debtor: The party who owes money.

Decision: The determination of a case of matter by a judicial body.

Deductible: The unrecoverable portion of insurance proceeds.

Defamation: An oral or written statement communicated to a third party that impugns a person's reputation in the community.

Default judgment: An award rendered after one party fails to appear in a lawsuit.

Defendant: The person or entity who is sued in a lawsuit.

Defense: The defendant's justification for relieving himself or herself of fault.

Definite term of employment: Employment of a fixed period of time.

Deposition: A pretrial proceeding in which one party is questioned, usually under oath, by the opposing party's lawyer.

Disclaimer: A clause in a sales, service, or other contract that attempts to limit or exonerate one party from liability in the event of a lawsuit.

Discovery: A general term used to describe several pretrial devices (e.g., depositions and interrogatories) that enable lawyers to elicit information from the opposing side.

Dual capacity: A legal theory, used to circumvent workers' compensation laws, that allows an injured employee to sue his or her employer directly in court.

Due process: Constitutional protections that guarantee that a person's life, liberty, or property cannot be taken away without the opportunity to be heard in a judicial proceeding.

Duress: Unlawful threats, pressure, or force that induces a person to act contrary to his or her intentions; if proved, it allows a party to disavow a contract.

Employee: A person who works and is subject to an employer's scope, direction, and control.

Employment at will: Employment by which an employee has no job security.

Employment discrimination: Conduct directed at employees and job applicants that is prohibited by law.

Equity: Fairness; usually applied when a judicial body awards a suitable remedy other than money to a party (e.g., an injunction).

Escrow account: A separate fund where lawyers or others are obligated to deposit money received from or on behalf of a client.

Estoppel: A legal bar to prevent a party from asserting a fact or claim inconsistent with that party's prior position that has been relied on or acted on by another party.

Evidence: Information in the form of oral testimony, exhibits, affidavits, etc., used to prove a party's claim.

Examination before trial: A pretrial legal device; also called a deposition.

Exhibit: Tangible evidence used to prove a party's claim.

Exit agreements: Agreements sometimes signed between employers and employees on resignation or termination of an employee's services.

Express contract: An agreement whose terms are manifested by clear and definite language, as distinguished from agreements inferred from conduct.

False imprisonment: The unlawful detention of a person who is held against his or her will without authority or justification.

Filing fee: Money paid to start a lawsuit.

Final decree: A court order or directive of a permanent nature.

Financial statement: A document, usually prepared by an accountant, that reflects a business's (or individual's) assets, liabilities, and financial condition.

Flat fee: A sum of money paid to a lawyer as compensation for services.

Flat fee plus time: A form of payment in which a lawyer receives one sum for services and also receives additional money calculated on an hourly basis.

Fraud: A false statement that is relied on and causes damages to the defrauded party.

General denial: A reply contained in the defendant's answer.

Ground: The basis for an action or an argument.

Guaranty: A contract in which one party agrees to answer for or satisfy the debt of another.

Hearsay evidence: Unsubstantiated evidence that is often excluded by a court.

Hourly fee: Money paid to a lawyer for services, computed on an hourly basis.

Implied contract: An agreement that is tacit rather than expressed in clear and definite language; an agreement inferred from the conduct of the parties.

Indemnification: Protection or reimbursement against damage or loss. The indemnified party is protected against liabilities or penalties from that party's actions; the indemnifying party provides the protection or reimbursement.

Infliction of emotional distress: A legal cause of action in which one party seeks to recover damages for mental pain and suffering caused by another.

Injunction: A court order restraining one party from doing or refusing to do an act.

Integration: The act of making a contract whole by integrating its elements into a coherent single entity. An agreement is considered integrated when the parties involved accept the final version as a complete expression of their agreement.

Interrogatories: A pretrial device used to elicit information; written questions are sent to an opponent to be answered under oath.

Invasion of privacy: The violation of a person's constitutionally protected right to privacy.

Judgment: A verdict rendered by a judicial body; if money is awarded, the winning party is the "judgment creditor" and the losing party is the "judgment debtor."

Jurisdiction: The authority of a court to hear a particular matter.

Legal duty: The responsibility of a party to perform a certain act.

Letter of agreement: An enforceable contract in the form of a letter.

Letter of protest: A letter sent to document a party's dissatisfaction.

Liable: Legally in the wrong or legally responsible for.

Lien: A claim made against the property of another in order to satisfy a judgment.

Lifetime contract: An employment agreement of infinite duration that is often unenforceable.

Liquidated damages: An amount of money agreed on in advance by parties to a contract to be paid in the event of a breach or dispute.

Malicious interference with contractual rights: A legal cause of action in which one party seeks to recover damages against an individual who has induced or caused another party to terminate a valid contract.

Malicious prosecution: A legal cause of action in which one party seeks to recover damages after another party instigates or institutes a frivolous judicial proceeding (usually criminal) that is dismissed.

Mediation: A voluntary dispute resolution process in which both sides attempt to settle their differences without resorting to formal litigation.

Misappropriation: A legal cause of action that arises when one party makes untrue statements of fact that induce another party to act and be damaged as a result.

Mitigation of damages: A legal principle that requires a party seeking damages to make reasonable efforts to reduce damages as much as possible; for example, to seek new employment after being unfairly discharged.

Motion: A written request made to a court by one party during a lawsuit.

Negligence: A party's failure to exercise a sufficient degree of care owed to another by law.

Nominal damages: A small sum of money awarded by a court.

Noncompetition clause: A restrictive provision in a contract that limits an employee's right to work in that particular industry after he or she ceases to be associated with his or her present employer.

Notary public: A person authorized under state law to administer an oath or verify a signature.

Notice to show cause: A written document in a lawsuit asking a court to expeditiously rule on a matter.

Objection: A formal protest made by a lawyer in a lawsuit.

Offer: The presentment of terms, which, if accepted, may lead to the formation of a contract.

Opinion letter: A written analysis of a client's case, prepared by a lawyer.

Option: An agreement giving one party the right to choose a certain course of action.

Oral contract: An enforceable verbal agreement.

Parol evidence: Oral evidence introduced at a trial to alter or explain the terms of a written agreement.

Partnership: A voluntary association between two or more competent persons engaged in a business as co-owners for profit.

Party: A plaintiff or defendant in a lawsuit.

Perjury: Committing false testimony while under oath.

Petition: A request filed in court by one party.

Plaintiff: The party who commences a lawsuit.

Pleading: A written document that states the facts or arguments put forth by a party in a lawsuit.

Power of attorney: A document executed by one party allowing another to act on his or her behalf in specified situations.

Pretrial discovery: A legal procedure used to gather information from an opponent before the trial.

Process server: An individual who delivers the summons and/or complaint to the defendant.

Promissory note: A written acknowledgment of a debt whereby one party agrees to pay a specified sum on a specified date.

Proof: Evidence presented at a trial and used by a judge or jury to fashion an award.

Punitive damages: Money awarded as punishment for a party's wrongful acts.

Quantum meruit: A legal principle whereby a court awards reasonable compensation to a party who performs work, labor, or services at another party's request.

Rebuttal: The opportunity for a lawyer at a trial to ask a client or witness additional questions to clarify points elicited by the opposing lawyer during cross-examination.

Release: A written document that, when signed, relinquishes a party's rights to enforce a claim against another.

Remedy: The means by which a right is enforced or protected.

Reply: A written document in a lawsuit conveying the contentions of a party in response to a motion.

Restrictive covenant: A provision in a contract that forbids one party from doing a certain act, e.g., working for another, soliciting customers, etc.

Retainer: A sum of money paid to a lawyer for services to be rendered.

Service-letter statutes: Laws in some states that require an employer to furnish an employee with written reasons for his or her discharge.

Sexual harassment: Prohibited conduct of a sexual nature that occurs in the workplace.

Shop rights: The rights of an employer to use within the employer's facility a device or method developed by an employee.

Slander: Oral defamation of a party's reputation.

Small-claims court: A particular court that presides over small disputes (e.g., those involving sums of less than $2,500).

Sole proprietorship: An unincorporated business.

Statement of fact: Remarks or comments of a specific nature that have a legal effect.

Statute: A law created by a legislative body.

Statute of frauds: A legal principle requiring a party to commence a lawsuit within a certain period of time.

Stipulation: An agreement between the parties.

Submission agreement: A signed agreement whereby both parties agree to submit a present dispute to binding arbitration.

Subpoena: A written order requiring a party or witness to appear at a legal proceeding; a *subpoena duces tecum* is a written order requiring a party to bring books and records to the legal proceeding.

Summation: The last part of the trial wherein both lawyers recap the respective positions of their clients.

Summons: A written document served on a defendant giving notification of a lawsuit.

Temporary decree: A court order or directive of a temporary nature, capable of being modified or changed.

Testimony: Oral evidence presented by a witness under oath.

"Time is of the essence": A legal expression often included in agreements to specify the requirement of timeliness.

Tort: A civil wrong.

Unfair and deceptive practice: Illegal business and trade acts prohibited by various federal and state laws.

Unfair discharge: An employee's termination without legal justification.

Verdict: The decision of a judge or jury.

Verification: A written statement signed under oath.

Waiver: A written document that, when signed, relinquishes a party's rights.

Whistle-blowing: Protected conduct where one party complains about the illegal acts of another.

Witness: A person who testifies at a judicial proceeding.

Workers' compensation: A process in which an employee receives compensation for injuries sustained in the course of employment.

Index